Assessing Outcome
in Clinical Practice

Benjamin M. Ogles
Ohio University

Michael J. Lambert
Brigham Young University

Kevin S. Masters
Utah State University

Allyn and Bacon
Boston • London • Toronto • Sydney • Tokyo • Singapore

To MO and the kiddos.   (BMO)

To Maddie, Spencer, and Zippy, who brighten my life.   (MJL)

To Jill, Sierra, and Hilary,
thank you for gifts I cannot measure but can only feel.   (KSM)

Copyright © 1996 by Allyn & Bacon
A Simon & Schuster Company
Needham Heights, Massachusetts 02194

Library of Congress Cataloging-in-Publication Data

Ogles, Benjamin M.
   Assessing outcome in clinical practice / Benjamin M. Ogles,
  Michael J. Lambert, Kevin S. Masters
     p.   cm.
   Includes bibliographical references and index.
   ISBN 0-205-19353-6
   1. Psychotherapy—Evaluation—Methodology.   2. Outcome assessment
(Medical care)—Methodology.   I. Lambert, Michael J.   II. Masters,
Kevin S.   III. Title.
   [DNLM: 1. Outcome and Process Assessment (Health Care).
2. Psychotherapy.   3. Evaluation Studies.   WM 420 035a 1996]
RC480.5.0385   1996
616.89′14—dc20
DNLM/DLC
for Library of Congress   95-38901
                                                CIP

Printed in the United States of America

10   9   8   7   6   5   4   3   2   1   00   99   98   97   96

Contents

Preface

This book has four related goals: (1) to identify a select group of outcome instruments that can be readily used in practice and research as a result of their demonstrated utility, ease of administration and implementation, and psychometric adequacy; (2) to describe a conceptual process that clinicians can use to help them identify pertinent outcome assessment devices for practical use; (3) to add a support beam to the precarious bridge spanning the gap between psychotherapy researchers and practitioners; and (4) to encourage explicit accountability for treatment outcome among practitioners in a time of increasing pressure from policy makers, third-party payers, and consumers.

As psychotherapy research evolves, studies are becoming more and more clinically relevant. One of the interesting offshoots of therapy research is the instruments that were originally developed to measure change in studies of psychotherapy outcome. Administration of these research-based instruments in clinical settings can have an immediate impact on clinical practice. Nevertheless, clinicians generally do not have access to these instruments nor the time to set about collecting data on their use. Similarly, the wide variety of instruments available makes it difficult for practitioners to know which instruments might be the most appropriate for assessing change in their particular area of practice. As a result, we set out to select a handful of instruments that may be used in clinical practice. Here, indeed, is a research-based strategy for obtaining clinically useful information.

The collection of instruments provided in this book will not be sufficient to meet all the needs of practitioners wishing to evaluate the effectiveness of their ongoing practice. As a result, a method for evaluating and selecting from other potentially useful instruments is presented. The conceptual and organizational scheme provides a way for clinicians to categorize outcome instruments based on certain key characteristics of outcome assessment devices. It can then be used to guide the development and selection of other outcome measures that are not described in this book. Clinicians can then make more informed choices concerning which instruments will provide the most useful outcome information for their ongoing practices.

By selecting pertinent instruments along with describing a conceptual scheme for selecting outcome assessment devices, we hope to make psychotherapy research methods available for practical application. Psychotherapy research has been criticized for its lack of relevance to clinical practice (see Goldfried, Greenberg, & Marmar, 1990). Yet, pragmatic and useful research-based methods are available for relatively easy implementation in many clinical settings. We hope *Assessing Outcome in Clinical Practice* will help narrow the gap between clinical research and practice.

Not only was this book guided by the desire to make clinical research useful in applied settings but it also is a response to the ever-increasing pressure from outside sources to demonstrate the efficacy of psychological interventions on an ongoing basis. Since the writing of the original proposal for this book (January 1991), a virtual explosion of demand has occurred in the public sector regarding the evaluation of outcomes in several areas, including education, medicine, and mental health, among others. Seemingly every program announcement includes a section on outcome evaluation, and government officers are increasingly asking for outcome evaluation to ascertain where taxpayers' dollars are most effectively used. Insurance companies, health maintenance organizations (HMOs), and the like are also attempting to gather data regarding the effectiveness of medical and mental health treatments so that informed decisions can be made concerning the most cost-effective strategies of intervention. Particularly in light of current proposals to modify the health care system, the issue of treatment effectiveness is becoming increasingly important.

In addition to public and private agencies, therapy researchers are interested in developing a "core battery" of outcome instruments to use in research. The Society for Psychotherapy Research recently organized a core battery discussion group at three consecutive annual meetings. From this foundation, the American Psychological Association along with Vanderbilt University sponsored a workshop on developing a core battery of outcome assessment devices in the areas of depression, anxiety, and personality disorders. While these efforts are primarily directed at developing consistency in measurement across research studies, the focus on outcome measurement has increased parallel to the heightened awareness of outcome assessment in the public and private sectors. The instruments presented here are based in the mainstream outcome assessment yet will assist practitioners in their efforts to evaluate treatment efficacy, to demonstrate the need for additional resources to intervene effectively, or to make termination decisions based on empirical evidence of improvement.

We do not purport to be comprehensive in our coverage of potential psychotherapy outcome instruments. Several books already cover a variety of areas of assessment and measurement that are applicable to the assessment of psychotherapy outcome in clinical practice, including: *The Assessment of Psychotherapy Outcome* (Lambert, Christensen, & DeJulio, 1983), *Behavioral Assessment* (Bellack & Hersen, 1988), *Measures for Clinical Practice* (Corcoran & Fischer, 1987), *Measuring Mental Illness: Psychometric Assessment for Clinicians* (Wetzler, 1989), *Mea-

surement Strategies in Health Psychology (Karoly, 1985), *Psychotherapy Change Measures* (Waskow & Parloff, 1975), *The Psychotherapeutic Process: A Research Handbook* (Greenberg & Pinsoff, 1986), *The Scientist-Practitioner: Research and Accountability in Clinical and Educational Settings* (Barlow, Hayes, & Nelson, 1984), and others. A complete description of all possible methods of assessment that are directly or indirectly related to therapy outcome would not be practical or possible in a reasonably sized book and would likely not be pertinent to the everyday practitioner. As a result, we have painstakingly selected instruments that are commonly used, psychometrically sound, potentially useful, or quickly and easily implemented in clinical practice. We hope that this book will influence clinicians to conduct and become consumers of clinical research (Cohen, Sargent, & Sechrest, 1986; Goldfried, Greenberg, & Marmar, 1990).

We apologize to any who are offended by the instruments we have included or excluded. Some good outcome measures are not included for one reason or another. Because they appear promising, we included some recently developed instruments that have received minimal empirical support. In most cases, however, we presented instruments that have a long history of research and/or clinical use. To any who feel slighted by being left out, they can send a copy of their instrument with any related research regarding the instrument to Benjamin M. Ogles at Ohio University for future reference and potential inclusion in future related works.

In our effort to include a variety of practical instruments, we necessarily omitted details concerning the arduous task of development. We hope our scholarly friends will not be offended by our brevity. Perhaps the utility of this book will make up for any perceived lack of rigor. We believed it was important to include, at a minimum, information concerning the reliability and validity of the instruments chosen. Similarly, we occasionally felt obligated to include additional statistical details because of the newness of the methods or the need for clarification. We hope our clinical friends will tolerate these brief excursions and find the clinically relevant material they desire.

In one sense, we are not presenting any "new" information. Rather, we are repackaging the instruments that have been used consistently for several years in a way that will hopefully be appealing to practitioners. Previous attempts to encourage the evaluation of outcome in practice (e.g., Barlow, Hayes, & Nelson, 1984) have been largely unsuccessful. We hope that the time is right for outcome evaluation to be integrated with clinical practice and that this book will help contribute to that integration.

As is the case with any book, this one is the product not only of the authors but of the many people in supporting roles. We thank them for their encouragement, effort, and thoughtful participation. Special thanks go to Dan Cohen, Jaime Cunningham, Sterling Johnson, Cheryl Yatsko, Holly Wilson, Jodi Aronoff, and Kirk Lunnen, who reviewed and summarized instruments, made figures, and helped collect and double-check references. Thank you also to the following reviewers for their useful suggestions: Simon H. Budman, Harvard Community Health Plan, Boston, MA; Gary R. VanderBos, American Psychological Association; and Carol Yoken, Northern Illinois University. In conclusion, we also appreciate the efforts of Chris France and Edward Anderson, who made insightful comments after reviewing earlier versions of the book.

About the Authors

Benjamin M. Ogles received his Ph.D. from Brigham Young University in 1990 after completing a predoctoral clinical internship at the Indiana University Medical School. He is currently an assistant professor at Ohio University and a part-time clinician at Health Recovery Services in Marietta, Ohio.

Michael J. Lambert received his Ph.D. from the University of Utah in 1971. He has been a practicing clinician for the past 25 years. He is currently a professor of psychology at Brigham Young University. He is the author of numerous articles and books on the effects of psychotherapy on client outcome.

Kevin S. Masters received his Ph.D. from Brigham Young University in 1989 after completing a predoctoral internship at the Duke University Medical Center. He is currently an assistant professor of psychology at Utah State University. Dr. Masters has practiced in a variety of hospitals and community mental health centers and has published research in the areas of health psychology, sports psychology, and psychotherapy outcome.

Chapter 1

Why Measure Change?

"Quit smoking in just one week!" "Find greater happiness and success by following our do-it-yourself plan." "Learn relaxation skills in three easy lessons." "Within three months you can erase painful memories, regain control of your feelings, and be free to love again." Consumers are increasingly bombarded with these and other such claims that promote self-help psychological methods as effective agents of change. Similarly, individuals with widely varying degrees of academic and clinical experience (or lack thereof) are becoming involved in the business of trying to help people change. A quick look through the Yellow Pages of your local telephone book will reveal a diverse group of individuals who purport to have the expertise to facilitate human growth toward mental health.

While the methods of behavior change continue to proliferate, relatively little evidence is provided, apart from client and practitioner testimonials, to demonstrate the effectiveness of this bewildering array of interventions. Still, many individuals continue to practice with a firm belief that their methods work. However, some policy makers, third-party payers, and consumers continue to doubt the need for and effectiveness of psychological interventions. Perhaps they have good reason to be skeptical, since many treatments lack empirical evidence for their effectiveness. Certainly, quality research has been conducted to demonstrate that a narrow range of psychological interventions, broadly termed *psychotherapy*, are effective (Lambert & Bergin, 1994). Yet the creation of "new" supposedly earth-shattering interventions seems to occur on a daily basis with little or no empirical support for the efficacy of these interventions.

While researchers continue to bemoan the fact that many contemporary methods of practice are unsupported, clinicians argue that they cannot wait for randomized studies of every possible helping method, especially when treating the client who is sitting in their office today. Besides, research is often seen as clinically irrelevant, poorly conducted, and contradictory.

Nevertheless, increasing pressure is being placed on service providers to meet the needs of those seeking their services and simultaneously to demonstrate that their treatments are working. Policy makers expect demonstrations of treatment effectiveness if they are to provide funds for service provision. Third-party payers are becoming increasingly restrictive with payments for service. Consumers, likewise, are becoming more informed and selective regarding psychological services. And even if they resist external coercion, practitioners still have an ethical obligation to ensure that their methods are helpful.

Pressure from policy makers, third-party payers, and consumers can be bothersome. There is extra paperwork and payment restrictions for clients who have genuine needs. At the same time, however, the movement toward greater accountability can be a blessing in disguise. Clinicians who take steps to ascertain whether treatment is working with an individual client will also be better informed about that client's condition. In fact, Barlow, Hayes, and Nelson (1984) suggest three reasons for clinicians to assess outcome: (1) to improve treatment, (2) to enhance clinical science, and (3) to provide accountability. We would add to this list the ethical responsibility practitioners share for the welfare of their clients.

Clinicians who assess client improvement at regular intervals can adapt their treatment methods based on the feedback they receive. Resources may also be saved by early detection of unproductive interventions. In addition, because clients who are receiving psychological interventions do not always receive them in the manner that was intended, collecting data regarding the purity of treatment delivery may also improve ongoing interventions. For example, a measure of treatment integrity may enlighten the clinician to any treatment deviations and subsequently enhance the intervention (Barlow, Hayes, & Nelson, 1984).

Furthermore, as clinicians participate in the collection of outcome data, the breadth of clinically relevant research findings will increase. Using well-designed outcome measures with individual cases can provide valuable information that may lead to an expanded knowledge of therapy processes and to more effective techniques. These data may also lead to better planned and practically informed clinical trials by providing detailed descriptions of treatment processes that may lead to more precise discrimination of problems and treatments.

Third-party payers are increasing pressure on practitioners to produce evidence that their methods are effective before guaranteeing additional funding. They often expect to receive treatment progress reports that include objective evidence of specific change related to specific treatment goals, as well as a justification for continued treatment. Clinicians will have an easier time convincing third-party payers that their interventions are effective, or that there is a need for continued treatment, if they routinely use psychometrically sound outcome instruments.

Finally, clients seeking treatment expect quality service that is based on the best theories and empirical efforts. The highest standards of ethical practice are satisfied when clinicians explore and verify the effectiveness of their treatment methods. It is doubtful that clients' best interests are truly being served if clinicians do not continuously evaluate their ability to provide high-quality interventions. Practitioners not only have an ethical responsibility to clients, but also to the profession as a whole. Naturally, outcome evaluations should take the form of standardized assessment rather than unsystematic therapist impressions of client improvement.

With the changing health care system, the time is right to begin collecting outcome data. We hope that this book will encourage clinicians in a variety of mental health professions to begin the process of collecting outcome data. We also hope this book will provide sufficient information regarding procedures and instruments to make the process more bearable. Prior to introducing the clinician to a variety of commonly used outcome assessment instruments, we discuss the evolution of outcome measurement. We then present an organizational and conceptual scheme that can be used to guide the selection or evaluation of outcome instruments used in research or practice (Chapter 2). We then make practical suggestions for using the organizing scheme along with presenting concrete examples (Chapter 3). Next, we describe commonly used research-based outcome instruments that can be used by the clinician. For the sake of convenience, the instruments are discussed in four separate chapters: measures of global change (Chapter 4), measures of specific change (Chapter 5), measures of idiographic or personalized change (Chapter 6), and measures of moment-to-moment change (Chapter 7). We then include a chapter covering the clinical significance of psychotherapy outcome measurement (Chapter 8). Finally, we discuss ethical (Chapter 9) and methodological issues (Chapter 10), followed by some brief concluding remarks (Chapter 11).

C h a p t e r 2

An Organizational and Conceptual Scheme for Measuring Change

When implementing evaluation procedures into existing clinical settings, the method of outcome assessment becomes a key ingredient for determining client improvement and successful treatment. Which instruments should be used? By whom should they be rated? And when should the administration occur? These are all potentially difficult questions to answer. A highly sophisticated treatment evaluation program can be useless if the outcome assessment devices are unreliable, impractical, or invalid.

Although we are committed to the idea of helping clinicians evaluate their own work, we are not addressing this book to all components of evaluation procedures (e.g., experimental design). Our focus remains on the methods used to assess the outcome of therapy. In this chapter, we describe the evolution of therapy outcome assessment in research, the resultant chaos regarding multidimensional change, and an organizational and conceptual scheme that has been developed to guide the future application of outcome assessment in both research and practice.

Evolution of Outcome Assessment

Measuring change in or outcome of psychotherapy has proven to be a central and complicated, multidimensional issue in psychotherapy research. Table 2–1 proposes several dimensions upon which assessments have varied since the focus of initial research to the present and offers a hint of what the future may hold.

Early investigations characteristically relied solely on therapist ratings of client improvement (see Fenichel, 1930). These therapist ratings were frequently not based on published rating scales with operationally defined anchor points, but rather on

TABLE 2-1   Evolution of Outcome Assessment

Then	Now	Future
Therapist-rated change	Multiple sources	Most important sources
Ratings of global change	Specific change/ Multiple technologies	Clinically significant changes
Bound to theoretical orientation	Practically important/ symptomatic	Practical and theoretical within disorder
Change is unidirectional	For better or worse	Predicting better and worse
Change is unidimensional	Change is multidimensional	Most important dimensions
Changes are stable	Changes are unstable	Predicting patterns

clinical impressions. Consequently, similar definitions of improvement were not applied from one study to the next nor even from one patient to the next.

The next step was to use *standardized* therapist rating scales to measure general improvement. These therapist rating scales typically had anywhere between three and seven points, with each point being associated with a particular description (e.g., improved, much improved, very much improved). Measures were often taken prior to and just after treatment. Although the early versions had serious limitations (Lambert, 1983), more recent scales have addressed many of these concerns (see Chapter 5). Standardized therapist ratings continue to have an important and useful contribution to make toward the evaluation of therapy outcome, both in research and in everyday clinical practice. At the same time, the possibility of bias has led to the creation of additional measures that provide another perspective on client change.

Following the use of therapist ratings came an emphasis on patient self-reports. Again, in the early stages, these measures were often global judgments of the value of therapy. The measures were only collected at the end of therapy since it made no sense to evaluate therapy prior to its implementation. Later efforts have included many structured personality tests, symptom rating scales, and the like, usually collected in a pre/posttreatment manner (e.g., MMPI [Hathaway & McKinley, 1983], Symptom Checklist-90 [Derogatis, 1983], Beck Depression Inventory [Beck, Ward, Mendelson, Mock, & Erbaugh, 1961]). Self-report measures provide a unique and important source of information regarding change occurring during psychotherapy. Self-report measures are particularly appealing in clinical practice where customer satisfaction is more important than research aims. In addition, self-report measures require less clinician time. Some concern remains, however, regarding the exclusive use of patient self-report as a means of evaluating treatment outcome. As a result of being an integral part of the therapy process, clients may have a limited perspective about changes occurring during treatment. In short, self-report measures provide an important yet potentially biased report of therapy outcome.

In an attempt to overcome the problems of therapist- and client-rated measures, many researchers turned to the use of persons not involved in therapy who were blind to treatment status as raters of outcome. These independent raters utilized scales of both global and specific natures. In addition, many of the rating scales targeted overt behaviors, which was particularly important for evaluating the effectiveness of behavioral therapies.

In a similar vein, investigators continued to search for "objective" measures as they utilized physiological indices and environmentally generated data (e.g., student grades, hospital readmissions). However, like their predecessors, these measures had many difficulties. For example, change in subjective experience often did not correspond with change in physiological measures. Environmental data were subject to a host of confounding influences, including policy decisions and other factors that were extraneous to therapy and generally considered to be irrelevant to measuring treatment outcome.

Another common trend has been for therapy researchers to employ measurement devices that are strongly affiliated with their particular theoretical position. Instruments rooted in Freudian dynamic psychology (e.g., Rorschach, TAT, etc.) represented the first manifestation of this tendency. Today, however, these tests have largely been discarded as measures of outcome (Lambert, Shapiro, & Bergin, 1986; Lambert, 1983). Following the dynamically based assessments came the use of devices consistent with client-centered theory (e.g., Q-sort technique). Finally, with the growth of behavioral and cognitive orientations to therapy came measures established in these traditions. Today, most clinicians and researchers recognize the need to go beyond the exclusive use of measures intimately associated with a particular theory. It is clear, however, that theoretical concerns still play a major role in determining what clinicians value as outcome appraisers (Cohen, 1980). Many researchers include multiple measures of outcome in order to include both theoretical and atheoretical perspectives on change. They intend to measure what is practically important as well as theoretically meaningful.

As can be seen, the measurement of psychotherapy outcome has substantially evolved from unstandardized, global, unidimensional, unidirectional assessment to assessment of multiple perspectives using standardized rating scales for specific treatment-related issues. Current research is much improved and generates useful information from a variety of sources regarding multiple potential outcomes of psychological treatments. These changes in research-related measures of outcome can be of substantial benefit to the clinician. The evolution of outcome measurement in research has resulted in several high-quality instruments that have good psychometric qualities, along with data for comparison with both clinical and normative samples while maintaining a level of brevity to make them practical for clinical use. We will present several of these instruments in Chapters 4 through 8. Before presenting these instruments, however, an organizational and conceptual scheme for considering the instruments is presented.

Multidimensional Chaos

Although the evolution of outcome measurement has created numerous positive changes in the way therapy outcome is viewed, the multidimensional assessment of therapy outcome also brings with it several problems. For example, multidimensional assessment in some research studies unfortunately consists of administering several different self-report instruments while leaving other sources of information (e.g., trained observers, significant others, therapists) untapped. In addition, measuring multiple *sources* of outcome data does not guarantee that the richness and complexity of change occurring during therapy will be adequately captured. Multidimensional assessment of outcome has also started to disintegrate into an infinite number of dimensions as each investigator develops and uses his or her own measure of each therapy-related variable. In fact, much of what occurs in outcome research appears to be lacking in any conceptual or organizational consistency, and there is still a wide range of opinion among practicing clinicians concerning desirable patient change measures.

Adding to this lack of diversity of opinion is the multitude of measures available. Froyd and Lambert (1989) surveyed instruments and procedures currently in use as techniques for measuring psychotherapy outcome and were startled to discover the seemingly endless number of measures. In a review of 348 studies published in 20 journals between 1983 and 1989, 1,430 outcome measures were found. Amazingly, of this total, 840 measures were used a single time! The blow is softened by noting that the review considered a wide variety of patient diagnoses, treatment modalities, and therapy types (Froyd & Lambert, 1989). At the same time, the number of measures that are in use could be expanded if one considers that some measures such as the Hamilton Rating Scale for Depression (Hamilton, 1967) is actually not a single scale, but a scale with many variants (Grundy, Lunnen, Lambert, Ashton, & Tovey, 1994)

In part to address this issue, a subsequent review was conducted that examined only studies of agoraphobia outcome published during the 1980s (Ogles & Lambert, 1989; Ogles, Lambert, Weight, & Payne, 1990). In the 106 studies located, 98 unique outcome measures were found. This is truly remarkable when one considers that the area of investigation (i.e., agoraphobia) is well defined and limited and is treated with an equally narrow range of interventions, mainly behavioral and cognitive/behavioral therapies.

This lack of organization and direction for current practices and procedures is striking, and outcome measurement has become increasingly chaotic. There are probably many reasons for this, including the fact that clients often participate in multifaceted treatments and that change is a multidimensional phenomenon. It is much too simple to routinely expect clients to show invariable and integrated improvement as a result of therapy. Consequently, methodological divergence is to be expected and, within limits, encouraged. Yet the extreme lack of consistency, replication, and organization that characterizes outcome measurement is disheartening and slows progress in the field. How can clinicians be expected to apply research findings when the research itself is characterized by such confusion? Which, if any, of the multitude of outcome measures currently used in research should clinicians choose when they are interested in evaluating the effectiveness of their own practice? The chaotic state of measurement in research serves to weaken the confidence that practitioners have in research and consequently provides an obstacle for the practical application of research findings.

It is clear that there are many different perspectives and issues to be considered when addressing outcome measurement. The patient, family, therapist, and society all have an established interest and potentially valuable perspectives from which to view therapy outcome. Additionally, matters pertaining to values and theory will influence the choice of therapeutic goals and consequently what is considered to be a desirable outcome (Bergin, 1980). These factors are important in the choice of measures (Schacht & Henry, 1992). Not surprisingly, conclusions about the effects of therapy may depend heavily on the particular measure that is used in assessing patient change.

Several interested parties have attempted to bring order to the disarray that has been rampant in conceptualizing outcome measurement. For example, as early as 1975, the National Institute of Mental Health (NIMH) sponsored an outcome measures project culminating in the publication of *Psychotherapy Change Measures* edited by Waskow and Parloff (1975). This text suggested a core battery of assessment procedures to be used in addressing patient change. Unfortunately, this important and well-meaning effort to bring consistency to outcome assessment has not resulted in widespread use of the core battery. In hindsight, it appears that few researchers or practitioners adopted the recommendations of the NIMH consultants in the ensuing years.

In addition to Waskow and Parloff (1975), several others have attempted to bring more order to the assessment of change. Curious readers are referred to works by Strupp and Hadley (1977), Gelso (1979), Ciarlo, Edwards, Kiresuk, Newman, and Brown (1981), Lambert (1983), Lambert, Ogles, and Masters (1992), and Elliot (1992). These efforts to organize the assessment of outcome have been largely motivated by the need to create a body of research studies that all use similar instruments. However, consistency in outcome measurement in research will also lead to increased utility of research instruments for practitioners.

In the rest of this chapter, we present an organizational and conceptual scheme for considering outcome measures. The scheme can be used as a framework for considering a variety of outcome measures in order to select those that may be the most appropriate for clinical applications. The scheme originated in reviews of the psychotherapy outcome literature (Bergin & Lambert, 1978; Lambert, Shapiro, & Bergin, 1986; Lambert, Christensen, & DeJulio, 1983) and has continued to evolve (Lambert, 1983; Lambert & Hill, 1994; Lambert, Masters, & Ogles, 1991, 1992; Lambert, Ogles, & Masters, 1992). As a result of our interactions with other professionals and reconsideration of primary issues, we have continued to modify the basic scheme. What is presented here is the most recent version.

An Organizational and Conceptual Scheme

Given the divergent processes that occur during psychotherapy and the complexity of human functioning and change, multiple assessments of psychotherapy outcome are necessary. But how should one go about choosing the most appropriate outcome measures? As a guide to answering this question, we offer the scheme depicted in Table 2–2. It is an idealistic scheme designed to give purpose and direction to the selection of a final assessment package. Of course practical limitations such as time,

TABLE 2–2   Organizational and Conceptual Scheme

Content	Social Level	Source	Technology	Time Orientation
Cognition	Intrapersonal	Self	Global	Trait
1	1	1	1	1
2	2	2	2	2
•	•	•	•	•
Affect	Interpersonal	Therapist	Specific	State
1	1	1	1	1
2	2	2	2	2
•	•	•	•	•
Behavior	Social Role	Trained Observer	Observation	
1	1	1	1	
2	2	2	2	
•	•	•	•	
		Relevant Other	Status	
		1	1	
		2	2	
		•	•	
			•	
		Institutional		
		1		
		2		
		•		

money, and client comfort must also be considered and in the final analysis will often place severe limitations on the type of measures that may be used in outcome assessment. Most practicing clinicians are going to rely largely on measures that utilize therapist or self-report sources of information. However, in some settings (e.g., medical centers), opportunities for more diversified measurement exist and should be taken advantage of. We are asking clinicians/investigators to be open to the possibilities that exist within the field of measurement and thereby to incorporate instruments that adequately cover the domain of interest. In essence, by using this scheme, researchers and clinicians will be better able to organize the measurement of therapy outcome.

Apart from guiding clinicians/researchers in the conduct of their ongoing and future investigations, the scheme has many additional uses. For example, clinicians may find it helpful to think in terms of the scheme as they conduct the routine assessments that are part of their consultation or treatment duties. Clinicians will also benefit by coming to understand better the specific effects produced by their interventions. The scheme should help them in this area. For example, clinicians who learn that their clients evidence strong cognitive change but weak behavioral change may choose to revise their treatments accordingly. At the agency level, use of the scheme may help in the formulation of record-keeping requirements and may also serve as a basis for staff development. It will also assist reviewers as they compare the results of many studies that use a variety of instruments. This will allow clinicians to learn more about what they specifically do and do not know.

In some instances, one will likely find holes in the assessment net where certain types of measures have not been used frequently enough with certain disorders. Forgetting to measure particular aspects of the disturbance may greatly limit what can be said about the overall effects of therapies. In one study that utilized the scheme for this purpose, Froyd and Lambert (1989) found that in major journals over a five-year period the typical study included 3.5 measures that most often assessed the intrapersonal social level, using self-report ratings, and symptom-specific measures. Alternatively, by demonstrating that some kinds of instruments are empirically related, the need for measuring each possible element of outcome can be eliminated in future studies. In any case, by consistently employing the scheme, one can come to know more about the state of the art/science of psychotherapy outcome and thereby be in a better position to draw reliable and accurate conclusions.

Used for didactic purposes, students could employ the scheme to conceptualize the limitations of proposed or existing studies by listing measures according to the specified dimensions. This will help them to be clear in their thinking and purposeful in their measurement. Students who have been taught to use the scheme in their classes will also be more likely to base their subsequent investigations and conclusions from the literature on its dimensions. We believe that this could have a decided impact on the profession.

The Schematic Dimensions

The specific dimensions included in this system include content, social level, source, technology, and time orientation. Although they are not completely independent, we believe the dimensions provide a precise, consistent, and, most importantly, useful way to organize assessments.

Content

The content dimension answers the question: What psychological area is being measured? This includes consideration of behavioral, cognitive, and affective faculties. Some may consider the physiological category to reflect a separate realm (Elliot, 1992); however, we include it as behavior. This is not to downplay physiological measures. We recognize that they are currently viewed as being particularly important for certain areas of psychology (e.g., health psychology) and are of at least some importance to most psychological investigations. However, as Kaplan (1990) has correctly and insightfully demonstrated, it is easy to become fascinated with physiological measures and their apparent "objectivity" at the expense of behavioral assessment. He argues convincingly that physiological measures are only important insofar as they predict or relate to some behavioral outcome. Since, strictly speaking, physiological functioning reflects behavior of the organism, we believe that it is both desirable and correct to include physiology as a subset of behavior.

Social Level

The social level dimension represents a continuum depicting the degree to which an instrument measures intrapsychic (internal) attributes of the client versus more broadly defined characteristics of the client's interpersonal (external) world. We have somewhat arbitrarily included three anchor points. These indicate that some instruments are developed to assess outcome that is primarily intrapsychic—for example, measures of mood, self-concept, self-control, negative cognitions, behavioral deficits, and so on. Interpersonal measures reflect the client's adjustment in areas of friendship and intimacy. Specific instruments in this area include marital adjustment scales, some aspects of social adjustment rating scales, and measures of sexual adjustment. The largest or most broad social level includes the client's adjustment to his or her social role performance within the society at large. Measures in this area could entail adjustment at work, in school, as pertaining to socially appropriate behavior (e.g., delinquency, antisocial conduct), and the like.

Source

The dimension considering source of outcome information answers the question: Who is making the assessment? It is divided into five categories: client self-report, therapist rating, relevant others (e.g., spouse, friend, work mate), trained observers or judges, and institutional referents (e.g., work and hospitalization records, public records of arrest, etc.). This dimension approximates a hierarchy of participation in treatment, beginning with the most involved sources (i.e., client and therapist) and moving to the more remote ones (i.e., others and institutions).

Obviously, this is a fluid dimension; depending on the particular setting and circumstances of the individual(s) involved, the exact ordering of these sources (particularly the observers, others, and institutions) could vary. But it is clear that they represent different points of view and likely different levels and types of motivation that could influence ratings. The ultimate significance or meaning of the information gained from these different sources will vary for each individual researcher or clinician. For example, involvement in therapy has been viewed alternately as both positive and negative for outcome assessment. On the one hand, it is the most involved sources (i.e., clients and therapists) who are the most informed about the details of change and perhaps the most important informants regarding the success of treatment (see Beutler & Crago, 1983; Newman, 1983). On the other hand, some consider these sources to be the most reactive sources of outcome information (Smith, Glass, & Miller, 1980), since the data are obtained from those who have the most to gain or lose from the results of the evaluation. By weighing the advantages and disadvantages involved in using each source category, outcome measurement will be tailored to the needs of each clinician's need for information.

Technology

The fourth dimension has proven difficult to precisely name and has undergone previous revision. Presently, we are calling it the technology dimension because instruments vary in terms of their methodology or technology of data collection. In addition, the measures tend to vary based on the degree to which they produce large or small effects in studies of outcome. For example, it is probable that a global measure asking the client to give a gross estimate of improvement will produce a relatively large effect (Smith, Glass, & Miller, 1980; Lambert & Hill, 1994). Examples of this kind of instrument include postservice questionnaires aimed at rating the effectiveness of service and quality of therapy provided at a clinic. Measures, such as the Symptom Checklist-90-R (Derogatis, 1983) or the Beck Depression Inventory (BDI; Beck, Ward, Mendelson, Mock, & Erbaugh, 1961) that ask for an evaluation of current symptomatology use a slightly different technology and will tend to be more rigorous. Observer ratings fall next on the continuum followed by status data. Status data are the final technology category, which includes a heterogeneous group of measurements, such as weight, electromyograph readings of muscle tension, blood levels of drugs, and so on, along with other current status indicators (e.g., separated, divorced, hospitalized, etc.).

A few comments regarding this last dimension may help to reduce confusion and clarify our intent. Less rigorous measures using one technology are not necessarily less valuable, whereas more rigorous measures using a different technology are not necessarily more valuable. The particular purposes and values of the person assessing the outcome, practical limitations, unique characteristics of the setting and clients, and the intended audience will all affect decisions relevant to selecting measures. Nevertheless, it is important to know that certain measures are more likely to depict strong effects than are other measures. The best evidence of a powerful treatment will occur when there are results showing hardy outcomes from a variety of points along this technology or rigor dimension. There is also some overlap among the anchor points of this dimension with those of other dimensions. Despite this impurity, however, the technology dimension should include all of the categories depicted in order to serve its purpose as a guide.

Time Orientation

The final dimension included in this conceptual scheme is time orientation. The time orientation dimension reflects the degree to which the instrument attempts to measure a stable, trait-like characteristic versus an unstable, state-like characteristic. Ultimately, of course, it is an empirical question as to whether a particular attribute maintains consistency across time and situations and astute investigators will attend to this issue. Nevertheless, many instruments are constructed and established with this dimension in mind and have demonstrated the trait-or state-like qualities of the constructs being measured. Consequently, we believe that time orientation may serve as a useful guide in choosing outcome measures. Ultimately, of course, the merit of this dimension, as well as that of the whole scheme, will be determined by its heuristic, organizational, and practical consequences.

Each outcome instrument can be rated and classified on all five dimensions. For example, the Beck Depression Inventory (BDI) would be considered primarily an affective *content* measure (although both behavior and cognition are included) assessing the intrapersonal *social level* utilizing self as the *source* with a *technology* typical for specific measures and a state-like *time orientation*. In actual practice, the identification of categories covered by different instruments may help individuals to choose instruments based on their unique or overlapping qualities. Some may use the conceptual scheme to select the one most efficient method for evaluating outcome in their practice. Others may purposely choose two or more instruments that address the same categories in an effort to demonstrate the reliability of the assessment or as part of an empirical comparison of the alternatives. In other circumstances, individuals may use the scheme to select outcome assessment methods that come from different categories as a way of representing different axes of multidimensional change. Reviewers may use the scheme as a way of evaluating outcome assessment over a large number of studies in a particular area (e.g., Froyd & Lambert, 1989; Lambert, Ogles, & Masters, 1992; Ogles, Lambert, Weight, & Payne, 1990). In any case, great care should be exercised in the choice of measurement instruments, and the conceptual scheme may provide a useful organizing context for assisting the selection process.

A Final Note Concerning the Role of Theory

Our scheme, by design, ignores psychotherapy theories or orientation. This is not, however, meant to imply that theory should be excluded from consideration when choosing outcome measures. Instead, theory could play a prominent role in the choice of outcome assessment instruments. Theoretical considerations are of great importance to those who subscribe to their particular doctrine. Furthermore, the results of outcome studies can be used to improve theories. Nevertheless, narrow and exclusionary use of theoretically based instruments will *not* prove convincing to the large body of parties interested in the effectiveness of various forms of psychotherapy.

The scheme suggests that theorists pay attention to the many types of assessments necessary to obtain adequate and convincing results. We posit that theoretical research should attempt to show that changes in clients can be observed by instruments associated with both large and small effects, utilizing a variety of sources, across numerous content areas and social levels, with varying time orientations. Then researchers and practitioners can truly say that their theories of change have been supported and that the treatment was effective. This kind of result could not help but influence third-party reimbursers, academicians and clinicians, as well as the public at large.

Chapter 3

Measuring Change
in Practice

Research designed to investigate the effectiveness of psychotherapy has dramatically changed over the past 80 years. Research designs are more sophisticated, measurement methods are more psychometrically sound, more measures are used to address multiple dimensions of change, and the hypotheses are more specific. Despite these improvements, psychotherapy research has had a minimal impact on the practice of psychotherapy. Oftentimes, the research is loaded with heavy statistics or theoretical questions that are too abstract or irrelevant to practicing clinicians. Another problem is the use of analog situations or populations with little similarity to patients seen in practice. With increasing pressure from external sources to demonstrate treatment effectiveness, however, researchers may finally have a useful if not necessary tool to offer the clinician. The psychotherapy outcome instruments reviewed later in this book can be used in practice to demonstrate client change, provide useful pretherapy information, and perhaps lead to broader theories of change. In addition, when the instruments presented in this book are not sufficient, the organizational and conceptual scheme will provide a method for considering other potentially useful measures. The choice, however, remains in the hands of practitioners. Outcome instruments will not be helpful if they are never used.

As clinicians, we understand the difficulties of implementing our own suggestions. Clients often have numerous forms to complete and may resist completing additional questionnaires. The last thing any therapist needs is more paperwork to do in the supposed 10-minute gap between clients. Certainly, the prospect of hiring trained judges to rate client progress or to conduct diagnostic interviews is fiscally impossible in most instances and at best pragmatically difficult in others.

But clinicians are being faced with increasing pressure to demonstrate and evaluate client benefit from treatment. We believe that practitioners can implement many of our suggestions with minimal headaches. Once the evaluation mechanisms are in place, they may well generate enough practical information to outweigh the cost. In many clinical settings, once an outcome evaluation plan is implemented, it will take care of itself.

Guidelines

To assist in the initiation of this process, this chapter includes recommendations for selecting and implementing the assessment of therapy outcome based on the differing practical problems faced by practitioners in a variety of clinical settings. Each outcome device has practical advantages and limitations. To aid the clinician in sorting out the details, the conceptual scheme is used to evaluate the practical utility of each class of instruments. The organizational and conceptual scheme includes five dimensions: content, social level, source, technology, and time orientation. Each instrument can be classified on all five of the dimensions. The Fear Questionnaire (Marks & Mathews, 1978), for example, is a self-report (source) instrument that taps an unstable (time orientation), intrapersonal (social level) characteristic in the cognitive/affective content area (content). The Fear Questionnaire is generally used as a pretest/posttest or specific assessment method (technology). By selecting instruments using the organizational and conceptual scheme, clinicians can identify areas of assessment that will minimize organization-specific implementation costs and maximize the production of practical information. Several guidelines will assist the process.

1. *Identify the content area, social level, and time orientation.* Clinicians and organizations who are selecting outcome assessment devices will value different types of information. Some clinicians are most interested in behavioral change, whereas others may be interested in cognitive or emotional change. A clinician who routinely conducts family and marital therapy will be more interested in interpersonal change than the "depth" psychotherapist who would also like information regarding intrapersonal change. In contrast, the case manager may request an outcome assessment device that evaluates changes in social role performance (e.g., vocational status or living arrangements). Similarly, some organizations may use instruments that assess unstable characteristics such as mood, whereas those involved in long-term psychotherapy may be more interested in the assessment of outcome using measures of stable personality traits. The point is that three dimensions of the organizational scheme—content area, social level, and time orientation—are a matter of preference. Each clinician can select those instruments that assess the areas and levels that tap dimensions he or she values most. Of course, administrative personnel and third-party payers may desire information regarding a specific outcome. In this case, an appropriate instrument can be selected to obtain the required data.

2. *Select nonredundant instruments.* In general, selecting a variety of instruments while considering each dimension will be the most useful method for evaluating change. For example, a self-report instrument that assesses unstable, intrapersonal characteristics in the affect content area used before and after treatment should *not* be accompanied by a second instrument that does the same. A better choice might be a therapist report instrument that rates stable, interpersonal characteristics in the behavioral content area both before and after treatment. Of course, there are circumstances where category overlap is preferred, such as when investigating the concurrent validity of an instrument or when attempting to establish the effectiveness of an intervention from the perspective of both the parent and child. In most clinical settings, however, choosing a variety of instruments across dimensions will generate the broadest range of usable information. In some clinical situations, only one instrument will be selected to reduce cost and time. When only one instrument is selected, careful consideration should be given to finding an instrument that provides information regarding the desired categories from each dimension.

3. *Examine the source by technology matrix.* Whereas the content area, social level, and time orientation are primarily a matter of personal preference or administrative mandate, the source and technology dimensions have a clear impact on the daily operation of a practice or clinic. Determining if an instrument should be completed by the client, the therapist, or a trained judge has important ramifications for any clinical organization. Time and money are both at stake. The limitations of using a particular source or technology, therefore, are important to consider. At the same time, there are advantages to using certain sources or technology categories that must also be considered. Tables 3–1, 3–2, and 3–3 were developed to assist readers in considering these advantages and disadvantages. In Table 3–1, an example instrument is listed from each category using the source by technology matrix. In Tables 3–2 and 3–3, some of the advantages and disadvantages of these categories are described.

As can be seen, there are advantages and limitations for each category in the matrix. It is impossible to select the one "best" method of assessing client outcome. Rather, there are a variety of ways to assess outcome, each with advantages and limitations. For a large mental health outpatient clinic, postservice questionnaires may

TABLE 3–1   Example Outcome Measures for the Technology by Source Matrix

| Source | Technology | | | |
	Global	*Specific*	*Observation*	*Status*
Self	CSQ-8	BDI	Panic Diary	Employment status
Therapist	Global rating of client improvement	HRSD	In-class behavioral observation	Diagnosis
Trained observer	GAS—Judge rated	SADS-C	Behavioral Approach Test	Need for medication
Relevant other	Global rating of marital adjustment	CBCL—Teacher rated	Bedwetting frequency	Divorce
Institutional	Successful completion of program	Absenteeism data	Nursing notes	Recidivism

TABLE 3–2   Disadvantages of Instruments by Cell in the Technology by Source Matrix

| Source | Technology | | | |
	Global	*Specific*	*Observation*	*Status*
Self	Halo effect	Drop out	Client reliability (e.g., lying, distortion, denial)	Tougher to show changes
Therapist	Lacks detailed information	Requires therapist time; may require session time	Often not amenable to office setting	May require some detective work to collect
Trained observer	May not include assessment of pretest characteristics	Need more than one staff member involved with each client	Cost ($)	Time consuming
Relevant other	Others may not cooperate	Requires clinician time to oversee completion of instruments	May require travel; time consuming; expensive	Difficult to acquire data
Institutional	Difficult to pin down "causes"	May contain useless or uninformative data	Difficult to compile or organize unless an existing database exists	Affected by client mobility

be the most cost-effective method of assessing client satisfaction and perception of change. Of course, postservice questionnaires do not reflect pre- to posttreatment change as accurately as other methods of assessment. Similarly, the questionnaires may be completed only by a portion of those who received service. Finally, postservice questionnaires do not include other perspectives on client change (e.g., therapist, significant others). Nevertheless, postservice questionnaires can be easily collected, can reach a large number of individuals, and will reflect the attitude of the consumers who respond to the survey. These advantages may be the perfect match for some outpatient organizations.

On the other hand, a clinician in the private practice, who has more control over the number of clients entering treatment and the amount of intake information collected, may decide to select a short battery to administer to each client at the beginning and end of treatment. This battery may include measures such as the Symptom Checklist-90-R, Beck Depression Inventory, or Fear Questionnaire. Again, there are problems with this approach. Not all clients will return to complete the posttreatment battery because of dropout or for other reasons. Some clients may have issues that are not reflected in the selected measures. And like the postservice questionnaire, the self-report battery will not include other individuals' perceptions of client change. However, the advantages of a self-report battery that can be quickly completed by the clients may outweigh these disadvantages.

TABLE 3–3   Advantages of Instruments by Cell in the Technology by Source Matrix

| Source | Technology | | | |
	Global	Specific	Observation	Status
Self	Generally shows change; reaches large numbers	Easily administered	Prima facie evidence of change	Reflects clinically relevant change
Therapist	Ease of administration	Evidence of pre/post change	Involves actual behaviors	Often includes components of quality of life
Trained observer	Quick administration	Usually standardized	Easily tailored to the individual	Reflects professional viewpoint
Relevant other	Extra data source	Good evidence of generalization to other settings	Encourages involvement of others	Reflects society's viewpoint
Institutional	Easily compiled	Norms may be available	Generally produced as a part of routine procedures	Not as affected by rater bias (nonreactive)

For research endeavors aimed at getting the most reliable and valid data, instruments are generally selected that have a more rigorous methodology. Pre- and posttesting is favored over retrospective ratings of improvement (Waskow & Parloff, 1975; Beutler & Crago, 1983), and independent observer ratings are important to include in addition to therapist and client ratings. These types of outcome measures will also be extremely useful in some clinical settings. Again, however, every instrument has practical limitations. Judge ratings may be expensive and time consuming to obtain. Therapist ratings require additional paperwork by the therapist. Pre/post ratings, as opposed to post only ratings, require more patient time and extra data collection forms. Each clinician will need to weigh the costs and benefits of obtaining outcome information from different sources using a variety of methodologies before determining which instruments will be the most practical.

4. *Consider nonreactive or unobtrusive data sources.* Recent public policy is directed at increasing accountability among service organizations operated by governmental agencies. This accountability is often referred to in the context of collecting outcome data. Public servants want services that are efficient and high quality, and that put the consumers first. However, outcome data collected using standardized outcome instruments are sometimes considered to be irrelevant in this arena. For example, diagnoses, MMPI scores (Hathaway & McKinley, 1983), and Child Behavior Checklist scores (CBCL; Achenbach, 1978) are not generally understood by consumers or public administrators. As a result, outcome information that is closer to the source may be required. For example, days in school, current residential status, days on the job, suicide attempts, or number of hospitalization days are all considered practical ways of gauging the effectiveness of treatments for people with chronic mental disturbance. Unobtrusively collected data regarding client behaviors may be particularly useful when dealing with legislators and lay consumers because of the immediate utility of the information. In mental health centers, some of these data may be routinely collected. For the private practitioner, however, unobtrusive data may be difficult to collect. Nevertheless, creative ways of collecting data may be helpful for demonstrating the effectiveness of treatment.

A Clinical Example

To further aid in the application of the scheme, a brief example is presented using a private practitioner as the guide. Suppose that you are in a group or private practice in which you would like to begin evaluating the outcome of clients who receive outpatient therapy. Further suppose that you have no measurement instruments in mind that might help to assess change. Turning to our model, the first issue is to select preferred content, time, and social level categories. If the outpatient practice is geared toward specific types of clients (e.g., clients with eating disorders, clients with headaches, etc.), instruments may need to cover the specific affective, cognitive, and behavioral content areas that are involved with this type of client. If the practice is a more general practice, a more broad instrument that covers a range of behavioral, cognitive, and affective content areas may be selected. Social level categories can also be selected to match the patient population. Therapists who work in employee assistance programs (EAPs) may prefer an instrument that addresses functioning at work. Similarly, therapists who are involved in marital therapy will want an instrument that assesses satisfaction with or level of functioning within an intimate relationship. In addition, the stability of the instrument should also be considered so that the instrument will be sufficiently sensitive to measure changes occurring during treatment.

Once preferred content, social role, and time orientation categories are selected, instruments can be identified to match these needs. If more than one instrument is to be used with each client, you can attempt to limit the redundancy of the instruments by examining their ratings on the various scheme categories. In many cases, only one instrument will be selected for each client. Perhaps all clients will receive the same global measure or, in some cases, one of several specific measures (e.g., one for people who are depressed, one for people with relationship problems, etc.). In some circumstances, no existing measure will cover the preferred content or social role categories. In this case, you can develop a measure to fit the need or select a measure from an alternative category.

After selecting instruments that cover preferred categories, the field can be narrowed by examining the source by technology matrix. For example, the Beck Depression Inventory (BDI; Beck et al., 1961), the Hamilton Rating Scale for Depression (HRSD; Hamilton, 1960, 1967), the Zung Self-Rating Depression Scale (ZSRDS; Zung, 1965), and the Inventory to Diagnose Depression (IDD; Zimmerman & Coryell,

1987) all cover depressive symptoms to some degree. Three (BDI, ZSRDS, and IDD) of the instruments are rated by the client, and one is rated by a judge or therapist (HRSD). Three (BDI, ZSRDS, and IDD) of the instruments use a specific technology, whereas the fourth (HRSD) is rated by a trained observer. Based on an evaluation of the source by technology categories while considering preferred categories of content, social role, and time orientation, an instrument or instruments can be selected for use in your practice.

In addition to collecting outcome data using traditional measures, nonobtrusive data (e.g., absenteeism for EAP clients or truancy for adolescent clients) can also be considered and collected as an index of outcome for some clients. Particularly for practitioners working in mental health centers or facilities that routinely collect other data, nonreactive data may be easily collected and practically important.

The conceptual scheme can guide practitioners to instruments that cover specific areas of outcome that they would like to assess. It will be particularly useful when the clinician has no predefined direction for selecting instruments or when choosing among a variety of existing instruments. In the next portion of the book, a number of existing practical methods for assessing outcome will be presented. The instruments represent a select group of instruments that are used in research and that have promise in the clinical arena. At the same time, a variety of instruments are presented so organizations with different needs will retain several options. In each chapter, the instruments presented will be described as well as placed within the organizational framework.

Summary

By selecting nonredundant instruments that consider user-preferred content, time, and social level categories, and by using the most cost-effective sources and methodologies of information while considering unobtrusive data collection methods, each practitioner can develop a reasonable system for collecting outcome data. Of course, each system will have limitations, yet outcome information with limitations is better than no outcome information at all. Similarly, there will be difficulties with the implementation of such a system. However, the benefits will, in time, outweigh the costs. Besides, outcome evaluation may soon be mandatory, so initiation of the procedures now is good preventive medicine.

C h a p t e r 4

Global Measures of Outcome

The inclusion of outcome assessment devices in clinical settings can make their most important contribution by allowing clinicians to evaluate if clients are benefiting in some global fashion from treatment. Are clients generally improved following treatment? Are there subsets of clients who do not improve? Are there particular services (e.g., group, individual, family) that are more successful than others? Do specific therapists have higher improvement rates with certain populations? These and similar questions may be addressed by using global outcome assessment devices. In the average clinical practice, a simple pre/postassessment of global improvement is likely to be the most common. This chapter highlights some of the more frequently used research instruments that include a global measure of improvement.

Deciding which instruments to present in this chapter was a difficult task, and there are adequate measures that will not be described. In addition to the criteria used for all measures selected for presentation, as stated in the Preface (e.g., commonly used, psychometrically sound, potentially useful, and quickly and easily implemented in practice), measures selected for this chapter provide a global measure of an area of importance to many practitioners such as behavioral adjustment, general symptomatology, or marital satisfaction. For example, even though it has specific scales, the Marital Satisfaction Inventory (Snyder, 1981) was included because it provides a global measure of marital satisfaction. Similarly, the Symptom Checklist-90-Revised was included because it has three global scales of distress in addition to the nine specific scales. For each instrument, we will provide basic information to assist readers in making an informed judgment as to whether they would like to gather additional information regarding the instrument. Each of the instruments and its conceptual scheme ratings is presented in Table 4–1. Additional information regarding all instruments reviewed in this book is presented in the Appendices.

TABLE 4–1   Global Measures of Outcome with Category Ratings

| | Conceptual and Organizational Scheme Categories | | | | |
Measure	Content	Social Level	Source	Technology	Time Orientation
SCL-90-R	Mixed	Intrapersonal	Self	Specific	State
BSI	Mixed	Intrapersonal	Self	Specific	State
SCL-90 Analog	Mixed	Intrapersonal	Rater	Specific	State
MSI	Mixed	Interpersonal	Self	Specific	State
GAS	Mixed	Intrapersonal	Therapist/rater	Global	State
CGAS	Behavior	Intrapersonal/ interpersonal	Therapist/rater	Global	State
SCID	Behavior	Intrapersonal	Therapist/rater	Status/global	Trait
SADS-C	Mixed	Intrapersonal	Therapist/rater	Status/global	Trait
KAS	Mixed	Interpersonal	Self/other	Specific	State
SAS	Mixed	Interpersonal	Self	Specific	State
Health Sickness Rating Scale	Mixed	Intrapersonal	Therapist/rater	Global	State
OQ	Mixed	Intrapersonal	Self	Specific	State

Review of Instruments

The Symptom Checklist-90-Revised (SCL-90-R) and Related Measures

The SCL-90-R (Derogatis, 1983) is a 90-item self-report symptom inventory. It was originally developed as the Hopkins Symptom Checklist (Derogatis, Lipman, Rickels, Uhlenhuth, & Covi, 1974), after which the instructions and a few items were minimally changed to create the SCL-90-R. Each item is rated on a 5-point scale of distress (0 = not at all; 1 = a little bit; 2 = moderately; 3 = quite a bit; 4 = extremely). There are nine primary symptom dimensions (somatization, obsessive-compulsive, interpersonal sensitivity, depression, anxiety, hostility, phobic anxiety, paranoid ideation, and psychoticism) and three global indices of distress of which the most important is the Global Severity Index (GSI). The GSI is the best single indicator of the current level or depth of disturbance. The GSI is based on all 90 items and is often used as a single global measure of outcome since it combines information on the number of symptoms and the intensity of the perceived distress.

The SCL-90-R was intended as a measure of current psychological symptom status and not as a measure of personality. It may be used repeatedly to document trends or as part of a pre/posttreatment evaluation. The time frame involved in making the ratings is for the "past seven days including today." It may be administered to nonpatient normal respondents, medical patients, and psychologically disturbed individuals who are at least 13 years old. Obviously, it is limited to use among those capable of completing a self-report inventory. This would exclude mentally retarded, illiterate, or floridly psychotic individuals.

The instrument requires approximately 12 to 15 minutes to complete, although on rare occasions it may take as long as 30 minutes. If the patient is disabled, it may be administered in narrative mode where the examiner reads the items and the patient responds by using a 3 × 5 card that is given to him or her that contains a numbered description of the response scale. Recently, a Hispanic version has been made available through National Computer Systems, although the test's other publisher (Clinical Psychometric Research, Inc. of Riderwood, Maryland) notes that the test has been translated into over 20 languages.

Scoring may be done by hand or microcomputer, or through a scoring service. Hand scoring requires approximately 15 to 30 minutes and entails the possibility of clerical errors. A more reliable but slightly more expensive scoring method involves purchasing microcomputer software that allows for 100 ($175) or 500 ($250) scorings and provides only raw scores and T-scores with graphic profiles. More expensive software may be purchased that will provide a clinical narrative. The current price is 25 reports for $125, 50 for $200, or 100 for $300. Data entry requires less than 10 minutes and may take only a few minutes. National Computer Systems also offers its own scoring and report service.

The SCL-90-R was one of the original instruments recommended by Waskow and Parloff (1975) as a measure that should be included in a core battery of instruments for assessing the outcome of psychotherapy. It has also received some use in clinical settings, although it is much less prominent there than in research programs (Piotrowski & Keller, 1989). In terms of psychometric qualities, the SCL-90-R has demonstrated internal consistency and test-retest reliability and there are numerous studies supporting its criterion and construct validity (Derogatis, 1983). Additionally, clinically significant cutoff points have been established (see Chapter 8). For the GSI, a T-score greater than or equal to 63 is considered important. This was established based on research with medical patients, psychiatric patients, and normals, producing a hit rate of 85 to 87 percent.

Brief Symptom Inventory

Two instruments have been developed from the SCL-90-R as well. The Brief Symptom Inventory (BSI; Derogatis & Melisaratos, 1983) is a brief form of the SCL-90-R that reflects the same nine symptom dimensions and three global indices but has only 53 as opposed to 90 items. The time required to administer the test is also shortened by a few minutes. Correlations between the BSI and SCL-90-R scales range from .92 to .99, suggesting that the two scales are measuring the same constructs. Thus, the BSI may be a handy instrument to use when time is of the essence, although, the time savings is, in absolute terms, rather small. Consequently, we suspect that the SCL-90-R can be used in most instances.

SCL-90 Analogue Scale

The other instrument to come from the SCL-90-R is the SCL-90 Analogue Scale (Derogatis, 1983), which is a clinical observer's scale designed for health professionals who do not have detailed training or knowledge in psychopathology (e.g., nurses, clinical interviewers, physicians, etc.). It is a graphic or analogue scale since each of the nine primary symptom dimensions from the SCL-90-R, along with a global psychopathology scale, are represented on a 100mm line, extending from "not-at-all" to "extremely." The clinical observer is required to place a mark on each line, which is judged to be proportional to the degree of that symptom manifested in the patient. Brief defining paragraphs for each dimension are presented on the back of the scale for easy reference and clarification. The test requires about one minute to complete and interrater reliability studies conducted on outpatients produced coefficients ranging from .78 to .96. Obviously, this instrument will have the most widespread use in institutional settings where clinical observers are likely to interact with the patient. It could, however, also be used by therapists, paraprofessionals, and others in outpatient settings.

Marital Satisfaction Inventory (MSI)

The MSI (Snyder, 1981) is designed for couples to use in making both general and specific evaluations of their relationship. The test is for use with individuals who are married or living together for at least six months. Administration requires 30 minutes to an hour for each spouse. The inventory consists of 280 true/false items organized into 11 different scales. The last 41 items deal with dissatisfaction with children or conflict over child rearing. Couples who do not have children may stop after question 239 and save time. Included in this group could be couples whose children are either quite young or who have already left home. Another difficult issue arises when one or both partners have children from a previous relationship. Generally speaking, if the couple has had any common interaction regarding one or more children in their home, both should complete the entire inventory.

The MSI is available through Western Psychological Services (WPS). The actual test and test manual may be purchased for a nominal fee. There are several alternatives for scoring the inventory. WPS offers a microcomputer disk that may be used for administration, scoring, and computerized interpretation. Further, the computerized interpretation may be tailored for either clinical or pastoral settings. Perhaps the most economical method is to hand score the inventory. Hand-scoring keys and answer sheets are reasonably priced. As always, hand scoring requires staff time and leaves open the possibility of clerical errors.

The individual scales provide a multidimensional self-report that identifies separately for each spouse the nature and extent of marital distress along nine specific dimensions of their relationship. A tenth scale is somewhat analogous to a validity scale (Conventionalization) in that it indicates the individuals' tendencies to respond in a socially desirable direction when evaluating their marriage. However, the scale of most interest for the present chapter is the Global Distress Scale (GDS), which measures individuals' overall dissatisfaction with the marriage. The item content of the GDS reflects global marital discontent, chronic disharmony, desire for marital therapy, and thoughts regarding separation or divorce. It consists primarily of two dimensions: general unhappiness with the marriage and uncertain commitment to the relationship. There are 43 items on this scale.

The psychometric qualities of the MSI are quite good. Internal consistency of the scales ranges from .80 to .97, with the GDS achieving .97. Test-retest reliability over a six-week interval depicts a range from .84 to .94, with the GDS at .92. The validity of the inventory is also impressive. GDS termination scores predicted marital status (i.e., married vs. divorced) four years later. By using a cutoff of equal to or above 60T for a couple's average GDS score at termination, the probability of divorce four years later was .42, or three times the probability of subsequent divorce (.14) for those with termination GDS scores below 60T (Snyder, Wills, & Grady-Fletcher, 1991).

This demonstrates the appropriateness of clinically significant cutoff points on the MSI. In general, scores below 50T indicate closeness to one's spouse, commitment to the relationship, and an absence of pervasive problems. Scores in the 50 to 60T range represent increasing likelihood of dissatisfaction and thoughts of separation or divorce. Scores above this range signify strong feelings of anger, a long history of problems, and increasing probability of separation or divorce. Finally, the MSI has a bounteous and distinguished track record of use in both clinical and research settings.

Global Assessment Scale (GAS)

The GAS (Endicott, Spitzer, Fleiss, & Cohen, 1976) is a clinical rating measure evaluating a hypothetical continuum ranging from psychological sickness to health. Ratings are made to represent the client's lowest level of functioning within a specified time period, usually one week. A numerical rating is entered on a scale from 1 to 100. This range is divided into 10 equal intervals. Each interval is described in some detail. For example, the interval 61–70 contains the following description: "Some mild symptoms (e.g., depressive mood and mild insomnia) OR some difficulty in several areas of functioning, but generally functioning pretty well, has some meaningful interpersonal relationships and most untrained people would not consider him 'sick'" (Endicott et al., 1976, p. 768). Raters are encouraged to use intermediate levels when appropriate (e.g., 45, 72, 23).

Lower scores on the GAS indicate more severe pathology. A score of 1 indicates that the client is in need of constant supervision, whereas 100 represents superior functioning in a wide range of activities. GAS ratings cover three main dimensions of psychopathology: (1) impairment in daily functioning, (2) impairment in reality test-ing, and (3) potential for suicide or violence. Raters should take into account both the degree of pathology and the urgency for treatment. Information for the ratings can come from a variety of sources, including patient interview, case reports and records, or an informant. When ratings are based on case records without face-to-face contact with the client, raters are likely to overestimate the level of functioning for the client (Dill, Eisen, & Grob, 1989). This is due to inconsistent and sometimes inaccurate doc-umentation in the record. Consequently, raters must adjust accordingly.

To make an actual GAS rating takes only a few moments, but the data collection process preceding this rating may take considerably longer. Rater training for the GAS takes approximately 75 minutes. A manual with more complete examples and descriptive information for each range of scores is available along with two self-study sessions (Kuhlman, Sincaban, & Bernstein, 1990). The cost of obtaining the instru-ment is minimal. The GAS itself, along with instructions, case vignettes, and a key of correct responses may all be purchased for under $5.

The GAS may be used in a variety of situations. In the next couple of pages, we will discuss some of the interview protocols that utilize the GAS. We also recommend that the GAS be used to assess change. The scale is sufficiently sensitive and time lim-ited to allow for relatively precise measures that accurately reflect a client's changing status. As expected, overall severity measures show greater sensitivity to change than do measures of single symptom dimensions.

Interrater reliability is greater when based on face-to-face interviews rather than secondary sources. Intraclass correlation coefficients for raters using records was .69, whereas those using interviews were .76 to .91. Validity has been based on the mod-erate correlations between the GAS and other rating measures of global severity, re-lationship to rehospitalization, and sensitivity to change. Using the GAS to predict re-hospitalization has provided mild evidence of validity for those with scores below 40. The GAS shows substantial sensitivity to change when ratings are made by both re-searchers and therapists (Endicott et al., 1976).

Kuhlman and colleagues (1990) reported an interesting adaptation of the GAS for team use. Each individual of the clinical team made a weekly patient rating and then these were averaged to provide the patient's GAS score for that week. Reliabil-ity and validity data supported this method.

The GAS has a long history of use in both clinical and research settings. It has often been employed as a measure of treatment outcome, and we recommend its continued use, assuming that raters will take the time to become sufficiently trained in the proper application of the scale.

Before continuing, we should make some comparison of the GAS with the Global Assessment of Functioning (GAF) scale that appears in *DSM-IV* (APA, 1994). Since the GAF is based on the GAS, the two are quite similar; however, there are two differences. First, the GAF is designed to make ratings for two time periods: current (i.e., time of the evaluation) and past year. It is the highest level of functioning dur-ing the past year that is assessed rather than the lowest level. Second, the GAF scale ranges from 1 to 90, whereas the GAS ranges from 1 to 100.

Children's Global Assessment Scale (CGAS)

The CGAS (Shaffer, Gould, Brasic, Ambrosini, Fisher, Bird, & Aluwahlia, 1983) is an adaptation of the GAS developed to rate a child or adolescent's lowest level of functioning during a certain time period. It is designed for individuals ranging in age from 4 to 16 years and it shares the same scale range (i.e., 1–100) and designated intervals as the GAS. The descriptive anchors, however, have been adapted for the target population so that they depict behavior and situations applicable to youngsters. For example, interval 61–70 states "some difficulty in a single area, but generally functioning pretty well (e.g., sporadic or isolated antisocial acts such as occasionally playing hooky or petty theft); consistent minor difficulties with school work; mood changes of brief duration; fears and anxieties which do not lead to gross avoidance behavior; self doubt(s); has some meaningful interpersonal relationships; most people who do not know the child well would not consider him/her deviant but those who do know him/her well might express concern" (Shaffer et al., 1983, p. 1229). Normal functioning is indicated by a score above 70.

Interrater reliability is very good, as indicated by an intraclass correlation coefficient of .84. Test-retest (six months) stability produced a coefficient of .85 (Shaffer et al., 1983). There was a significant difference between CGAS scores of outpatients and inpatients, providing an indication of discriminant validity. In a review of child global rating scales, Sorensen, Hargreaves, and Friedlander (1982) noted that the CGAS was preferred over the Children's Impairment Scale and that it is useful to both clinicians and researchers as a complement to syndrome-specific scales.

Structured Clinical Interview for DSM-III-R (SCID)

The SCID (Spitzer, Williams, Gibbon, & First, 1989) is a semi-structured interview designed to render a diagnosis on *DSM-III-R* Axis I. The SCID-II provides the same service for Axis II. Both the SCID-I and SCID-II may be given to psychiatric patients, medical patients, or nonpatients. They are most appropriate for adults and were included here for a couple of reasons. First, they provide a determination as to whether the patient is in the pathological population or in the normal population, and in this sense is an obvious measure of clinical change. Second, the SCID uses an adaptation of the Global Assessment of Functioning (GAF) to provide a global indication of functioning that complements the diagnostic material. In addition, there are specific versions of the SCID for use with different populations such as psychiatric patients (SCID-P) and nonpsychiatric patients (SCID-NP).

The SCID manual (Spitzer et al., 1989) provides information regarding administration, instructions, and specific mistakes to avoid. Before using the SCID, professionals are instructed to read carefully through the manual and the instrument itself. They should then practice reading the questions aloud to become skilled in their verbalization. Recitation with a role-playing colleague is also suggested.

Additionally, observing an eight-hour training videotape or attending a two-day workshop are suggested.

In order to administer the SCID, the interviewer first obtains a general overview of the patient, including a history and information on the present state of the illness. The interviewer then makes a tentative differential diagnosis. All the questions are open ended so as to capture the subject's own words. The next section is the main part of the SCID. The interviewer asks questions that are in the booklet and is instructed to follow the directions precisely. After asking a set of questions, the interviewer must make a clinical judgment and decide if a diagnostic criterion has been met. Each criterion is rated on a four-point scale consisting of: (?) indicating not enough information to code; (1) absent/false—does not meet criteria for diagnosis; (2) subthreshold—threshold for criterion is almost met; and (3) threshold/true—criterion is met. At the end, a summary score sheet is completed to record the diagnoses and the severity of the illness. It is also determined if a diagnosis on Axis I has been present in the past and if it is presently current (in the last month). The GAF is completed at this time. Administration requires 60 to 90 minutes.

The SCID-II is given after the SCID-I because certain Axis I diagnoses may confound Axis II. It also begins with a brief overview to give information about the individual's capacity to self-reflect. The SCID Personality Questionnaire is a self-report instrument wherein clients indicate whether a statement describes how they usually have felt or behaved over the past several years. Each item corresponds to a SCID-II question. The test provides a crude screening device with a high rate of false positives. Administration requires approximately 20 minutes. Clients who have difficulty completing the Personality Questionnaire will probably not be good candidates for a SCID-II evaluation. The interviewer then asks only about the criteria on SCID-II that correspond to the "yes" responses on the Personality Questionnaire. The "no" responses are pursued if there is a clinical basis for suspecting the item is true or if the number of endorsed ratings on the SCID-II is within one item of the diagnostic threshold. The SCID-II can be conducted without using the screening instrument, but this would take more time.

The psychometric qualities of the SCID are good. Kappas for Axis I are similar to those obtained from the Diagnostic Interview Schedule (Robbins, Helzer, Croughan, & Ratcliff, 1981) and from the Schedule for Affective Disorders and Schizophrenia (SADS; Endicott & Spitzer, 1978). Test-retest reliabilities are acceptable but not outstanding. Kappa for the presence or absence of a personality disorder for separate interviews equals .66, and for a simultaneous interview by two raters it is equal to .70.

The validity of the SCID is difficult to determine since it is highly dependent on the validity of the *DSM-III-R*. As is eloquently discussed in the SCID manual, there is really no gold standard to use when assessing the validity of psychological diagnoses. If diagnoses based on clinical interviews serve as the standard to validate a procedure such as the SCID, there is obvious conceptual difficulty since the purpose of the SCID is to advance diagnostic accuracy beyond what a general, unstructured interview can do. To address this issue, Spitzer proposed the LEAD standard. This involves longitudinal assessment (L), done by expert diagnosticians (E), incorporating all data (AD) that are available from all sources. Skodol, Rosnick, Kellman, Oldham, and Hyler

(1988) have attempted such a study, resulting in low agreement between the SCID-II and the LEAD standard.

Although the SCID is a time-consuming measure to administer and is surely inappropriate for multiple or continuous assessment, it produces a wealth of information that may be useful to the clinician beyond the actual diagnosis or GAF rating. Consequently, we can imagine situations where the SCID may have such practical usefulness that it can easily be included as part of a pre/posttreatment assessment package. Not all clinicians are going to be interested in this approach, but some should be. This scale may help to assess adequately the effects of psychotherapy—although it should not serve as the sole criterion.

Schedule for Affective Disorders and Schizophrenia-Change Version (SADS-C)

The SADS-C (Spitzer & Endicott, 1978) consists of a subset of 45 items taken from the SADS that are rated for their presence during the past week. Consequently, it is much shorter than the original SADS (which may require between 1½ to 2 hours to administer) and is more useful for outcome assessments since it is aimed at a relatively discrete and recent time period. Often, the SADS-C is administered after treatment is completed (as opposed to the original SADS, which is administered at pretreatment), although it is acceptable, and perhaps desirable, to administer SADS-C at both the onset and termination of treatment. In fact, Endicott, Cohen, Nee, Fleiss, and Sarantakos (1981) suggest that the SADS-C may be used initially instead of the regular SADS to provide a measure of the level of severity of psychopathology. Both the SADS and SADS-C utilize the GAS to provide a global rating of the individual's lowest level of functioning for the past week.

In order to understand SADS-C, we should briefly discuss the parent instrument, SADS, which was developed to reduce information variance in descriptive and diagnostic evaluations (Endicott & Spitzer, 1978). The SADS is a structured interview that assesses current functioning and also aims at getting a diagnosis by eliciting detailed information about the individual. This requires examination of current and past disturbances. The items progress in a systematic fashion, ruling in and out various diagnostic considerations along the way. Standardized questions to rate the severity of the disorder are also included. Judgments are based on all available sources.

When all is said and done, the SADS-C yields several kinds of information. First is a diagnosis based on the Research Diagnostic Criteria (RDC; Spitzer, Endicott, & Robins, 1975). Second is a severity rating of individual symptoms on a scale from 0 (not at all) to 6 (extreme). The symptoms are those primarily associated with schizophrenic and affective disorders, thus limiting its usefulness with less disturbed individuals. Third, a rating on the GAS is made. And finally, summary scale scores for the various symptom dimensions are also calculated.

The administration of the SADS-C is relatively straightforward; however, it is best if administrators are first trained in administering the complete SADS. To be qualified in administration of the SADS, individuals first need to be experienced interviewers. They must also become intimately familiar with the instrument by reading through the manual and practicing the questions. Familiarity with the RDC is an additional prerequisite. Finally, there are SADS training tapes with vignettes accompanied by a key with consensus ratings and diagnoses and discussion. The tapes are 1½ to 2 hours in length and are designed for specific versions of the SADS, including the original and the SADS-C. They are available only in VHS format and presently cost $65 plus postage and handling. A letter describing the way in which the tapes will be used, who will be viewing them, and including a statement that the tapes will not be copied must also accompany the order. The actual cost of the SADS or SADS-C is minimal.

The SADS and SADS-C have been used as measures of change and show sufficient sensitivity, although probably not as much as other instruments. The symptom ratings and global rating in particular show promise as measures of change in practice. The instruments have also demonstrated acceptable psychometric properties (Matarazzo, 1989; Endicott & Spitzer, 1978).

Katz Adjustment Scale (KAS)

The KAS (Katz & Lyerly, 1963) was designed to measure both the patient's community functioning and the kind and degree of psychopathology. There are two versions: KAS-S is a self-report version given to the patient and KAS-R is completed by a close friend, relative, or someone who has been in relatively close contact with the patient for a period of at least two to three weeks. This person should be sufficiently involved with the patient to be able to provide information regarding the patient's behavior at home as well as in the community. Each scale (i.e., KAS-S and KAS-R) is further divided into five forms. Four of these forms contain the same items on both KAS-S and KAS-R, the only difference being the source of information (i.e., patient or significant other). The first form differs in content (as described here) as well as source. The derived scores permit evaluation of the client's adjustment in clinical, social, and personal areas.

Form R1 provides the significant other's ratings of patient symptoms and social behaviors. There are two major divisions of this form. The first assesses all psychiatric symptoms as comprehensively as possible and is worded in everyday language. The second measures social behavior. Each of the 127 items is rated on a 4-point scale, ranging from almost never (1) to almost always (4). From these items, 13 clusters were formed (belligerence, verbal expansiveness, negativism, helplessness, suspiciousness, anxiety, withdrawal and retardation, general psychopathology, nervousness, confusion, stability, bizarreness, and hyperactivity) and these were subsequently factor analyzed into three major dimensions (social obstreperousness, acute psychoticism, and withdrawn depression). Form S1 is completed by the patient and consists of a modification of the Johns Hopkins Symptom Distress Checklist (Parloff, Kelman, & Frank, 1954). A total score of symptom discomfort is obtained.

Form R2 provides a measure of the level of performance of socially expected activities as viewed from the perspective of the significant other. It consists of 16 items each rated on a 3-point scale (is not doing, is doing some, is doing regularly). Form R3 uses the same 16 items (and a similar 3-point scale) but asks the rater to indicate whether he or she had or had not expected the patient to be doing this within a reasonable time following treatment. For R2 and R3, a simple total is calculated. Thus, a comparison between R2 and R3 will provide an index of the significant other's level of dissatisfaction.

Form R4 assesses level of free-time activities, again from the significant other's perspective. It uses 23 items each being rated on a 3-point (frequently, sometimes, practically never) scale. Form R5 asks the evaluator to rate his or her level of satisfaction with what the patient is doing on each of the items. Although ratings are made on a 3-point scale, for summation only a 2-point scale (representing satisfaction and dissatisfaction) is used. Totals are again calculated for R4 and R5. Forms S2 through S5 are identical except that the client completes them concerning himself or herself.

The KAS requires that the client and relative be able to read, but they only make a check mark for each response. It takes 25 to 45 minutes to complete and is written in such a manner as to be easily comprehended by most individuals. Respondents are to base their ratings on the past two to three weeks.

The KAS-R and KAS-S have acceptable evidence of reliability and validity. Initial information was reported by Katz and Lyerly (1963), and Hogarty (1975) has summarized much of the subsequent work. In 1971, Hogarty and Katz normed the KAS with 450 nonpsychiatric community residents and found that all scores significantly differentiated between residents and patients. Additionally, the KAS-R has been used cross-culturally (Katz, Gudeman, & Sanborn, 1969) and with nonpsychotic psychiatric patients (Shaffer, Perlin, Schmidt, & Himelfarb, 1972). It also seems to be sufficiently sensitive to change (Wallace & Haas, 1983). Waskow and Parloff (1975) included the KAS in their core battery of psychotherapy outcome measures. The KAS is easy to administer, covers a wide range of symptomatic behaviors, and although it may be most appropriate for use with chronically mentally ill patients, it may be used with many populations. A sixth-grade reading level is necessary for standard administration but the items may be read to those unable to read. We conclude that the KAS-R and KAS-S are both useful and important measures and recommend their use in future investigations and clinical practice. Although the length of time required to administer the scales may prohibit several repeated administrations, the scales could be used in a pre/posttreatment manner. It is also possible to break the KAS down and administer only parts of it. This would provide for a large time savings.

Social Adjustment Scale (SAS)

The SAS (Weissman & Paykel, 1974) is a semi-structured interview that assesses the client's adjustment in the role areas of work (including worker, housewife, or student roles), social and leisure activities, extended family relationships, spousal role, and parental capabilities. There is also an item dealing with economic sufficiency. In each of these areas, a series of individual items are utilized and total (actually mean per number of items scored) scores may be obtained. Each item is rated on a scale ranging from 1 to 5. Most item ratings are based on the client's actual behavior in the context of all the information available (e.g., demographic, background, etc.) rather than purely on the client's perception of it. The items that ask for patients' feelings are, however, based only on the patients' report. There are also ways of combining the items to form scores based on qualitative categories (i.e., performance, interpersonal behaviors, friction, feelings and satisfactions, overall evaluations) and factor analysis (work performance, interpersonal friction, inhibited communication, submissive-dependency, family attachment, anxious rumination). The factor scoring system seems to be most frequently used.

Of greatest interest for the present chapter are the global ratings. Utilizing a 7-point scale (with lower scores indicating more favorable adjustment), ratings for each role area are made. Finally, an overall adjustment rating, also using a 7-point scale, is made.

The SAS interview takes approximately 45 to 90 minutes to complete. It focuses on the last 2 to 2½ months of the client's life. Theoretically, a bachelor-level individual trained and experienced in conducting the interview may be capable of performing it. We would recommend, however, that a trained clinician conduct the interview. An instruction booklet is available through the Yale University Department of Psychiatry Depression Clinic, although an appreciable amount of information can be found in Weissman and Paykel (1974).

The psychometric qualities of the SAS are quite good. Interrater reliability scores have averaged about .83 (Auerbach, 1983). The instrument has been able to distinguish between depressed women and normals, women when acutely depressed and when recovered, and psychotherapy patients from others. It is also sensitive to change. Platt (1981) has offered a number of criticisms of the instrument, some of which were responded to by Auerbach (1983). Generally, we believe that the SAS adequately measures social adjustment and can be utilized for making such ratings.

Since the advent of the SAS, two related forms have developed. The SAS-SR is a self-report version developed for economical and administrative reasons. It is oriented toward only the past two weeks. The SAS-II was developed for use with schizophrenic populations for whom social adjustment ratings may be particularly important.

Health Sickness Rating Scale

Luborsky's (1962) Health Sickness Rating Scale attempts to order each of seven client characteristics along a continuum, from "health" to "sickness." The Menninger Clinic's research team developed the scale by rating 34 client cases, then asking five independent clinicians to rank these cases. The cases they did not agree on were discussed further (Luborsky, 1975). These discussions produced the following seven client characteristics:

1. The client's need to be protected and/or supported versus his or her ability to function autonomously
2. The seriousness of the client's symptoms
3. The degree of the client's subjective distress
4. The client's effect on his or her environment (causes danger, discomfort, etc.)
5. The degree to which the client can utilize his or her abilities

6. The quality of the client's interpersonal relationships
7. The breadth and depth of the client's interests

Each of these characteristics is rated on a 100-point continuum (1= the most sick to 100 = the most healthy). The seven characteristics are typified by case examples at different points along the continuum. To use the scale, one identifies case examples that match the current client for each of the seven characteristics. Finally, the rater is asked to "balance" subjectively these seven ratings to come up with an overall global rating. Luborsky (1975) reports that various research projects have demonstrated the reliability and validity of the Health Sickness Rating Scale. A trained rater can rate a client using the Health Sickness Rating Scale in just a few minutes.

The Outcome Questionnaire

The Outcome Questionnaire (OQ; Lambert, Lunnen, Umphres, Hansen, & Burlingame, 1994) is a 45-item scale designed to measure patient progress in therapy by repeated administration during the course of treatment and at termination. Patient progress is measured along several important dimensions, based on Lambert's (1983) conceptualization suggesting that three aspects of the patient's life should be monitored: (1) subjective discomfort (intrapsychic functioning); (2) interpersonal relationships; and (3) social role performance. These areas of functioning suggest a continuum from how the person feels inside, how the person is getting along with significant others, and how he or she is doing in important life tasks such as work and school. In addition, the OQ can be used as a baseline screening instrument with application for gross treatment assignment decisions.

The OQ was designed to be available at low cost, sensitive to change over short periods of time, and brief—while still maintaining a high level of reliability and validity. Items address commonly occurring problems across a wide variety of disorders and tap the symptoms most likely to occur. The items also measure personally and socially relevant characteristics that affect the quality of life of the individual. The number of items was limited to 45 so that administration of the OQ assists, rather than hinders, customary clinical practice, is tolerable to patients, and is suitable for repeated testing while providing clinicians with data that can be used for decision making.

The OQ is self-administered and requires no instructions beyond those printed on the instrument itself. Under usual circumstances, subjects will complete the scale in under 10 minutes.

Scoring the OQ is a straightforward procedure involving simple addition of item values. Each item is scored on a 5-point likert scale (0 = never, 1 = rarely, 2 = sometimes, 3 = frequently, 4 = almost always). The OQ provides a total score and three individual subscale scores. The *total score* (TOT) is calculated by summing the patient's ratings across all 45 items. This yields a TOT range from 0 to 180. The *symptom distress score* (SD) is calculated by summing the patient's ratings on 22 select items. The SD has a range of 0 to 88. The *interpersonal relations score* (IR) is calculated by summing the patient's ratings on 11 select items. The IR has a range of 0 to 44. The *social role score* (SR) is calculated by summing the patient's ratings on 9 select items. The SR has a range of 0 to 36. Templates to facilitate scoring have been designed and a computer scoring program is in development.

To use the OQ clinically, the creators suggest considering three elements. First, the subject's responses to certain select items should be evaluated. Items on suicide potential, substance abuse, and violence at work should be investigated further if any rating other than 0 (never) is given by the subject.

Second, the total score should be evaluated. A high score suggests that the subject is admitting to a large number of symptoms, interpersonal difficulties, social role difficulties, and lower overall life satisfaction. A low score suggests that the subject is no more disturbed than the general population. Comparison of the subject's TOT with the different normative samples established for the OQ provides clinically useful information.

Finally, the subscale scores should be considered. These scores provide information on specific areas of difficulty. The SD rates anxiety disorders, affective disorders, adjustment disorders, and stress-related illness. A high SD indicates that the subject exhibits problems in these areas, and a low SD indicates either an absence or denial of any such symptoms. The IR rates complaints such as loneliness, conflicts with others, and family/marriage problems. A high IR indicates problems in these areas, and a low IR suggests both the absence of such problems as well as general satisfaction with the quality of the subject's interpersonal relationships. The SR measures the extent to which difficulties (conflicts, fatigue, distress, and inefficiency) in the social roles of worker, homemaker, or student are present. A high SR indicates difficulty in social roles, and a low SR indicates adequate social role adjustment.

Adequate internal consistency is reported for the TOT as well as the three subscales (TOT: $\alpha = .93$; SD $- \alpha = .92$; IR $- \alpha = .74$; and SR $- \alpha = .70$. Test-retest values for the total scale and all three subscale were significant at the .01 level. Concurrent validity was estimated by correlating the OQ TOT and subscales with their respective counterparts on the Symptom Checklist-90-R (SCL-90-R; Derogatis, 1983), Beck Depression Inventory (BDI; Beck et al., 1961), Zung Self-Rating Depression Scale (ZSRDS; Zung, 1965), Zung Self-Rating Anxiety Scale (ZAS; Zung, 1971), Taylor Manifest Anxiety Scale (TMA; Taylor, 1953), State-Trait Anxiety Inventory (STAI; (Spielberger, 1970, 1983), Inventory of Interpersonal Problems (IIP; Horowitz et al., 1988), and Social Adjustment Scale (SAS; Weissman & Bothwell, 1976). Concurrent validity for the TOT and all three domains with the criterion measures were all significant at the .01 level.

Although still in development, the OQ seems to be a practical and cost-effective instrument that represents global outcome.

Practical Applications

The global outcome measures presented in this chapter can be incorporated into existing clinical practice for a variety of purposes. Some of the most useful applications include:

1. *Assessing pretreatment severity.* Global measures are particularly useful for assessing the overall severity of distress prior to treatment. Although the content area of the distress may vary depending on the focus of the measure (e.g., social relationships, intimate relationships, global symptomatology, etc.), the rating of overall or global severity can be quite useful. Particularly when a normative sample has been collected using the instrument, pretreatment scores of clients can be compared to the norm group to assess the level of severity.

2. *Assessing session-to-session change.* Global measures can be used to track the progress of clients from session to session. Particularly the brief measures can be easily and quickly administered to clients in the waiting room. For example, one community mental health center is currently administering the OQ to all outpatient clients just prior to every outpatient session. Global measures are most useful when a heterogeneous group of clients is being served. When a more limited and homogeneous group is being served, specific measures described in the next chapter may be useful.

3. *Assessing pre- to posttreatment change.* Global measures can also be administered at just two occasions—before and after treatment to assess the amount of change that has occurred during treatment. Even more lengthy measures can be used for this purpose. Again, global measures are most useful when clients with a wide variety of symptoms or problems are being served.

4. *Evaluating the clinical significance of change occurring in psychotherapy.* Measures that have normative data can be used to evaluate the clients' end of treatment level of functioning by comparing their scores with the norm group. More will be said about this topic in Chapter 8.

5. *Evaluating for the presence or absence of symptoms representative of a specific diagnosis.* The diagnostic interviews can be administered before and after treatment to assess for the presence or absence of a specific diagnosis. Hopefully, clients will improve to the extent that any pretreatment disorders are no longer present following treatment. Obviously, this will depend on the disorder, the treatment, the duration of treatment, and a number of other considerations. Nevertheless, diagnostic assessment is one potential method for evaluating the effectiveness of treatment.

Summary

There are, of course, many other instruments that we could have referenced in this section. In keeping with our model, we have tried to present a variety of measures that utilize different sources and data points. Some are more practical than others, some have a more substantial history than others, and some have better psychometric properties than others. However, all are worthy of consideration. We hope that this chapter will provoke serious contemplation among clinicians as they consider assessing their clients for both research and clinical purposes.

Chapter *5*

Assessment of Outcome in Specific Populations

In 1975, Waskow and Parloff, in conjunction with current psychotherapy experts, developed a core battery of psychotherapy change measures for use in research and practice. Unfortunately, the core battery never received widespread use. One reason for the failure of the core battery concept is that it attempted to define assessment procedures that would be applicable across a wide range of psychological disorders. Probably the most useful substitute for a core battery would be the proposal of multiple core batteries, each appropriate for specific disorders. Even these more limited batteries, however, do not exist at present. In fact, Ogles, Lambert, Weight, and Payne (1990) found that even with actively researched problems such as agoraphobia, researchers cannot agree to use a single measure to assess change, let alone a battery of measures. Therefore, the research literature is limited with regard to specifying the way in which clinicians should measure changes in patients whose diagnosis might imply the use of standard assessment procedures.

Nevertheless, several useful books on the topic of outcome assessment that have chapters devoted to assessing outcome by diagnostic category have been published. Some of these were noted in the Preface. The interested clinician whose practice encompasses an abundance of patients within a diagnostic category will find many comprehensive batteries within these texts. For our present purposes, it is more useful to suggest several tests that can be used across many patient populations regardless of diagnosis. Therefore, we now highlight several measures that have utility for the therapist who wants a limited number of procedures for outcome measurement in general psychological practice.

Besides the criteria mentioned in the Preface, the selection of instruments presented in this chapter was guided by several additional principles. First, we selected instruments that are appropriate for specific problems. Second, we selected measures that dealt with frequently occurring problems in outpatient practice, including adjustment disorders, mood disorders, anxiety disorders, substance abuse, marital problems, and child behavioral problems. Third, we selected measures on the basis of their common use in outcome research based on surveys of this literature (Lambert & Hill, 1994). Fourth, we selected measures that are or could be commonly used in a private practice as well as community settings. Fifth, we selected measures that would allow the measurement of outcome from a variety of viewpoints: self-report, therapist, clinician, and relevant others.

With these considerations in mind, we compiled a short list of measures that can be recommended for assessing treatment outcome for specific problems. Since depression and anxiety are common symptoms in most patient samples, we have provided two standardized scales measuring each dimension. Depression measures include the Beck Depression Inventory (self-report) and the Hamilton Rating Scales for Depression (clinician rating). Anxiety measures include the State-Trait Anxiety Inventory (self-report) and the Hamilton Anxiety Rating Scale (Hamilton, 1959) (clinician judged). Measures of interpersonal relationship include the Dyadic Adjustment Scale (self-report, significant other) and the Inventory of Interpersonal Problems (self-report). In addition to these instruments, we have included a measure of addictive behavior (the Addiction Severity Index; clinician rated), a measure for agoraphobia (the Fear Questionnaire; self-report), and a measure of child problems (the Child Behavior Checklist; parent or other rated). These instruments are now briefly described and reviewed. Later in this book, we present some interesting data on cutoff scores that will make the use of some of these instruments even more appealing to the clinician.

Review of Instruments

Beck Depression Inventory

The Beck Depression Inventory (BDI) is a 21-item self-report inventory of common depressive symptoms and attitudes including mood, pessimism, sense of failure, lack of satisfaction, guilt, sense of punishment, self-dislike, self-accusation, suicidal wishes, crying, irritability, social withdrawal, indecisiveness, distortion of body image, work inhibition, sleep disturbance, fatigability, loss of appetite, weight loss, somatic preoccupation, and loss of libido (example items are shown in Table 5–1).. These symptoms and attitudes were chosen because they are frequently found in depressed psychiatric clients and infrequently in nondepressed psychiatric clients (Beck, Steer, & Garbin, 1988). Each symptom is rated for intensity from 0 to 3. A shorter, 13-item form also exists, as well as several computerized forms. The original (1961) version was modified in 1978 and is usually self-administered.

Beck, Steer, and Garbin (1988) summarized the research regarding the reliability and validity of the BDI. Internal consistencies for psychiatric populations range from .76 to .95, whereas nonpsychiatric populations' internal consistencies range from .73 to .92. In regard to validity, the BDI covers six of the *DSM-III*'s criteria for major depression, partially covers two of these criteria, and does not include one at

TABLE 5–1   Specific Measures of Outcome with Category Ratings

Conceptual and Organizational Scheme Categories

Measure	*Content*	*Social Level*	*Source*	*Technology*	*Time Orientation*
BDI	Affect	Intrapersonal	Self	Specific	State
HRSD	Affect	Intrapersonal	Therapist/rater	Trained observer	State
STAI	Affect	Intrapersonal	Self	Specific	State
HARS	Affect	Interpersonal	Therapist/rater	Trained observer	State
DAS	Behavior	Intrapersonal	Self	Specific	State
IIP	Behavior	Intrapersonal	Self	Specific	State/trait
COMPASS	Affect/ behavior	Mixed	Self/therapist/	Specific	State/trait
ASI	Behavior	Intrapersonal	Therapist/rater	Trained observer	State
FQ	Affect/ behavior	Intrapersonal	Self	Specific	State
CBCL	Affect/ behavior	Mixed	Parent/self/ rater	Specific	State

all (psychomotor agitation). Correlations between the BDI and other measurements of depression are variable: correlations with clinical ratings range from .55 to .96; correlations with the Hamilton Rating Scale for Depression range from .41 to .86; correlations with the Zung Self-Rating Depression Scale range from .62 to .86; correlations with the MMPI Depression Scale range from .41 to .75; and correlations with the Multiple Affect Adjective Checklist Depression Scale (Zuckerman, 1960) range from .59 to .66. Beck, Steer and Garbin (1988) also report several studies demonstrating the ability of the BDI to successfully differentiate psychiatric from nonpsychiatric groups; however, the BDI appears to be less successful in discriminating among depressive disorders.

The BDI is the most frequently used measure of client improvement in psychotherapy outcome studies with depressed clients (Nietzel, Russel, Hemmings, & Gretter, 1987) and is quickly and easily completed. The BDI is also frequently used in clinical practice as a client assessment device (Piotrowski & Keller, 1989). Overall, the BDI is a practical instrument for assessing depressive symptoms with an impressive research history and adequate psychometric properties.

The Hamilton Rating Scale for Depression

The Hamilton Rating Scale for Depression (HRSD), like the Beck Depression Inventory, is an instrument designed to assess the severity of depressive symptomatology. However, the HRSD is a clinician's rating tool. A patient's score on the HRSD is not dependent on the patient's self-appraisal as with the BDI, but on the observations and perceptions of a skilled and experienced clinician based on the information available about the patient.

The HRSD is a 17-item protocol (although many versions are used; Grundy et al., 1994). Each item has either three or five grades of severity represented by statements that the rater must choose from to best describe the patient. A score on an item will range from 0 to 4 or 0 to 2, depending on its length. The overall score is the sum of the scores for all 17 items. Mowbray (1972) provides a guideline for interpreting the HRSD scores. These guidelines are summarized in Table 5–2.

Because of the nature of the HRSD, the measure of reliability that is most appropriate is interrater reliability. The brevity of the scale makes a split-half correlation difficult, and the dynamic nature of depression renders a long-term test-retest measurement inconclusive for reliability. Hamilton's (1960) original article introducing the HRSD reported interrater reliability between .84 and .90. Ziegler, Meyer, Rosen, and Biggs (1978) reported high interrater correlations using videotapes of patients. Measurements were obtained from clinicians who saw the patients personally or via video. When the results were compared, the reliability of the ratings was above .95, showing extremely strong agreement between raters.

The HRSD shows high concurrent validity with other measures of depression. Hammen (1980) shows a .80 correlation between the HRSD and the Beck Depression Inventory. Even higher agreement was found between the HRSD and independent clinical ratings (see Bech, Gram, Dein, Jacobsen, Vitger, & Bolwig, 1975; Knesevich, Biggs, Clayton, & Ziegler, 1977). This high agreement is expected because in both cases the clinician is the primary source of data. The HRSD shows high construct validity also. It represents well all the aspects of depression described in the *DSM-III* (Moran & Lambert, 1983). The HRSD may be more sensitive to differential degrees of depressive pathology than other methods of depression assessment (Moran & Lambert, 1983), and a computerized administration version of the HRSD has also been developed (Kobak, Reynolds, Rosenfeld, & Griest, 1990).

The Hamilton Anxiety Rating Scale

The Hamilton Anxiety Rating Scale (HARS; Hamilton, 1959) is a clinical interview designed to assess levels of anxiety as rated by a clinician. This instrument is perhaps the most frequently used observer rated scale of anxiety. The HARS was first pre-

TABLE 5–2 A Summary of Mowbray's Guidelines for Interpreting the HRSD

HRSD Score	Severity of Depressive Symptomatology
0–10	Normal mood
10–20	Mild depression
20–25	Moderate depression
25–35	Severe depression
35+	Very severe depression

Source: Moran & Lambert, 1983.

sented by Max Hamilton in 1959 as a 13-item scale. Guy (1976) included an additional item, making the HARS 14 items long. The 1976 version is now considered the standard HARS and is often used in both clinical and research settings, especially in psychopharmacological research aimed at determining the efficacy of anxiolytic drugs.

Although the HARS is widely used, it is subject to criticism. Researchers have shown that the HARS is unable to discriminate accurately between anxiety and depression (a problem that is common in anxiety and depression assessment) or between specific subtypes of anxiety. Much of the problem with the HARS lies in the construct of anxiety, as outlined in the *DSM* classification. When the scale was devised in 1959, the *DSM* had fewer subtypes of anxiety and was less specific about particular symptoms than is now the case with the *DSM-IV*. Yet, rather than abandoning this popular instrument, we suggest here a reliable method for obtaining a more accurate diagnosis with the Hamilton Anxiety Rating Scale.

Anxiety and depression assessments may often measure the same symptoms. Tension, insomnia, agitation, gastrointestinal disturbances, hypochondriasis, and somatic ailments are some of the characteristics that are common between the two disorders. The HARS and the Hamilton Rating Scale for Depression (HRSD) overlap in their assessment of these symptoms. Riskind, Beck, Brown, and Steer (1987) have recently developed a restructured form of both the HARS and the HRSD that successfully differentiates between anxiety and depression. The new 16-item restructured Hamilton Anxiety Rating Scale (R-HARS) contains items from both original Hamilton scales and yields a more precise diagnosis and measure of outcome.

Riskind and colleagues (1987) report a Cronbach's alpha coefficient of .83, an improvement over the older scale, showing greater interitem agreement. These researchers also report that the R-HARS has greater discriminant validity than could be obtained previously. There is also greater agreement between the R-HARS and clinical assessment of anxiety. The separation of anxiety from depression is evident by the low correlation ($r = .15$) between the R-HARS and the reconstructed Hamilton Depression Rating Scale; this indicates that the two scales are independent from one another and measure different disorders. Construct and concurrent validity between the R-HARS and other measures of anxiety has not been firmly established.

The scoring of the R-HARS is essentially the same as with the original version. The items are rated on a 5-point scale from 0 to 4, with a higher score representing more severe levels of anxiety. The total score of the 16-item scale ranges from 0 to 64. The R-HARS can be given often and is sensitive to changes in anxiety. Although the R-HARS is a promising measure of outcome for clients with anxiety disorders, the instrument is in need of more validation studies and comparisons with other measures of anxiety.

The State-Trait Anxiety Inventory

The State-Trait Anxiety Inventory (STAI; Spielberger, Gorsuch, & Lushene, 1970) is a self-report instrument that differentiates between general feelings of anxiety (trait anxiety) and current feelings of anxiety (state anxiety). This instrument is the most widely used outcome measure for measuring changes in anxiety. The STAI, originally published in 1970, immediately found popularity and widespread use in research and clinical applications. But in 1983, the STAI was revised in an effort to improve factor content and remove psychometrically ambiguous questions. It has now been used in thousands of studies and has been published in over 30 languages.

The STAI is a single-page self-report protocol consisting of two scales. The trait scale is on one side of the page and the state scale is on the reverse. Each scale is composed of 20 items, making a total of 40. On the state scale, each item consists of a statement such as "I feel calm" followed by a 4-point intensity scale with the phrases "not at all," "somewhat," "moderately so," and "very much so." The phrases are numbered 1 through 4 and the respondent must mark the one that best describes his or her feelings "right now." The trait scale is of a similar format and each statement is followed by the phrases "almost never," "sometimes," "often," and "almost always." Two scores are computed (one for state and one for trait anxiety). The overall score for each scale is a simple summation of the scores for the 20 items and ranges from 20 to 80. A higher score reflects a greater level of anxiety for that particular scale. Specific scoring guidelines and procedures are discussed in detail in the manual for the inventory.

Spielberger found internal consistency estimates to range from .89 to .91 for the trait scale and .86 to .95 for the state scale. Test-retest reliability for the trait scale using a sample of high school and college students ranged from .65 to .86. As the length of time between test and retest increased (one hour to 104 days), the reliability coefficient decreased (see Spielberger, Gorsuch, & Lushene, 1970). Test-retest correlations have also been reported in the literature for the state scale, but because of the transient nature of state anxiety, test-retest correlations may not be informative.

Construct validity is quite high for both scales, showing that the STAI measures the theoretical constructs of state and trait anxiety. For example, Oei, Evans, and Brook (1990) demonstrated the factorial validity of the STAI. They found that 18 of the 20 items on the state scale showed salient loadings on factor one, and all 20 of the trait items showed salient loadings on factor two. It should be noted that their study used the original form X version of the inventory. Both items on the state scale showing nonsalient loadings were replaced on the 1983 form Y revision of the STAI.

The STAI takes less than 10 minutes to complete and can be administered individually or to groups. Of the two scales, the state scale seems to be the most useful. It is sensitive to change and can be administered repetitively over short intervals.

The Fear Questionnaire

The Fear Questionnaire (FQ) is the most frequently used standardized scale for measuring client outcome in studies of treatments for agoraphobia (Ogles et al., 1990). It was developed by Marks and Mathews (1978) to assess phobic clients' perceptions of fear before and after treatment. The FQ includes 21 items that are rated on a 9-point Likert scale, from "Would not avoid it" to "Always avoid it," and from "Hardly troublesome at all" to "Very severely troublesome." Fifteen of the items are summed to create three subscales: agoraphobia, blood-injury phobia, and social phobia. Five additional items measure anxiety and depression associated with the client's phobia. The final item is a global phobia index.

Normative data are available (Mathews, Gelder & Johnston, 1981; Mizes & Crawford, 1986; Nietzel & Trull, 1988) and are discussed in Chapter 8. Corcoran and Fischer (1987) report test-retest reliabilities ranging from .79 to .93. In terms of validity, they also describe studies demonstrating the ability of the Fear Questionnaire to discriminate between phobics and nonphobics, and to be sensitive to treatment interventions. Mizes and Crawford (1986) report that the advantages of the Fear Questionnaire include the brevity of the instrument, the emphasis on common rather than rare phobic items, the inclusion of agoraphobic items, and the emphasis of agoraphobia and social phobia items over simple phobia. Oei, Moylan, and Evans (1991) suggest that the Fear Questionnaire can be used to discriminate agoraphobics from social phobics by using the agoraphobia and social phobia subscales. They also report normative data for individuals in four diagnostic categories: agoraphobia, social phobia, generalized anxiety disorder, and panic disorder without agoraphobia. Finally, they provide additional evidence to support the psychometric soundness of the Fear Questionnaire. Overall, the Fear Questionnaire is a widely used, brief measure of outcome for treatment involving phobic symptoms.

Inventory of Interpersonal Problems

The Inventory of Interpersonal Problems (IIP; Horowitz, Rosenberg, Baer, Ureno, & Villasenor, 1988) is a self-report instrument that is designed to measure the level of distress arising from interpersonal sources. This instrument is one of few measures of interpersonal functioning and is perhaps the more revealing of the interpersonal assessment instruments because it focuses on behavior and assesses a broad range of interpersonal problems. The IIP has 127 items divided into two types that assess "the most common ways that people express complaints during intake interviews" (Horowitz, Rosenberg, Baer, Ureno, & Villasenor, 1988). The items used in the inventory were derived from complaint statements made by clients during interviews with therapists. Statements beginning with the phrases "I can't" or "I have to" or similar phrases were recorded and evaluated. The 127 items on the IIP are those that reflect the most common interpersonal problems based on the complaint statements. The first 78 items begin with the phrase "it is hard for me to . . . ." The next 49 items begin with the phrase "These are things I do too much." The respondent must determine the level of distress from each item posed to them on a scale from 0 (not at all distressing) to 4 (extremely distressing).

Normative data for the IIP were collected from 103 outpatient clients in the San Francisco area. Factor analysis revealed six subscales of the inventory as well as an overall complaint factor or tendency. The six subscales are H. Assertive (hard to be assertive), H. Sociable, H. Intimate, H. Submissive, T. Responsible (too responsible), and T. Controlling. The score on each scale is computed by averaging all the ratings of the items in the subscale. A high average indicates greater levels of distress.

The measures of reliability that have been applied to this inventory are test-retest reliability and the alpha coefficient of reliability. The IIP rates high on both. Test-retest reliability at 10 weeks on a waiting list is reported at .98 for the overall inventory and ranges from .80 to .87 for the subscales. These numbers represent good stability in the inventory. The alpha coefficient of correlation ranges from .82 to .94, showing good internal consistency among the items.

Construct validity of the IIP has been documented but remains to be replicated. Horowitz and colleagues (1988) compared selected subscales of the IIP to three other measures of interpersonal problems: the UCLA Loneliness Scale, the Rathus Assertiveness Schedule, and the Interpersonal Dependency Inventory. All three had high agreement with the corresponding subscale of the IIP. The SCL–90-R, a measure of distress associated with mainly noninterpersonal sources, was also compared to the IIP. Both of these instruments seemed to measure an overall complaint tendency. But when the complaint tendency was controlled for, the correlation between the two instruments was quite low, showing that each instrument deals with a different construct of distress. Overall, the IIP is a worthwhile addition to assessment batteries that seek to measure interpersonal aspects of functioning to a greater degree of quality than was previously possible.

COMPASS Outpatient Tracking

The COMPASS outpatient tracking system is a unique combination of global and specific outcome evaluation measures developed for the ongoing evaluation of therapy progress. The instrument includes four client-rated scales (Well-Being–4 items, Current Symptoms–40 items, Current Life Functioning–24 items, and Therapeutic Bond–12 items) based on the phase model of psychotherapy (Howard, Leuger, Maling, & Martinovich, 1994) and therapist ratings of the client on the Global Assessment Scale plus client level of functioning in each of six areas (family; health and grooming; intimate relationships; self-management; social relationships; and work, school, household functioning; 1 item for each area). The Well-Being, Current Symptoms, and Current Life Functioning Scales are scored separately or combined to create an overall Mental Health Index. Similarly, the therapist-rated scales are rated separately or combined to create a Clinical Assessment Index. Reliabilities for each of these scales are displayed in Table 5–3. As can be seen, both internal consistency and test-retest reliabilities are adequate for the patient and therapist scales (internal consistencies are not applicable in some cases).

Validity information is available for the patient scales and the therapist-rated GAS. Two of the three patient scales correlate with theoretically or practically important scales of similar constructs. For example, the Well-Being scale correlated .79 with the General Well-Being Scale (Dupuy, 1977). Similarly, the Current Symptoms scale correlated .91 with an abbreviated version of the SCL-90-R. The Current Life Functioning Scale correlated .74 with GAS ratings, and the work, intimacy, and health subscales correlated .31, .41,. and .46, respectively, with their respective counterparts on the Social Adjustment Scale. Validity data for the GAS have already

**TABLE 5–3   Reliabilities for the COMPASS
Outpatient Tracking Scales**

Scale	Internal Consistency	Test-Retest Reliability
Client Rated		
Subjective Well-being	.79	.82
Current Symptoms	.94	.85
Current Life Functioning	.93	.76
Mental Health Index	.87	.82
Therapeutic Bond	.88	.62
Therapist Rated		
Global Assessment Scale	NA	.69 to .91
Life Functioning Scales	NA	.58 to .70
Clinical Assessment Index	.84	.77

Summarized from Howard, Brill, Lueger, O'Mahoney, & Grissom, 1993.

been discussed in Chapter 4, and no data are reported for the validity of the therapist-rated Life Functioning Scales.

The COMPASS tracking system is sold as a service to health maintenance organizations (HMOs) or other mental health service providers and will soon be available to private practitioners via fax technology. Clients and therapists complete the measures at intake and every four to six sessions thereafter. After completing the instruments, the therapist must send them to the COMPASS organization where the scales are scored and a four-page report is generated. The report provides useful information regarding both the current status of the client and treatment progress. A graph depicts the client's change since intake using both the Mental Health Index and Clinical Assessment Index. Similarly, the therapeutic bond score is depicted graphically over time. Client changes on each of the individual scales is displayed in a table where the overall amount of change is reported along with percentile scores so that the client's scores can be compared with a normative sample. Finally, individual items that the client endorses as extremely, considerably, or moderately troublesome are displayed.

The COMPASS tracking system is meant to provide ongoing evaluation of therapy progress as a way of both monitoring treatment success and providing feedback so that necessary midcourse changes can be made when necessary. Advantages of the method include the information concerning current status of the client in relationship to a normative sample, immediate feedback regarding client progress, creation of a report that can be used as a clinical record, and minimal work required from the clinician (e.g., all scoring, reporting, and so on is conducted by the

COMPASS personnel). Disadvantages include the lack of information regarding the validity of the therapist-rated Life Functioning Scales and lack of independence in administration and scoring (e.g., the COMPASS system is proprietary and must be purchased from them on a per use basis).

Overall, the COMPASS system is an excellent example of the outcome assessment advocated in this book. Clinicians can purchase a useful service that can inform them about client level of functioning at intake, progress during treatment, and ultimate benefit from treatment.

Dyadic Adjustment Scale

The Dyadic Adjustment Scale (DAS) is a self-report measure of relationship satisfaction in married or cohabitating couples. Developed by Spanier (1976), the DAS has become one of the most widely used scales in marriage research, and is perhaps the instrument of choice in the clinical setting. The 32 items on the DAS were the best out of an original 200-item pool that differentiated between married and divorced individuals.

The DAS can be used as either a general measure of satisfaction in a relationship or as a measure of satisfaction in four different aspects of a relationship: dyadic satisfaction, dyadic cohesion, dyadic consensus, and affectional expression. These four aspects were derived from a factor analysis of the 32 items by the developer of the scale: 10 items from the scale represent dyadic satisfaction, 5 items represent dyadic cohesion, 13 items deal with dyadic consensus, and 4 items from the scale address affectional expression. Although Spanier reported strong evidence favoring the presence of four subscales, subsequent factor analyses have shown differing results, giving only weak support for four subscales. These studies strongly suggest that the DAS is composed of a single factor—a general measure of relationship satisfaction (Sharpley & Cross, 1982; Kazak, Jarmas, & Snitzer, 1988).

Scores from 0 to 151 are possible on the DAS, with higher scores reflecting a better relationship. A Likert-type scale is used for almost all of the items excepting two "yes" or "no" questions. Most of the 32 items use a 7-point scale ranging from "always agree" to "always disagree" or from "all the time" to "never." Six items use a 5-point Likert scale and one item has a 6-point scale. The normative data involved 218 married and 94 divorced men and women.

Spanier (1976) originally reported an alpha coefficient of .96, showing strong internal consistency. This finding was supported in two additional studies (see Sharpley & Cross, 1982; Spanier & Thompson, 1982). The alpha coefficients for the subscales originally reported by Spanier (1976) were .94 for dyadic satisfaction, .81 for dyadic cohesion, .90 for dyadic consensus, and .73 for affectional expression.

High concurrent validity of the DAS has been found by comparing the scale to the Locke-Wallace Marital Adjustment Test. These correlations were .86 for married people and .88 for divorced people. Construct validity can be considered high, as the scale reliably discriminates between divorced and married individuals. Whisman and Jacobson (1992) compared the DAS with the Global Distress Scale of the Marital Satisfaction Inventory as measures of treatment outcome for couples who completed a behavioral marital therapy program. They suggest that the Global Distress Scale of the MSI is a more conservative estimate of change because several items on the GDS assess historical satisfaction with the relationship and do not change as a result of treatment.

The Child Behavior Checklist

The Child Behavior Checklist (CBCL; Achenbach & Edelbrock, 1983) is a well-crafted checklist designed to assess the competencies and behavioral problems of children and adolescents between the ages of 4 and 16. The CBCL is completed by parents or parent surrogates. These respondents rate their child in two general areas: social competence and behavioral problems.

The social competencies portion of the checklist consists of 20 items distributed into three scales: activities, social, and school. The behavioral problems portion of the checklist contains 118 items and several subscales (see Achenbach & Edelbrock, 1983, for a complete description of the CBCL and the various scales of the behavior problems). The respondents are asked to give each item a score between 0 and 2. The scores from each scale can be figured by summing the scores from the scale's individual items. Generally, low scores on the social competence scales indicate a lack of social competence, and high scores on the behavioral problems scale show greater levels of problem behaviors. The raw scores from each scale are used to construct an individual profile from which interpretation and comparison with normative and clinical profiles can be made. Normative data for the CBCL and the profiles (revised) were obtained from a randomly selected sample of 1,400 children and their parents in the Washington, DC, area. Clinical data have been derived from 2,300 children from 42 clinics in the eastern United States. To reflect sex and age differences, Achenbach constructed six different editions of the profile, one for each of the different groups. The group divisions are as follows: boys age 4 and 5, boys age 6 to 11, boys age 12 to 16, girls age 4 and 5, girls age 6 to 11, and girls age 12 to 16. The procedure of comparing individual profiles to group profiles can be done either by hand or with the assistance of a computer. Instructions and computer software are available from the publisher.

The reliability measures of the CBCL have shown the instrument to be stable. Achenbach and Edelbrock (Achenbach, 1978; Achenbach & Edelbrock, 1979) reported test-retest correlations at one week to range from .82 to .97. Long-term stability (12 months) for boys age 6 to 11 averaged at .63. The other groups showed reasonable long-term stability with correlations ranging from .42 to .55. Interparent agreement was adequate, ranging from .54 to .87.

The clinical population of children had scores significantly different from the normal data, showing the CBCL to have excellent discriminative validity. High concurrent validity has also been reported (Hodges, McKnew, Cytryn, Stern, & Klein, 1982; Romano & Nelson, 1988).

The CBCL now is available in several different formats. There is the Teacher Report Form that assesses the child's classroom behavior, the Direct Observation Form that assesses behavior across several 10-minute samples of observation, and the

Youth Self Report Form that allows the older child to report his or her own perceptions of behavior and social competence.

The Addiction Severity Index

The Addiction Severity Index (ASI) is a 180-item structured clinical interview developed to assess the severity of drug and alcohol addiction. The ASI is designed for repeated administration. The protocol takes less than 40 minutes to administer and can easily be given by a technician. The ASI attempts to quantify the severity of an addiction in the context of seven different problem areas that commonly contribute to or result from addiction: medical, employment, alcohol, drug, legal, family/social, and psychiatric.

Objective questions are asked in each of the seven areas. The questions measure the extent and duration of addiction symptoms during the patient's lifetime and during the past month. The patient is also asked to report his or her attitude regarding problems in each of the seven areas. Two scores are tabulated from the data in each area: a severity rating and a composite score. The composite score is mathematically derived from specified items within each problem area. The severity ratings are an estimation of the need for additional treatment rated by the interviewer. The rating is on a scale from 0 to 9, and the interviewer must follow specified guidelines when making the rating. From these ratings, a patient profile is constructed for comparison and interpretation. Complete scoring information and interpretive guidelines are available from the ASI authors.

In a thorough analysis of interrater reliability, McLellan, Luborsky, Cacciola, Griffeth, Evans, Barr, and O'Brien (1985) found that the ASI did quite well, producing an overall coefficient of .89. Test-retest reliability at three days was greater than .92 in all cases. These measures show that the ASI is a stable instrument with low variability within the instrument.

McLellan and colleagues (1985) showed the seven scales of the ASI to be relatively independent of one another. That is, all seven scales provide useful information that does not overlap. Concurrent validity of the ASI was measured by comparing subscales of the instrument with other standardized assessment measures. The concurrent validity was shown to be exceptional. Discriminative validity was also quite high. The sample from which the validity and reliability were measured consisted of a predominantly male veteran population.

Although the ASI is a reliable, valid, and convenient protocol for the assessment of addiction severity, McLellan and associates (1985) recommend that the ASI not be used with the following three groups of patients: older alcoholics who show signs of cognitive impairment and may be unable to follow or understand what is asked of them; young adult substance abusers with criminal involvement who will often purposely falsify the information they give; and adolescents under 16 years of age being supported by parents (since the ASI is designed for older adolescents and adults).

The ASI may be administered by a technician and should always be given in interview form; questionnaire or computer administration of the ASI considerably reduces its reliability and validity.

Practical Applications

The specific outcome measures presented in this chapter are perhaps the most easily applied measures presented in this book. Here are some useful applications:

1. *Assessing pretreatment severity.* As with the global measures, specific measures are useful for assessing the severity of distress prior to treatment. With specific measures, however, certain groups of clients must be targeted for instrument administration. For example, a clinician in private practice may identify depressed clients in an initial interview and then administer the Beck Depression Inventory during or immediately following the interview. In this way, the level of depressive severity can be evaluated along with obtaining a pretreatment administration. Pretreatment administration of specific measures may also provide diagnostic information. For example, six of the nine diagnostic criteria for depression are touched on in the Beck Depression Inventory.

2. *Assessing session-to-session change.* The specific measures presented in this chapter are perhaps the most frequently used measures in studies of psychotherapy effectiveness with outpatient clients who have depression, anxiety, marital problems, child behavior problems, and substance abuse. In some of these studies, the outcome measures are administered at every session. For example, the NIMH Treatment for Depression Collaborative Research Program (Elkin et al., 1989) administered the Beck Depression Inventory to clients nearly every session. Clinicians can also use these instruments to track progress in psychotherapy.

3. *Assessing pre- to posttreatment change.* If administration of instruments at every session is impossible, specific instruments are still extremely useful for assessing pre- to posttreatment change. They differ from global measures in that clients must be identified who have the symptoms or problem areas assessed by the given instrument. Nevertheless, a clinician could identify several instruments that cover his or her typical client load then administer the appropriate instrument at the end of the initial session.

4. *Evaluating the clinical significance of change occurring in psychotherapy.* Just as the global measures can be used to assess clinical significance, specific measures that have normative data can be used to evaluate the clients' end-of-treatment level of functioning by comparing their scores with the norm group. More will said about this topic in Chapter 8, where normative data will be presented for several of the measures reviewed here.

Summary

As with the global measures of outcome, the specific measures included in our sample represent a small proportion of the numerous available instruments. For example, a myriad of brief self-report instruments (or rapid assessment devices) are available, with more being developed each year (Corcoran & Fischer, 1987). Yet, for the most part, these instruments are not used in treatment outcome studies. The degree to which they may contribute to outcome evaluation in the future will be governed by their demonstrated utility in pretest/posttest treatment outcome studies.

The instruments selected, however, have a long history of use in research and to some extent in practice. Their use in practice, however, usually involves diagnostic assessment rather than evaluation of treatment outcome. We hope that by including them in this book we can encourage clinicians to begin using them to assess outcome in practice. Of course, clinicians involved in more specialized practice with a narrow group of clients (e.g., chronic pain patients) may need to do additional work to find practical instruments. Our instruments may provide a good starting point for many clinicians involved in a general practice.

Chapter 6

Individualized Outcome Assessment

Even though contemporary research studies focus on seemingly homogeneous samples of patients (e.g., unipolar depression, agoraphobia), it is clear that each patient is unique and brings to treatment unique problems. For example, although the major complaint of a person may be summed up as "depression" and this person meets diagnostic criteria for major depression, this same patient can have serious interpersonal problems, somatic concerns, evidence of anxiety, financial difficulties, problems at work, problems parenting children, substance abuse, and so on. These problems often become a central focus of treatment, although they are not central to the definition of the depression—the ostensive reason for treatment.

Diversity also characterizes the symptomatic picture that can be present even within the disorder of interest. Williams (1985), for example, has documented considerable evidence that supports the position that even within the seemingly limited diagnosis of agoraphobia, there is significant diversity among patients. He notes, for example, that there is substantial variance in the kinds of situations that provoke panic across patients, including numerous phobias that appear often as simple phobias (e.g., fear of flying, heights). The typical agoraphobic will usually be severely handicapped in some situations, moderately handicapped in others, and not at all restricted in other situations. The most frequent panic-provoking situation (driving on freeways) was rated as "no problem" by nearly 30 percent of agoraphobics. "The configuration of fears in agoraphobics is so highly idiosyncratic that it is substantially true that no two agoraphobics have exactly the same pattern of phobias, and that two people with virtually no overlapping areas of phobia disability can both be called agoraphobic" (p. 112). Furthermore, agoraphobics have many fears that are common to social phobia as well as many somatic complaints for which they often and persistently seek medical consultation even after agoraphobia is diagnosed (Williams, 1985). They are also inclined toward associated problems such as generalized anxiety disorder, depression, obsessions, compulsions, and depersonalization.

Most clinicians will want an assessment of a client's idiosyncratic configuration of fears above and beyond a general measurement of anxiety. Moreover, most will also likely want to know about other "unrelated" problems that may be even more incapacitating or troubling. Comprehensive assessment of outcome may require that changes in all these problems be measured. This is obviously a demanding task—one that can not always be accomplished by application of multiple standardized scales. The use of individualized outcome measures may assist in resolving such dilemmas.

The complexity of agoraphobia is no greater than that apparent in other psychological conditions. People participating in psychotherapy have disturbances that need attention, and these disturbances go far beyond the diagnostic label or target behavior that may be the justification or apparent reason for treatment. Given the multitude of symptoms that any specific patient could present, we can only suggest that in addition to the dimensions tapped by standardized scales, clinicians attempt to measure change on a variety of treatment goals unique to a patient—the assessment of outcome may need to be individualized.

Should Individualized Measures of Change Be Employed?

The earliest studies of psychotherapy usually produced gross ratings of improvement drawn from clinical records. A clinician, usually the therapist, viewed the progress of an individual patient and noted improvement in relation to initial status. This was a highly individualized approach. Since the formulation of patient problems and symptoms was never clearly operationalized and reliably measured, this procedure has given way to more formal assessments. These more formal procedures can provide a clearer picture of change than informal therapist judgments.

Typical of these approaches is the *case-formulation method* advocated by Persons (1991). She has criticized psychotherapy outcome research for being incompatible with psychotherapy as it is actually practiced. Among her criticisms is the overreliance of research on standardized measures of outcome. She notes that even patients with a circumscribed disorder have a wide range of problems, and argues that the typical standardized assessment procedure ignores most of these difficulties, whereas the therapist does not. Persons further notes that the informal assessment procedures used by clinicians in psychotherapy are theoretically based, idiographic, and multifaceted, rather than standardized and limited to a single problem. She suggests that psychotherapy research would be more relevant to everyday clinical practice if it were individualized: Each patient will have a different set of problems assessed with a different set of measures. Persons' suggestions have not gone unchallenged (Garfield, 1991; Herbert & Mueser, 1991; Messer, 1991; Schacht, 1991; Silverman, 1991). She is hardly the first to make such recommendations, however. Strupp, Schacht, and Henry (1988), for example, have argued for the principle of problem-treatment-outcome congruence to increase the likelihood that outcome assessment would accurately reflect the actual targets of treatment. Strupp's proposal and Persons' proposal, however, have not yet faced the foreboding task of empirical application. And similar, if not more practical, approaches were undertaken in the 1970s and 1980s, with enough success to warrant recommendation of a few procedures.

In spite of the difficulties individualized assessment presents, we believe it deserves serious consideration. Three methods are presented next: Target Complaints, Goal Attainment Scaling, and Progress Evaluation Scales. Any one of these procedures can be adopted for everyday clinical practice and promise to systematize the individual assessment of patient outcomes. In keeping with our organizational scheme, Table 6.1 depicts the three measures described in this chapter along with their ratings on each of the dimensions. Note that the individualized outcome measures can be tailored to the client in such a way as to address any of the content, social role, or time orientation categories.

Target Complaints

The use of Target Complaints as criteria of improvement is discussed by Battle, Imber, Hoen-Saric, Stone, Nash, and Frank (1966). Their research suggests that Target Complaints are informative, make good sense to clinicians, and seem sensitive to the changes that result from psychotherapy. A sample form is presented in Figure 6–1. This measure is applied by having the patient state complaints and rate their severity or by having the therapist identify patient complaints and make the severity ratings. Sometimes both collaborate on the task.

The three target symptoms might obviously pertain to one central problem (being overweight, worrying about appearance, feeling inferior to other people) or might seem to be unrelated (compulsive eating, apprehensiveness with other people, not doing homework). The object of choosing symptoms is to allow the patient to define problems and set goals. Thus, neither the problems nor changes that might occur would seem obscure or irrelevant to the therapy.

The clinician should discuss complaints or symptoms in an initial interview, eliciting when they appeared, when last experienced, and their average frequency and duration. This information can help in making the rating of severity. Each subsequent estimate of severity should be undertaken without reference to initial ratings. Thus, the clinician may wish to make several copies of the problems prior to making initial

TABLE 6–1   Idiographic Measures of Outcome with Category Ratings

	Conceptual Scheme Ratings				
Measure	*Content*	*Social Level*	*Source*	*Technology*	*Time Orientation*
Target Complaints	Any	Any	Self/therapist	Specific	State/trait
Goal Attainment Scaling	Any	Any	Self/therapist	Specific	State/trait
PES	Mixed	Mixed	Self/therapist	Specific	State/trait

FIGURE 6–1   Target Symptom Rating Form

Client Name _____   Date _____

Therapist _____

Target Symptom #1 _____

_____

_____

_____

Judged Severity _____|_____|_____|_____|_____|_____
                    Absent   Trivial   Mild   Moderate   Severe

Target Symptom #2 _____

_____

_____

_____

Judged Severity _____|_____|_____|_____|_____|_____
                    Absent   Trivial   Mild   Moderate   Severe

Target Symptom #3

_____

_____

_____

Judged Severity _____|_____|_____|_____|_____|_____
                    Absent   Trivial   Mild   Moderate   Severe

severity ratings. The outcome score then becomes the simple difference between severity ratings at intake and subsequent ratings.

   In general, reliabilities have been reasonably high, and, perhaps more importantly, some validity evidence suggests that independent raters make judgments similar to therapists and patients (Strupp & Bloxom, 1975). One advantage to this procedure is that therapists may state the goals of treatment in their own language and in terms of their theoretical orientation. Experienced therapists certainly have ideas about what is wrong and what their therapy can reasonably hope to focus on. The

Target Complaints method is easily applied across a broad spectrum of patients and therapists, making it ideal for application in a general clinical practice.

The Target Complaints method has generated little research in the ensuing years since the proposal of its use in the NIMH core battery (Waskow & Parloff, 1975). We will defer further discussion of the limitations of Target Complaints to a later point because similar limitations apply to Goal Attainment Scaling, the next measure under discussion.

Goal Attainment Scaling

A method that has received more widespread attention and use is Goal Attainment Scaling (Kiresuk & Sherman, 1968). This measure requires that a number of mental health goals be set up prior to treatment. These goals may be formulated by an individual patient or a clinician. In large treatment settings, goals can be formulated by a combination of clinicians, client, and/or a committee assigned to the task. For each goal specified, a scale with a graded series of likely outcomes, ranging from least to most favorable, is devised. These goals are formulated and specified with sufficient precision that an independent observer can determine the point at which the patient is functioning at any given time. In everyday clinical practice, this allows the clinician to assess goal attainment reliably at anytime. The procedure also allows for transformation of goal attainment into a standard score.

The procedure for evaluating individual progress toward unique goals consists of six steps:

1. A set of goals is specified for the client. (This procedure is similar to that used in specifying Target Complaints, although it allows for more than three goals). Information about the client's background, available resources, level of motivation, and the like can be taken into account in the process of goal setting (Kiresuk & Serhman, 1968). In fact, this is explicitly stated in the training manual, and clinicians are encouraged to base their goals on social circumstances as well as client needs.
2. Each goal is weighted according to priority.
3. A continuum of possible outcomes by the end of the intervention period is specified. Unlike the Target Complaints method, patient improvement can be demonstrated not only by the absence of symptoms but the attainment of a more positive level of functioning.
4. Current or initial (intake) performance is specified.
5. Attained performance on each goal is rated by the therapist at the end of the intervention.
6. The extent of goal attainment is evaluated either through visual analysis or via statistical analysis. Standardized T-scores can be used or a weighted percentage improvement score can be calculated.

Table 6–2 illustrates goals that were set for a client who attended a Crises Intervention Center. Five goals were identified and weighted in terms of priority and

TABLE 6–2 Goal Attainment Scaling

Check whether or not the scale has been mutually negotiated between patient and CIC interviewer.	Yes ___ No ___ Scale 1: Education	Yes ___ No ___ Scale 2: Suicide	Yes ___ No ___ Scale 3: Manipulation	Yes ___ No ___ Scale 4: Drug Abuse	Yes ___ No ___ Scale 5: Dependency on CIC
Scale Attainment Levels					
a. most unfavorable treatment outcome thought likely −2	Patient has made no attempt to enroll in high school.	Patient has committed suicide.	Patient makes rounds of community service agencies demanding medication and refuses other forms of treatment.	Patient reports addiction to "hard narcotics" (heroine, morphine).	Patient has contacted CIC by telephone or in person at least seven times since her first visit.
b. less than expected success with treatment −1	Patient has enrolled in school, but at time of follow-up has dropped out.	Patient has acted on at least one suicidal impulse since her first contact with the CIC, but has not succeeded.	Patient no longer visits CIC with demands for medication but continues with other community agencies and still refuses other forms of treatment.	Patient has used "hard narcotics" but is not addicted and/or uses hallucinogens (LSD, Pot) more than four times a month.	Patient has contacted CIC 5–6 times since intake.
c. Expected level of treatment success 0	Patient has enrolled, and is in school at follow-up, but is attending class sporadically (misses an average of more than a third of her classes during a week).	Patient reports she has at least some suicidal impulses since her first contact with the CIC but has not acted on any of them.	Patient no longer attempts to manipulate for drugs at community service agencies but will not accept another form of treatment.	Patient has not used "hard narcotics" during follow-up period and uses hallucinogens between 1 and 4 times per month.	Patient has contacted CIC 3–4 times since intake.

Continued

TABLE 6–2 Goal Attainment Scaling

d. More than expected success with treatment	Patient has enrolled in school at follow-up and is attending classes consistently, but has no +1 vocational goals.		Patient accepts nonmedication treatment at some community agency.	Patient uses hallucinogens less than once a month.
e. Best anticipated success with treatment	Patient has enrolled in school at follow-up, is attending classes +2 consistently, and has some vocational goals.	Patient reports she has has no suicidal impulses since her first contact with the CIC.	Patient accepts nonmedication treatment and by own report shows signs of improvement.	At time of follow-up, patient is not using any illegal drugs.	Patient has not contacted CIC since intake.

Level at intake: 0
Level at Follow-up:*
Score at intake: −7.0
Score at Follow-up: 5.0

Reprinted from Zusman, J. & Wursten, C. R. (Eds.). (1975). *Program evaluation: Alcohol, drug abuse, and mental health services.* Lexington, Mass.: D.C. Heath.

importance. As can be noted, an attempt was made to reduce inference by phrasing expected levels of attainment in behavioral terms. Visual inspection of Table 6–2 indicates that this client improved substantially in a number of areas over the course of treatment. In addition, reading each set of goals provides a brief summary of important and diverse dimensions of the clients life that were the focus of treatment.

Goal Attainment Scaling allows for a good deal of flexibility in goal setting and can be used in combination with scales from standardized tests. In using this method for the treatment of obesity, for example, one goal could be the specification and measurement of weight loss. A second goal could pertain to reduction of depressive symptoms as measured by a single symptom scale such as the Beck Depression Inventory. Further, marital satisfaction could be assessed via the Marital Satisfaction Inventory if the patient has serious marital problems. The particular scales and behaviors examined could be varied from patient to patient, and, of course, one may include other specific operational definitions of improvement from additional sources of information.

One advantage of Goal Attainment Scaling is that not only is it applicable to individuals but it can also be used to express change in larger systems as well. Thus, it has been recommended for use in marital and family therapy (Russell, Olson, Sprenkle, & Alilano, 1983) and continues to be applied with families, as a way of expressing changes in the family as a whole rather than limiting assessment to the identified patient (Fleuridas, Rosenthal, Leigh, & Leigh, 1990). For example, Woodward, Santa-Barbara, Levin, and Epstin (1978) examined the role of Goal Attainment Scaling in studying family therapy outcome. In their study, which focused on termination and six-month follow-up goals, 270 families were considered. This resulted in an analysis of 1,005 goals. The authors, who seem to be advocates of Goal Attainment Scaling, reported reliable ratings that reflected diverse changes in the families studied. They also noted that ratings correlated moderately with other measures of outcome and thus seemed to be valid. This interesting, although somewhat uncritical, report is a good demonstration of the flexibility of Goal Attainment Scaling and the wealth of information that can result from using this idiographic procedure.

When used in comparative research studies, Goal Attainment Scaling suffers from many of the same difficulties as other goal-setting procedures such as Target Complaints. Some of these difficulties should be noted by clinicians who plan to adopt these methods for evaluation of outcomes. First, goal attainment is judged on a relative rather than an absolute basis, so that behavior change is confounded with expectations. Second, the correlations between goals seems to be around 0.65, raising the questions about their lack of independence. Do clients have separate goals or are the goals representative of some underlying dimension? Perhaps individualized goals and changes in Target Complaints, despite their specificity, measure only a general dimension such as patient subjective discomfort. Third, extremely easy or extremely difficult goals are chosen for analysis, raising questions about what has really changed (e.g., a particular clinician may persistently specify goals that are so easily obtained as to be meaningless). Fourth, because the choice and attainment of goals are related to client as well as therapist characteristics, interpretation of change is difficult: Goal Attainment Scaling progress may reflect better therapy, more modest goals, healthier clients, and so on. Fifth, although goal attainment emphasizes the uniqueness of each client, it does not properly balance idiographic goals with standard criteria of adjustment. The usefulness of this procedure is highly dependent on the clinicians' ability to project outcome accurately.

Calsyn and Davidson (1978) reviewed and assessed Goal Attainment Scaling as an evaluative procedure. These authors suggest that the reliability of Goal Attainment Scaling is more variable than standardized self-report measures. Interrater agreement (reliability) for goal attainment ranged from $r = 0.51$ to 0.85, indicating variability between those making ratings (e.g., therapist, client, expert judge). In general, studies that have correlated Goal Attainment Scaling improvement ratings with other ratings of improvement (such as MMPI scores, client satisfaction, and therapist improvement ratings) have often failed to show substantial agreement (Fleuridas et al., 1990). Suggestions for the use of Goal Attainment Scaling in psychotherapy research have been made by Mintz and Kiesler (1982). Since their review, Lewis, Spencer, Haas, and Di-Vittis (1987) have described methods of data gathering and scale construction that they feel increase the reliability and validity of Goal Attainment Scaling. They applied Goal Attainment Scaling in conjunction with family-based interventions with inpatients. Specific procedures for goal creation and later evaluation increased reliability and validity without reducing the advantages of individualized goals. Among the innovations suggested by these researchers was the use of Goal Attainment Scaling ratings only at follow-up, with evaluations of the *pattern of adjustment* built into goal expectations and evaluations.

Numerous questions continue to be raised about the reliability of creating and judging goals and about the weighting of goals. Clark and Caudrey (1986), for example, have suggested that the use of the T conversion formula proposed by Kiresuk and Sherman (1968) confuses "difficulty" and "importance" of a goal. They propose weighting each goal by its *difficulty* and *importance*.

Similar procedures used in the evaluation of mental health services include the Problem-Oriented System (Klonoff & Cox, 1975; Weed, 1969), and Projection Line System (Lloyds, 1983). These procedures suffer from some of the same deficiencies as Goal Attainment Scaling and Target Complaints; they remain only frameworks for structuring the statement of goals and do not assure that the individualized goals or problems that are specified will be more than poorly defined subjective statements made by patients or clinicians. A partial solution to this problem is to use a system that brings more structure to the task of goal setting. We next consider the Progress Evaluation Scales—just such a procedure.

Progress Evaluation Scales (PES)

A third method that can be advocated for use in individualizing goals is the Progress Evaluation Scales, developed by Ihilevich and Gleser (1979). The PES consists of seven scales, each measuring a particular area of functioning. The seven areas of functioning were chosen to express a broad range of disturbance that is typical of people who are having psychological problems. They include Family Interaction; Occupation (school-job, homemaking); Getting Along with Others; Feelings and Mood;

TABLE 6–3 Progress Evaluation Scales

Instructions: Please circle *one* statement in each column that describes best how you expect to be in _____ months.

Family Interaction	Occupation (School, Job or Homemaking)	Getting Along with Others	Feelings and Mood	Use of Free Time	Problems	Attitude toward Self
Often must have help with basic needs (e.g., eating, dressing).	Does not hold job or care for home or go to school.	Always fighting or destructive or always alone.	Almost always feels nervous, or depressed, or angry and bitter, or no emotions at all.	Almost no recreational activities or hobbies.	Severe problems most of the time.	Negative attitude toward self most of the time.
Takes care of own basic needs but must have help with everyday plans and activities.	Seldom holds job, or attends classes, or cares for home.	Seldom able to get along with others without quarreling or being destructive or is often alone.	Often feels nervous, or depressed, or angry and bitter, or hardly shows any emotion for weeks at a time.	Only occasional recreational activities or repeats the same activity over and over again.	Severe problems more of the time or moderate problems continuously.	Negative attitude toward self much of the time.
Makes own plans but without considering the needs of other family members.	Sometimes holds job, or attends some classes, or does limited housework.	Sometimes quarreling, but seldom destructive; difficulties in making friends.	Frequently in a good mood but occasionally feels nervous, or depressed, or angry for days at a time.	Participates in some recreational activities or hobbies.	Moderate problems most of the time, or mild problems almost continuously.	Almost equal in positive and negative attitude toward self.
Tries to consider everyone's needs but somehow decisions and actions do not work well for everybody in the family.	Holds regular job, or classes, or does housework (or some combination of these) but with difficulty.	Gets along with others most of the time; has occasional friends.	Usually in a good mood, but occasionally feels nervous, or depressed, or angry all day.	Often participates in recreational activities and hobbies.	Occasional moderate problems.	Positive attitude toward self much of the time.
Usually plans and acts so that own needs as well as needs of others in the family are considered.	Holds regular job, or attends classes, or does housework (or some combination of these) with little difficulty.	Gets along with others most of the time; has regular close friends.	In a good mood most of the time, and able to be as happy, or sad, or angry as the situation calls for.	Participates in, as well as creates, variety of own recreational activities and hobbies for self and others.	Occasional mild problems.	Positive attitude toward self most of the time.

59

Use of Free Time; Problems; and Attitudes toward Self. Each of these seven areas is divided into five levels that represent a continuum of adjustment, from the most pathological to the healthiest level observed in the community. Thus, the PES is directed toward not only the absence of pathology but also the presence of positive mental health. Four different versions of the scales are available and appropriate for either children, adolescents, adults, or the developmentally disabled. Goals can be set for each of the seven areas of functioning.

Table 6–3 presents scales of areas of functioning to give the reader a concrete sense of how these scales are used in clinical practice with adults. Development of the PES was heavily influenced by Kiresuk and Sherman's (1968) Goal Attainment Scaling. To use the scales, the therapist, client, or significant other is asked to indicate the item in each scale that best describes current functioning (e.g., behavior and experience during preceding two weeks). A separate rating sheet is used to set goals. These goals are set by the clinician or client or some combination of client, clinician, and significant other. Usually three-month goals are set and the client, therapist, and significant other make outcome ratings independently. The PES authors experimented with a variety of procedures before deciding on a two-week period of assessing functioning and a three-month period for goal setting. Clinicians will want to review their work before modifying the usual procedures.

The results of several studies published in the PES manual suggest that, once interviewers are experienced in the use of the scales, ratings can be made in one to two minutes following a routine diagnostic interview (Ihilevich & Gleser, 1979). Clients and significant others can typically complete the scales in five to eight minutes. According to the manual, the scales seem to have fair test-retest and interrater reliability. Interrater reliability estimates between clinicians rating the same goals ranged from .49 to .86, with a median reliability of .68. Validity has been supported by studies showing that the scales differentiate between normal subjects and patients, as well as more and less severely disturbed patients. The PES correlate with standardized rating scales and show satisfactory convergent and discriminate validity (Ihilevich & Gleser, 1982). The scales have rather low intercorrelations amongst themselves, suggesting that they tap distinct areas of functioning. Important for consideration here is the finding that they are sensitive to changes in level of functioning as assessed by patients, therapists, and significant others (Ihilevich, Gleser, Gritter, Kroman, & Watson, 1981).

Practical Applications of Individual Measures

Individualized measures can be extremely useful in clinical practice because of their versatility and ease of administration. Several practical suggestions regarding their use include:

1. *Selection based on desired focus*. The three methods presented vary in the degree to which they consume time and impose structure on the task of setting up and evaluating goals. For the clinician interested in the procedure that allows for the greatest freedom in specifying goals, the Target Complaints method is recommended. Unfortunately, Target Complaints is psychopathology oriented, measuring only the absence of psychopathology. For those who appreciate more structure and the imposition of a more psychometrically sophisticated approach—albeit one that is initially more time consuming—Goal Attainment Scaling is suggested. The most structured approach, in which therapy outcomes are just slightly individualized, is the Progress Evaluation Scales. This procedures requires very brief amounts of time commitment by the therapist or client while providing only modest individualization of personal goals.

2. *Use in conjunction with other measures.* The most serious disadvantage of using individualized measures in clinical practice is the lack of normative data. By definition, the individual approach does not facilitate comparison with other clients. As a result, the seriousness of the impairment or the size of change cannot be directly compared to a normative sample of treated or untreated clients. By using the individualized measure in conjunction with a global or specific measure that includes a normative group, the aims of both measures can be satisfied.

3. *Rate using more than one source.* All three methods can easily provide data from more than one source. Thus, the clinician as well as the patient (and significant others) can rate change on the same targets of treatment. This advantage is not present on most standardized scales.

4. *Previous applications.* Individualized measures have many of the advantages of global and specific measures, in that they can be used to track change over sessions, assess change pre- and posttreatment, and assess level of pretreatment subjective severity. To the extent that normative data are available, they can also be used to compare with a normative sample. These measures are not typically used, however, for making diagnoses.

Summary

Scales tapping individualized outcome are methods of assessment that have marked advantages for the clinician and for clinical practice. The major advantage is the way outcome is tailored to each client and each therapist. Most of the disadvantages of individualizing outcome are more of a concern in controlled experimental applications where interpretation of findings is hindered by the methodological problems associated with techniques in this area. We have presented what we consider to be the three best options for individualizing outcome assessment. Data generated by individualized goals can provide convincing evidence of change that is rich in meaning.

Chapter 7

Moment-to-Moment Change

Psychotherapy research has evolved over the years from determining *if* psychological treatments are effective to investigating *how* they are effective (Greenberg & Pinsof, 1986; Lambert & Bergin, 1994; Lambert, Masters, & Ogles, 1991). With this evolution, psychotherapy process studies have taken a more dominant role in the research literature (Lambert & Hill, 1994). Traditionally, process and outcome issues were kept separate as if they were technically and theoretically distinct except when attempting to identify the critical process variables that lead to positive outcome. However, psychotherapy process variables may be construed as mini- or micro-outcome measurements (Orlinsky & Howard, 1986). Certainly, most clinicians would agree that they can often identify specific therapy processes that alert them to potential problems or successes in the coming sessions and may be indicative of the final treatment result. For example, "patient involvement" during the first three sessions as measured by one of the scales on the Vanderbilt Psychotherapy Process Scale (VPPS) has been linked to successful outcome (Gomes-Schwartz, 1978). From one perspective, the measurement of patient involvement might be seen as an outcome measure since the degree to which the client becomes involved is related to the ultimate outcome. In this chapter, we hope to address briefly some of the most common methods used to assess psychotherapy process in clinical research and how these may be beneficially used by the practicing clinician to identify key components of therapy and modify their interventions with clients.

Selecting process instruments for this chapter was a difficult task. A myriad of client-, therapist-, and judge-rated instruments are available yet not all could be included (see Greenberg & Pinsof, 1986, for a more detailed review of selected instruments). Our goal was to choose process assessment methods that have a demonstrated relationship with therapy outcome and that meet the criteria stated in the Preface. Although numerous components of the therapy process are thought to be important and sometimes even necessary for change to occur, few process variables have clear research evidence for their support. In some cases, clinicians believe in the importance of a process variable and its instrumentality for change,

TABLE 7–1   Process Measures with Category Ratings

Measure	Content	Social Level	Source	Technology	Time Orientation
ES	Cognition/affect	Interpersonal	Rater	Observation	State
TSR	Cognition/affect	Interpersonal	Self/therapist	Global	State
VPPS	All	Interpersonal	Rater	Observation	State
HAQ	Cognition/affect	Interpersonal	Self	Specific	State
CALTARS	Cognition/affect	Interpersonal	Self	Observation	State
WAI	Cognition/affect	Interpersonal	Self	Specific	State
BLRI	Cognition/affect	Interpersonal	Self	Specific	State
CCRT	All	Intrapersonal	Rater	Specific	State
VNIS	Cognition/affect	Interpersonal	Rater	Observation	State

yet no empirical studies have been conducted relative to the variable. In other cases, a process variable has several operational methods for its assessment with a variety of findings concerning the occurrence and relationship of the construct to outcome and other process variables. For example, many clinicians believe that therapist empathy, respect, and warmth are necessary therapist contributions to the counseling process if change is to occur and several instruments have been developed to assess empathy and warmth. Empirical evidence suggests a relationship between empathy, respect (and warmth), and client change, but this relationship depends on the type of scale used to measure the process variables (Lambert, DeJulio, & Stein, 1978). We attempted to limit our selection of instruments to those with evidence for a direct relationship to therapy outcome.

The process evaluations that occur in research settings are typically made by the therapist or the client who makes ratings immediately following the session, or by a trained observer who rates transcripts, audiotapes, or videotapes of the session. In addition, one notable combination, Interpersonal Process Recall (IPR; Elliot, 1986), involves clients and therapists rating the videotapes of their own sessions immediately following the therapy hour. Clinicians can easily obtain client paper-pencil ratings immediately following the session or complete therapist-report instruments themselves. It may be difficult and impractical, however, to obtain recorded tapes of sessions and to train and pay independent judges to rate them. Despite these problems, we have included judge-rated scales in this chapter for those circumstances where time and money permit using observer ratings of the psychotherapy process. Perhaps clinicians who meet in treatment teams will learn to use process rating instruments as a group and then once a month or so they will exchange tapes so that each person gets an independent rating of a difficult case. The potential applications of process rating instruments are often limited only by one's creativity in applying them. In addition, therapists who are trained as independent observers will naturally attend to certain aspects of therapy process and may rate their own sessions using observer-based instruments even though the therapists' perspective may alter the results of the scale. At the same time, therapists rating their own sessions may gain valuable information regarding the progress of the client.

General Process Instruments

Experiencing Scale (ES)

The Experiencing Scale is a single 7-point ordinal scale that reflects increasing levels of client experiencing as determined by the client's verbal behavior (see Table 7–2). The intent of the ES is to assess the client's participation in therapy evidenced by the degree to which the client focuses on and expands on inner referents (Klein, Mathieu-Coughlan, & Keisler, 1986). The instrument is rated by trained judges using segments of transcripts, audiotapes, or videotapes. Originally, the scale was used to rate segments from individual client-centered psychotherapy sessions from 2 to 8 minutes in length, but the scale has been applied to group, couples, and monologue-type situations and to a variety of theoretical orientations (e.g., dynamic, gestalt, cognitive). While the theoretical framework of the ES is firmly grounded in client-centered theory and phenomenological philosophy, the scale is assumed to "define the basic and essential processes that lead to change and health" irrespective of theoretical orientation (Klein, Mathieu-Coughlan, & Keisler, 1986, p. 27). In other words, experiencing is viewed as the *method* by which the client explores his or her problems while the theoretical orientation of the therapist determines the *content* of the exploration.

The ES manual (Klein, Mathieu, Gendlin, & Kiesler, 1969) details the theoretical and research background of the ES and gives procedures and materials for

TABLE 7–2   Short Form of the Experiencing Scale (Patient)

	Stage Content	Treatment
1	External events; refusal to participate	Impersonal, detached
2	External events; behavioral or intellectual self-description	Interested, personal, self-participation
3	Personal reactions to external events; limited self-descriptions; behavioral descriptions of feelings	Reactive, emotionally involved
4	Descriptions of feelings and personal experiences	Self-descriptive; associative
5	Problems or propositions about feelings and personal experiences	Exploratory, elaborative, hypothetical
6	Felt sense of an inner referent	Focused on there being more about "it"
7	A series of felt senses connecting the content	Evolving, emergent

Reprinted by permission of Marjorie H. Klein, Philippa L. Mathieu, Eugene T. Gendlin, and Donald J. Kiesler.

conducting eight 2-hour rater training sessions. Raters are trained to rate each client statement using the 7-point scale. Summary ratings are tabulated by counting the frequency of statements in each category in order to identify the modal level of experiencing and the peak level of experiencing, regardless of the duration. In addition, practice ratings are included with a final assessment of rater reliability. Klein, Mathieu-Coughlan, and Keisler (1986) suggest rating at least two segments of a therapy sequence using middle or working sessions rather than the initial or termination sessions when relating the experiencing process to outcome. Obviously, random samples of the therapy sequence will result in better representativeness of the actual occurrences in the treatment.

Generally, the reliability of the ES is quite good. Interrater reliability coefficients are typically in the .80s and .90s when rating multiple cases and somewhat lower when rating single cases (Klein, Mathieu-Coughlan, & Keisler, 1986). Validity data suggest that the experiencing construct is representative of a reflective or self-observational style, a skill that can be taught, a process that is related to therapist interventions, and an important indicator of productive functioning that is ultimately related to therapy outcome (Klein, Mathieu-Coughlan, & Keisler, 1986).

Therapy Session Report (TSR)

An alternative method for studying the therapy process involves the collection of client and therapist reports of therapeutic events. Orlinsky and Howard's (1966) Therapy Session Report (TSR) was developed to study both the client's and the therapist's experience of the therapy session, and the interrelationships between the two. The test authors originally defended the validity of asking about clients' subjective experiences by claiming that although not all experiences can be expressed in words, and clients' verbal abilities differ, most clients can describe the most salient parts of their therapy experience if given sets of statements from which to chose (Orlinsky & Howard, 1966). They also note that analyzing the interrelationships among clients' responses can help circumvent problems of limited client insight. Finally, they argue that because psychotherapy is a self-reflective process for both client and therapist, asking them to reflect on their experience should not detract from, but rather clarify and intensify, their participation in therapy.

Both the client and the therapist forms of the TSR ask the participants how they felt about the session they just completed, what the client talked about, what problems or feelings concerned the client, and how the client felt during the session. They also both ask how the client and therapist related to one another, how the therapist felt during the session, how well the therapist understood the client, and how helpfully the therapist reacted to the client. Finally, the client and therapist forms both ask about the client's ideational/emotional arousal, self-evaluation, self-awareness, self-control, emotional and psychological functioning, sense of progress, and motivation for coming to the session. The client form alone asks what clients felt they got from the session and their motivation for the next session. The therapist form alone asks what aims for their client the therapist worked on during the session and what the therapist's motivations were for the session, self-disclosure, and personal reactions. Both forms take about 10 to 15 minutes to complete, and are filled out on computer answer sheets for quick scoring. After the questionnaire was designed, baseline data were collected on 60 clients (rating a total of 890 therapy sessions they participated in) and from 17 therapists (470 sessions total). Although most of the data were collected on individual psychotherapy clients and therapists, marital and group therapy were represented as well.

Two main uses for the TSR were proposed by Orlinsky and Howard (1966). First, the TSR was used to examine if therapists' and clients' experiences of therapy sessions agree. Therapists were found to agree with clients on what topics were discussed, on various aspects of the dialogue, and on how well the session went overall. Little agreement was found, however, between therapists' and clients' perceptions of client concerns, their aims in exchange, their behavior in terms of interpersonal relatedness, and their feelings. Second, and more importantly, the TSR was used to evaluate if therapists' feelings during therapy predict their clients' report of progress. When therapists felt that their clients were communicating effectively and had good rapport with the experiences of the client, clients reported making progress in therapy. On the other hand, when therapists felt bored and discouraged, clients felt that they were not getting much out of therapy.

In summary, the TSR is historically important for paving the way for other instruments assessing clients' subjective experience of therapy. Moreover, it is important in its own right for being a well-tested instrument providing clinically useful information on how well therapists' and clients' experiences agree, and on how therapists' feelings during therapy can help them predict their clients' sense of progress. In addition, the client report form may be used separately from the therapist rated form when therapist time is an issue.

Vanderbilt Psychotherapy Process Scale (VPPS)

Using the TSR as a starting point, Strupp, Hartley, and Blackwood (1974) developed the Vanderbilt Psychotherapy Process Scale (VPPS) to "obtain objective assessments of the characteristics of the (therapy) participants and their transactions" (O'Malley, Suh, & Strupp, 1983, p. 582). The final version of the VPPS is a clinical judge-rated scale consisting of 80 Likert-type items that are rated on a 1 ("not at all") to 5 ("a great deal") scale (Suh, Strupp, & O'Malley, 1986). The items are divided into eight factor analytically derived scales: patient participation, patient hostility, patient psychic distress, patient exploration, patient dependency, therapist exploration, therapist warmth and friendliness, and negative therapist attitude (see Table 7–3). Internal consistency estimates for the eight scales are excellent, ranging from .82 to .96 (median .92; O'Malley, Suh, & Strupp, 1983). Interrater reliabilities are adequate, ranging from .79 to .94 (median .92; O'Malley, Suh, & Strupp, 1983).

Suh, Strupp, and O'Malley (1986) suggest using 15-minute segments from audiotapes or videotapes to make VPPS ratings. Although the Vanderbilt researchers have used advanced clinical students or recent Ph.D. psychologists as raters, Suh, Strupp, and O'Malley indicate that a relatively low level of clinical experience is required to make reliable judgments and therefore students with a minimal level of

TABLE 7–3   Vanderbilt Psychotherapy Process Scale

Subscale	Description	Example Item
Patient Participation	Degree to which the patient is positively engaged in the therapeutic interaction	Patient took initiative in bringing up the subjects that were talked about
Patient Hostility	Rating of the more negative aspects of the patient's behavior and attitudes	Patient reacted negatively to the therapist's comments
Patient Psychic Distress	Rating of the patient's feelings of discouragement	Withdrawn
Patient Exploration	Level of patient self-examination	Patient tried to understand the reasons behind problematic feelings or behavior
Patient Dependency	Rating of patient's reliance on the therapist	Deferential
Therapist Exploration	Degree to which the therapist attempts to examine the patient's feelings and behaviors	Helped the patient to change and to try new ways of dealing with self and others
Therapist Warmth and Friendliness	Rating of overt therapist warm behaviors and emotional involvement	Showed warmth and friendliness towards the patient
Negative Therapist Attitude	Rating of therapist behaviors or attitudes that might threaten or intimidate the patient	Annoyed

Summarized from Suh, Strupp, & O'Malley, 1986.

clinical experience may be adequate judges. Studies using the VPPS have indicated that patient involvement (a composite including patient participation and patient hostility) consistently predicts treatment outcome irrespective of therapist orientation (Gomes-Schwartz, 1978) and that the relationship between patient involvement and outcome increases in strength across the first three sessions (O'Malley, Suh, & Strupp, 1983).

Measures of the Therapeutic Relationship

The measurement and description of the therapeutic alliance, working alliance, or therapeutic relationship as the "overarching general process variable that relates to outcome" has recently experienced a resurgence of interest (Goldfried, Greenberg, & Marmar, 1990, p. 670). Several process measures of the therapeutic relationship are available, four of which we have selected for presentation here: Penn Helping Alliance Rating Scales, California Therapeutic Alliance Rating System, Working Alliance Inventory, and Barrett-Lennard Relationship Inventory.

Penn Helping Alliance Scales

The Helping Alliance (HA) scales were developed at the University of Pennsylvania by Lester Luborsky and colleagues (Alexander & Luborsky, 1986). The system includes three instruments developed to assess the strength of the working relationship between client and therapist based on a psychodynamic formulation of the helping alliance. The three measures use similar items but three different formats: the Helping Alliance questionnaire (HAq—with two parallel forms for the therapist and client), a counting signs method (HAcs), and a rating scale (HAr). The Penn system is based on the assumption that the Helping Alliance is composed of two factors: (1) how helpful the client believes the therapist is or will be and (2) the client's perception of the collaboration between himself or herself and the therapist. The three main HA scales are each divided into these two main categories which are in turn divided into subscales.

The Helping Alliance questionnaire (HAq) consists of 17 items that are rated using a 6-point interval scale, ranging from +3 ("Yes, I strongly feel that it is true") to −3 ("No, I strongly feel that it is not true") with no 0 point. The items are written so that both clients and therapists can rate them. Total scores are obtained by summing the ratings. Alexander and Luborsky (1986) report that this method is the most cost effective and the least time consuming of the three methods.

The counting signs (HAcs) method subdivides the perceived helpfulness of the therapist category into four subscales: (1) the client perceives that the therapy and/or the therapist is helpful, (2) the client believes he or she is improving, (3) the client feels a rapport between himself or herself and the therapist, and (4) the client is confident that the therapist and/or the therapy will be helpful. The second category, the client's perception of his or her collaboration with the therapist, is divided into three subscales: (1) the client believes that he or she is working with the therapist toward jointly shared goals, (2) the client and the therapist agree about the reasons for the client's problems, and (3) the client and the therapist are similar to each other. The HAcs method involves an observer reading through the therapy transcript and identifying all of the client's statements or "signs" relevant to these subscales, recording which subscale each "sign" relates to, determining whether each is positive or negative (a negative sign is the opposite of one of the seven subscales—e.g., the client and therapist are not similar to each other), and, finally, rating the intensity of each "sign" on a 5-point interval scale. To determine a client's score, one adds the number of positive signs, or perhaps finds the difference between the number of positive and negative signs, weighting each by its intensity rating.

The rating (HAr) method is similar to the HAcs method, except that each subscale is in the form of a 10-point interval scale and three new subscales have been added. In addition to the subscales just cited, the therapist helpfulness category includes: (1) the client perceives the therapist as supportive and (2) the client believes that the therapist respects him or her. The third new subscale (3) the client perceives himself or herself as improving in the ability to understand his or her own behavior, has been added to the collaboration category. Like the HAcs, the HAr is observer rated. To obtain the client's score, the subscale ratings are added together.

All three Helping Alliance scales have parallel forms for the therapist. The Therapist Facilitative Behaviors' Counting Signs Method (TFBcs) and the Therapist Facilitative Behaviors' Rating Method (TFBr) are rated by trained judges, whereas the Therapist Facilitative Behaviors' Questionnaire Method (TFBq) is completed by the therapist. Each of these instruments has items that are parallel, respectively, to those of the HAcs, the HAr, and the HAq. Scoring is identical.

Regarding reliability, Luborsky and colleagues found that interrater reliabilities ranged from .75 to .88 for the HAr method, with satisfactory internal reliability for the subscales (coefficient alpha = .96; Alexander & Luborsky, 1986). For the HAcs method, judges were rather unreliable in locating the same "signs" or client statements relevant to the helping alliance; for example, using the same therapy session transcripts, one judge identified 120 "signs" while another identified 173. However, significant interrater agreement was found for total numbers of signs, with reliabilities ranging from .47 to .82. Interrater reliabilities for the TFBcs and the TFBr were generally in the .80s. HAq reliabilities across different occasions was .83.

Regarding validity, Alexander and Luborsky (1986) found that the two categories (therapist helpfulness and collaboration) correlated significantly with each other, r = .68 for the HAcs method and r = .91 for the HAr method. The two methods (HAcs and HAr) also correlate significantly with each other for positive signs (range from .57 to .86), though not for negative signs. Also, early HAcs HAr scores were positively related to outcome measures, with correlations around .5. The authors further report that the HAq and the TFBq predicted outcome in a study using veterans with drug dependency, with correlations ranging from .51 to .72. Overall, the Helping Alliance scales provide some useful methods for assessing the therapeutic alliance. The patient self-report version is particularly appealing given its brevity.

California Therapeutic Alliance Rating System (CALTARS)

The CALTARS (Marmar, Horowitz, Weiss, & Marziali, 1986; Marmar, Weiss, & Gaston, 1989) consists of 41 clinical judge-rated items: 21 patient items (11 positive and 10 negative contributions to the alliance) and 20 therapist items (11 positive and 9 negative contributions to the alliance). The items are grouped into five factor analytically derived scales: therapist understanding and involvement, patient hostile resistance, patient commitment, therapist negative contributions, and patient working capacity (Marmar, Weiss, & Gaston, 1989). Although the instrument was developed in studies of time-limited dynamic psychotherapy, the authors indicate that pilot studies appear promising in terms of applying the CALTARS to a broad range of clinical problems and therapeutic orientations (Marmar, Horowitz, Weiss, & Marziali, 1986). The clinical judges in the early work with this instrument were experienced clinicians or advanced trainees. The authors suggest, however, that experienced clinicians may be "more readily trained to a criterion of reliability" (Marmar, Horowitz, Weiss, & Marziali, 1986, p. 370). In studies of the CALTARS and its relationship to outcome and in-therapy behaviors, judges typically rate 20- to 25-minute videotaped segments of four different sessions, the segments are either the first 25 minutes of the session or a randomly selected 20-minute segment (first third, middle third, or last third).

The CALTARS items have also been rewritten and used as patient (CALPAS-P) and therapist (CALPAS-T) report measures of the alliance. For example, Gaston (1991) presents evidence of the reliability and criterion-related validity of the CALPAS-P. The CALPAS-P consists of 24 items divided into four scales that are rated by the client on a 1 ("not at all") to 7 ("very much so") scale. Gaston (1991) reported adequate internal consistency for the total scale (alpha = .84), with a range from .43 to .73 for the four subscales. The scales were also moderately correlated with one another. Gaston (1991) also reported that the CALPAS-P is negatively related to a pretreatment measure of symptomatology. This suggests that individuals with a greater intensity of disturbance have a more difficult time establishing a therapeutic alliance. Finally, the CALPAS-P scores were positively correlated with a measure of treatment satisfaction.

In sum, the various versions of the California Therapeutic Psychotherapy Alliance System present a promising and useful method of assessing the therapeutic alliance.

Working Alliance Inventory (WAI)

The WAI was originally developed to assess the Working Alliance as conceptualized by Bordin (1976). Bordin proposed that the Working Alliance consists of three distinct features: agreement on goals, concordance regarding tasks, and personal bonds. Based on these features, Horvath (1981) developed a self-report inventory to assess the three dimensions while considering three applications: (1) predicting therapy outcome, (2) identifying weaknesses in the alliance in clinical situations, and (3) investigating qualitative differences among alliances developed by therapists of a variety of orientations in research settings (Horvath & Greenberg, 1986).

The WAI includes 36 items rated on a 7-point Likert scale with 12 items on each of three dimensions. Horvath and Greenberg (1986) recommend administering the instrument after the third, fourth, or fifth session, although they indicate the instrument may be useful for long-term therapy cases as well. A therapist report version of the instrument was written so a multitrait-multimethod study of alliance constructs could be conducted (Horvath & Greenberg, 1986, 1989). However, developing the client report instrument appeared to be the primary focus of the research.

Internal consistency is good for all three scales on both the client and therapist forms, although there are some indications that the scales are not independent (Horvath & Greenberg, 1989). Mosley found correlations between the three scales to be quite high, especially between Goal and Task (.92). Similarly, Tracey and Kokotovic's (1989) factor analysis of the WAI indicates that although there are some differences among what the scales measure, the WAI is most strongly measuring one overriding general alliance factor. Safran and Wallner (1991) compared the relative predictive validity of the WAI and the CALPAS-P administered to 22 patients at the third session. They report that both instruments predicted outcome measured in a number of ways, although the CALPAS was predictive of a "slightly wider spectrum of outcome measures than the WAI" (Safran & Wallner, 1991, p. 188).

The major advantage of the WAI is the brief, self-report format. Clients and therapists can complete the instrument in just 5 to 10 minutes. In addition, the WAI is theoretically based and has been demonstrated to predict therapy outcome (Greenberg & Webster, 1982; Horvath, 1981). Evidence of the convergent and concurrent validity of the instrument have also been presented (Horvath & Greenberg, 1989).

Barrett-Lennard Relationship Inventory (BLRI)

The BLRI (Barrett-Lennard, 1959) has a long history of use in the psychotherapy literature as a measure of client-perceived therapist contributions to the therapy. Based on Roger's Client Centered Therapy, the BLRI includes four interspersed scales (empathic understanding, level of regard, unconditionality of regard, and congruence), each containing 16 items (8 worded positively, 8 worded negatively). Level of regard is defined as one's overall positive or negative affect toward another. Congruence is seen as the degree of consistency between one's total experience, one's conscious awareness, and one's overt communication. Incongruence can thus result from saying something one doesn't feel (inconsistency between conscious awareness and overt communication) or being unaware of one's true feelings (inconsistency between conscious awareness and total experience).

Several forms of the BLRI exist, two of which are most relevant to the present discussion: the OS, where one rates another's feelings toward oneself, and the MO, where one rates one's feelings toward another. The items are rated on an anchored 6-point scale ($+3$, $+2$, $+1$, -1, -2, -3). No 0 is used, based on the assumption that people give 0s to avoid deliberation. Although Barrett-Lennard concedes the possibility that for some items the most accurate response would be an "equally true and untrue" (0) response, he argues that given the balance between positively and negatively worded items, errors resulting from forced choice of $+1$ or -1 should cancel out. For each scale, the obtained score is the sum of all the ratings for the negatively worded items multiplied by -1, added to the sum of the ratings for the positively worded ones. Barrett-Lennard (1986) feels that at least three sessions need to have passed before one has enough experience of the helping relationship to be able to rate it meaningfully using the BLRI. Although no true norms exist for the BLRI, most of the scores lie on the positive side of zero. Scores tend to be highest for level of regard, lowest for unconditionality, with empathy and congruence falling in between.

The BLRI's internal consistency is quite good. Alpha's for the four scales range from .74 to .91. In addition, all four scales have good test-retest reliabilities, ranging from .80 for unconditionality to .85 for congruence. The BLRI shows good construct validity (especially for the OS form). A number of studies (reviewed in Gurman, 1977) show client ratings on the OS form to be positively correlated with therapy outcome. The lesser-used MO form has much lower predictive power, though it is not necessarily invalid. OS ratings by marriage partners were highly correlated with marital adjustment measures, and the greater the difference between individuals' OS ratings and their partners' MO ratings for them, the more marital conflict there was. A variety of intervention studies have also used the BLRI as a measure of change. According to Barrett-Lennard (1986), these studies have found the empathy, level of regard, and congruence scales to be correlated with intervention effects assessed in various ways. All in all, the OS form of the BLRI seems to be a good measure for assessing the quality of the helping relationship and for predicting outcome.

Verbal Response Modes

Classification of client and therapist utterances has been of interest to researchers since Rogers and Dymond (1954) conducted the first studies using audiotapes to record in-therapy events. With accurate records of therapist statements via transcripts or tapes, researchers could examine the impact of various types of therapist interventions or client modes of speaking. Several classification schemes have been developed (see Elliot, Hill, Stiles, Friedlander, Mahrer, & Margison, 1987), one of which we have chosen to describe: the Hill Counselor and Client Verbal Response Modes Categories.

Hill Counselor and Client Verbal Response Modes Categories (HVRM)

The HVRM includes two systems that classify counselor and client statements into categories. The counselor system includes 14 different categories: minimal encourager, silence, approval-reassurance, information, direct guidance, closed question, open question, restatement, reflection, interpretation, confrontation, nonverbal referent, self-disclosure, and other. The client system includes nine categories: simple response, request, description, experiencing, exploration of client-counselor relationship, insight, discussion of plans, silence, and other.

To use these systems, trained "unitizers" divide session transcripts into "response units," or sentences. Three trained judges then independently classify each response unit into one of the aforementioned categories. When all three judges disagree over the assignment of a unit, they discuss it until they can agree on a category.

Hill (1986) considers these systems pantheoretical, based on the fact that counselors from several different orientations agreed that the categories cover all of the possible verbal events that generally occur in therapy. She reports fairly high interjudge agreement, with kappas ranging from .68 to .79 for the counselor system and .71 to .92 for the client system. Content validity is established by the fact that the categories were based on existing category systems. Several studies have demonstrated that the systems match what we know about therapy sessions; for example, when used with intake interviews, most of the counselor data are classified as minimal encouragers, information, and closed questions. Also, the first two-thirds of intake sessions were classified as mainly minimal encouragers, closed questions, and restatements, whereas the last third were characterized more by information, direct guidance, and interpretation.

Other Instruments

The Core Conflictual Relationship Theme (CCRT) Method

The CCRT method is system designed to identify troublesome patterns in an individual's relationships with significant others. With strong ties to psychodynamic psychotherapy, this method assumes that clients repeat certain maladaptive patterns across their relationships with various significant others, including the therapist. Using the descriptions clients give about past and current relationships, either spontaneously in therapy or during "relationship anecdote paradigm interviews" (Luborsky & Crits-Christoph, 1990), a rater attempts to identify (1) the client's needs, wishes, or intentions in relation to a significant other; (2) the client's interpretation of the other's response to those needs or wishes; and (3) the client's response in return. The significant other's response and the client's return response can be coded as positive or negative. A positive response involves the actual or expected fulfillment of a wish or need, and a negative response involves an actual or expected lack of wish fulfillment. Judges simply identify the wishes, other's responses, and client return responses in therapy session transcripts, code the responses as positive or negative, and count the number of times each appears. The wish, other's response, and client return response that appear most often are considered to be the Core Conflictual Relationship Theme (Luborsky & Crits-Christoph, 1990).

A detailed description of the CCRT scoring method can be found in Luborsky and Crits-Christoph (1990). These authors also suggest other options for judging CCRTs, such as a 5-point rating scale for judging the intensity of the wishes and responses, recording the sequences of the various wishes and responses, and rating the extent to which clients are aware of their wishes and responses. Finally, Luborsky and Crits-Cristoph (1990) provide a list of standard categories of wishes and responses—for example, client's desires to approved of, to not be judged, or to be affirmed are standardized under the general category "to be accepted."

Luborsky and Crits-Cristoph (1990) find an average interrater reliability for non standardized wishes and responses of .79. Weighted kappas for standard category agreement range from .61 to .70. Regarding validity, these authors compared CCRT pervasiveness at the beginning of therapy with its pervasiveness at the end of therapy, assuming that fewer instances of maladaptive relationship patterns constitute client improvement. Clients improved, although nonsignificantly, in wish pervasiveness, and improved significantly in response pervasiveness. Although CCRT pervasiveness was unrelated to standardized symptom measures (the Hopkins Symptom Checklist and the Health Sickness Rating Scale) early in therapy, improvement in CCRT pervasiveness as therapy progressed was related to symptom improvement as measured by these instruments.

Vanderbilt Negative Indicators Scale (VNIS)

Initially based on surveys of clinicians, theoreticians, and psychotherapy researchers, the Vanderbilt psychotherapy research group developed several versions of the Vanderbilt Negative Indicators Scale (VNIS; Gomes-Schwartz, 1978; Hadley & Strupp, 1976; Strupp, Hadley, & Gomes-Schwartz, 1977; Strupp, Moras, Sandell, Waterhouse, O'Malley, Keithly, & Gomes-Schwartz, 1981). The current version consists of 42 items grouped into five subscales: Patient Qualities, Therapist Personal Qualities, Errors in Technique, Patient-Therapist Interaction, and Global Factors. The Global Factors subscale contains four items "designed to tap general clinical impressions of the session" (Suh, Strupp, & O'Malley, 1986, p. 305). Each of the subscales is further divided into conceptual categories. The total score can also be used.

The internal consistency of the subscales ranges from .26 to .81, with interrater reliabilities ranging from .58 to .88. Because the scales were formed conceptually rather than statistically, the low internal consistencies may be expected (Suh, Strupp, & O'Malley, 1986). The VNIS total score has been used to discriminate high from low outcome groups of clients when raters evaluated tapes of the third session (Strupp, Keithly, Moras, Samples, Sandell, & Waterhouse, 1980). Similarly, subscale ratings of the first three sessions were related to a composite index of client improvement (Sandell, 1981).

The VNIS is a promising instrument that attempts to assess an important if not critical dimension of the therapeutic process. Although there is a paucity of research regarding the correlates of the VNIS, we recommend that clinicians become familiar with its content and experiment with it in their practices. Suh and colleagues (1986) recommend that the VNIS be used only by experienced clinicians. Unlike other process measures, the VNIS requires a fair degree of inference and an applied frame of reference.

Adherence and Competence Scales

Rating systems have been developed in studies of psychotherapy outcome to assure that treatments are administered in a uniform or competent fashion. For example, Beck, Rush, Shaw, and Emery (1979) present a rating scale for cognitive therapy of depression to evaluate the degree to which the therapist is adhering to the cognitive model. Similarly, a second scale has been developed to rate the competence of the clinician by evaluating the degree to which he or she applies the model in a consistent and timely manner (JCCP special section on Manuals, 1984). This type of process rating instrument may be especially useful to clinicians who are involved in supervision.

Practical Applications of Process Instruments

What are the applications of process instruments for the practicing clinician?

1. *Peer review.* We can think of no better or more useful application of the many judge-rated process instruments than as tools for clinicians to use in mutual peer review. We are not referring to peer review in the quality assurance sense, although as empirical evidence demonstrates the necessity of meaningful process variables these instruments may be used for quality assurance, but for the personal growth of the therapist.

2. *Therapist adherence and competence.* For those therapists who are treating clients using systematic methods, adherence and competence rating scales may be extremely useful. These scales may also be useful to supervisors. Clinicians who supervise neophyte therapists have not taken advantage of the many treatment manuals that are developed by researchers to ensure treatment integrity, but as manuals become more commonly used and readily available, instruments for rating adherence and competence for the methods can also be integrated into training.

3. *Fine tuning.* Clinicians who learn rating systems will also be more attuned to relevant client signals of therapeutic progress. For example, a clinician who has used the VPPS may notice signs of reduced patient involvement during the early sessions of therapy and subsequently take steps to intervene appropriately. Similarly, clinicians trained in verbal response mode rating may be more aware of their typical patterns of communication. As clinicians become accustomed to listening through a rating scale framework, their interventions may be more appropriately matched to the level of client experiencing, the CCRT, the therapeutic quadrant, and so on.

4. *Description of micro-outcomes.* For those process characteristics that are related to posttreatment outcome, clinicians can report on micro-successes in therapy by obtaining and reporting process ratings. For example, the clinician may obtain a process rating that indicates the therapeutic alliance is alive and growing in a healthy fashion, even though no symptomatic change has occurred for the client yet. In this case, the positive alliance may be an indication that change is on the horizon and that continuation of the relationship is warranted. This information can be used in reports to insurance companies, in treatment team meetings, or for routine quality assurance evaluations. As clinicians take advantage of the relevant process instruments that are available, evidence of therapeutic progress can be gathered early in treatment.

5. *Training.* Process instruments provide a unique teaching tool that can be used when training psychotherapists. Supervisors can easily require neophyte therapists to rate transcripts or tapes of their own therapy sessions. And in fact, all three of us have participated in group psychotherapy practicums where a verbal response modes category rating system was used as a key ingredient for learning to listen to group therapy process. In addition, one of us (Ogles) was required to transcribe and rate a therapy session using a verbal response mode rating system as a part of a graduate school practicum course in individual psychotherapy. After examining the results, he identified a pattern of questioning that occurred whenever he intended to make an interpretive statement but felt reluctant to do so. Similar and meaningful learning has occurred for his students who are also required to make ratings. Again, the possible applications are limited only by one's creativity.

6. *Identification of negative signs.* Process instruments can be used to identify breeches in the therapeutic relationship. The VNIS was developed specifically for this purpose and may be helpful to therapists and counselors when treatment is seemingly ineffective. Hopefully, the ratings can occur quickly enough that the course of treatment can be adapted in such a way as to prevent negative outcome, but in other circumstances the rating scale may be useful for understanding past mistakes and preventing future reoccurences.

Chapter *8*

Clinical Significance

One of the continuing complaints of clinicians who attempt to make practical application of psychotherapy and counseling research is the lack of information regarding the clinical significance of research findings (Barlow, 1981; Barlow, Hayes, & Nelson, 1984; Jacobson, Follette, & Revenstorf, 1984; Kazdin, 1977; Persons, 1991). More specifically, researchers' consistent focus on group means and statistically significant results may lead to neglecting information regarding the variety of individual responses to treatments and the practical or clinical meaningfulness of individual change (Jacobson & Truax, 1991). Clinicians are unlikely to use outcome instruments just because researchers use them as dependent variables unless the measures are valid indicators of "real" change. In essence, clinicians query, "What clinically relevant change is demonstrated by a statistical difference between the mean scores for two groups?" and "How can statistically significant results that describe groups be translated into practice with my current client?" These questions are of particular relevance in a book considering the application of outcome measurement in clinical settings.

Two types of statistical significance may have little utility for the clinician. The first has to do with group differences, and the second has to do with individual change. When examining treatments for psychological disturbances, researchers often include a comparison group. Sometimes the design involves the comparison of a treatment group with a control group, whereas other studies compare two different treatments or a new treatment with the usual or standard treatment. Whatever the comparison, the investigators rely on statistics to inform them whether the two groups are significantly different after treatment. If the statistical test reveals that the two groups are different and the difference is in the expected direction (i.e., the treated group is better), the researcher has evidence that the treatment of interest is more effective than the comparison treatment or control. However, statistically significant differences between groups do not necessarily indicate practical, meaningful, or clinically significant differences between groups nor for individuals within the groups. For example, consider a weight-loss treatment that is compared with a control group.

Forty individuals who are at extreme risk for detrimental physical consequences related to their obesity are selected to participate in the study. The subjects are randomly assigned to either the treatment or the control group. After two months, those receiving treatment have lost an average of 8 pounds each. The comparison group, however, has lost on the average no weight during the elapsed time. The statistical test reveals a significant finding for the treatment group as compared to the control group. These statistical effects suggest that the differences between the groups are real as opposed to differences that are "illusory, questionable, or unreliable" (Jacobson & Truax, 1991, p. 12). However, the statistical test does not give information regarding the variety of responses to treatment within the treated group. With an average of 8 pounds weight loss, some individuals who received treatment may have lost 16 pounds while others who received treatment lost no weight.

Similarly, the statistical test gives us evidence that the performance of the treatment is unlikely to be the result of a chance finding, but it gives us no information regarding the "size, importance, or clinical significance" of the results (Jacobson & Truax, 1991, p. 12). As a group, the participants in the study remain classified as extremely obese. Even though the 20 treated individuals lost an average of eight pounds, many, if not all of them, remain extremely overweight and are likely to experience the physical consequences of extreme obesity despite treatment. In a pragmatic or clinical sense, the treatment and control groups may be considered identical after two months of treatment.

One method of evaluating the size of change involves the calculation of effect sizes or other similar statistics that report the degree or magnitude of the relationship between variables. A small effect would be indicative of a less meaningful result than a moderate or large effect. Even these numbers, however, do not give us information regarding within-group variation or the clinical relevance of group or individual change.

In order to evaluate the clinical relevance of this particular study, one must know how much weight each individual lost and one must then make some value judgments as well as empirical observations concerning that amount of weight loss for an extremely obese person. Is the quality of life for a person in the treated group improved? Does the person's weight loss make a difference in terms of the probability of negative physical consequences of obesity? Has the individual returned to a "normal" weight for his or her height and bone structure? Does the prospect of fluctuating weight loss and weight gain with its subsequent consequences appear detrimental? These and other similar questions must be considered. At the same time, a small weight loss may reflect a clinically meaningful change for an eight-week treatment program. The problem with this study is the duration of the treatment rather than the lack of meaningful change. The point is, however, that clinical studies are often uninformative with respect to the within-group variation or the clinical meaningfulness of differences in group means.

Similarly, individual change may be clinically meaningless. For example, consider an individual who is participating in a research study examining a treatment for depression. This individual is severely depressed and reports a Beck Depression Inventory score of 45 before treatment. After five months of treatment, the individual reports a BDI score of 31. Again, the difference may be statistically reliable while the clinical utility of a 14-point change on the BDI must be questioned. A clinician would immediately ask, "What differences in behavioral, social, occupational, or family functioning are reflected in the BDI?" Clearly, other information is necessary before one can determine the clinical utility of a 14-point change on the BDI. We realize that our statements discount the possibility that the BDI has been adequately linked to areas of functioning through numerous validity studies; however, most instruments used to measure the effectiveness of psychological treatments are not so sophisticated as to be clearly linked to behavioral functioning at every level, particularly when using standardized "nomothetic" instruments for individual applications (Cone, 1988).

One of the problems with determining the clinical significance of a 14-point decrease on the BDI is that it depends on the viewpoint of the person being asked. In fact, Strupp and Hadley (1977) suggest that three important yet different perspectives on outcome must be considered: the individual client, society, and the mental health professional. In this example, the client may be completely satisfied with the treatment being received and the progress being made, not to mention feeling happy that he or she has not committed suicide during the time period. At the same time, society may view the change as negligible, unless the client's symptoms are reduced to the point that he or she is functioning like the average or "normal" person and therefore has no need for additional therapy and the expense it entails. This would be typical of a teacher who wants a designated child client to be "just as cooperative as the other children" and no change will be meaningful until that end goal is reached. From the mental health professional's viewpoint, the change that has occurred may be quite impressive, but much more change will be needed before the person can be viewed as nondepressed, nonsuicidal, psychologically healthy, or inoculated against further depressive episodes from a theoretical point of view. Certainly, the values of the interested party play an important role in their view of positive and negative outcomes of treatment (Strupp & Hadley, 1977).

Clinical significance, therefore, remains an important concept to integrate into both research and practice. Several methods of considering clinical significance have been developed to further understand within-group variation and consequently address the concerns of practitioners. The remainder of this chapter will be directed at a thorough discussion of the methods developed by researchers for investigating the clinical and practical significance of research findings (organized by perspective) and the potential applications for clinicians who must constantly assess the utility of ongoing treatment.

The Consumer's Perspective

Strupp and Hadley (1977) suggest that the client is primarily concerned with being happy and feeling content. The client's definition of *meaningful change* might be called a subjective feeling of well-being that occurs as a result of treatment. Treatment is successful from the client's point of view if he or she feels better and is satisfied with the treatment whether or not the contentment is accompanied by behavioral, situational, or symptomatic change. Similarly, the client's contentment may occur independently of the treatment and as a result of extra-therapy events, yet client contentment would indicate clinical utility (Maisto & Connors, 1988; Bloom & Fischer, 1982).

Granted, clients may enter treatment with a specific behavioral goal in mind (e.g., to be more assertive, to procrastinate less, or to achieve orgasm), which becomes the criterion by which their subjective feelings of contentment are determined. However, in other cases, they may leave treatment feeling happy and satisfied with no corresponding behavioral or objectively observable evidence of change. In line with this argument, Baer (1988) surmises that researchers consider improvement in symptoms the method of quantifying change, whereas clinicians continue to conduct treatment in response to or as a reaction to consumer complaints. Baer suggests that because clinical practice is complaint driven, perhaps the assessment of changes in complaints should be considered the method of assessing clinical utility, or, in his words, the method of considering "social validity." Yet, few attempts have been made to assess change in the "complaints" of the consumer. Two attempts to evaluate client complaints include the assessment of client satisfaction with treatment and client target complaints.

Postservice Questionnaires

One of the commonly used measures of client satisfaction is a postservice questionnaire (PSQ). Many mental health clinics, retailers, and other service organizations (e.g., restaurants, hospitals, etc.) use customer-completed postservice surveys to gauge their effectiveness at providing efficient, useful, and high-quality services. Particularly in business environments, the happiness of the customer is the primary index of "treatment success." A variety of postservice or client satisfaction questionnaires are available with varying degrees of psychometric sophistication ranging from home-made one-item questionnaires to lengthy forms with demonstrated psychometric properties. For example, the Client Satisfaction Questionnaire (CSQ-8; Larsen, Attkisson, Hargreaves, & Nguyen, 1979; Attkisson & Zwick, 1982) is an eight-item measure developed to assess postservice client satisfaction (see the instrument in Appendix B). The CSQ-8 requires only a few minutes for the client to complete, has adequate psychometric properties, and has been reviewed favorably by several independent sources (Ciarlo, Edwards, Kiresuk, Newman, & Brown, 1985; Corcoran & Fischer, 1987; Berger, 1983). In addition, a Spanish version has been developed with equal psychometric evidence for its utility (Roberts & Attkisson, 1983; Roberts, Attkisson, & Stegner, 1983).

Other client satisfaction instruments are available. For example, Tanner (1982) presents the development of a multidimensional client satisfaction instrument that consists of five factors (satisfaction, helpfulness, accessibility, respect, and partnership) with five items on each factor. Similarly, Greenfield and Attkisson (1989) present the development of a multifactorial satisfaction scale that had two consistent factors—practitioner manner and skill, and perceived outcome satisfaction—and several weaker factors. Ciarlo and Reihman (1977) also present the development of a multidimensional program evaluation instrument that includes a five-item client satisfaction scale. Finally, many clinics and mental health centers have developed questionnaires that assess client satisfaction regarding institution specific intake and service procedures.

Although client satisfaction is an important indicator of clinical utility, it may not provide a complete picture of the effects of psychotherapy. "A program that is described by its consumers as well-liked or effective may not necessarily be either pleasant or effective" (Wolf, 1978, p. 212). Since client satisfaction is not always reflected in behavioral changes, the assessment of client satisfaction as the sole criterion upon which to base clinical meaningfulness is unwarranted. Clients may be entirely satisfied with the services provided while continuing to be concerned with ongoing symptoms of illness; a physician may provide timely, efficient, and high-quality service yet the client still has terminal cancer. In addition, some people may be entirely satisfied with highly questionable treatments (e.g., astrological, parapsychological, etc.) whether or not they are effective. Finally, some psychological problems (e.g., addictions, narcissism, psychopathy) include the denial of problems as a diagnostic symptom. Another treatment outcome perspective seems necessary to ascertain the effectiveness of treatment in these cases. Nevertheless, consumers have a unique perspective of their change and should be used as one of several sources of information regarding the clinical utility of psychological interventions (Wolf, 1978). If the definition of *clinical meaningfulness* includes the alleviation of the presenting problems or changes in functioning, however, it may not be enough to know that the client is satisfied with treatment. As a result, another dimension of the client's perspective might include his or her view of changes in symptoms, quality of life, or functioning that is a result of treatment. Nevertheless, an important dimension of clinical significance would include the assessment of the consumer's subjective feeling of satisfaction or contentment with treatment.

Symptomatic Change

Numerous self-report questionnaires are available to assess the client's view of his or her symptomatic change (see Chapter 4). In the context of this chapter, however, we are considering methods for determining clinically meaningful or useful change through an assessment of changes in symptoms. Clients who present with specific symptoms or goals may consider treatment clinically meaningful if the symptoms are ameliorated or the goals are met. In short, then, *clinical utility* is described grossly as the absence of the presenting problem following treatment. In practice, symptoms often continue yet treatment helps to reduce the frequency, intensity, or quality of their appearance. For example, few consumers, service providers, or researchers would expect a treatment for headaches to result in the absence of headaches for the client during the remainder of his or her life. And in fact, careful studies of college students report that only 0.7 percent of this population report having no headaches (Andrasik, Holroyd, & Abell, 1979). A consumer could reasonably expect, however, that treatment would result in a substantial reduction in frequency and intensity of headaches (Blanchard & Schwarz, 1988). The consumer may be satisfied with enough symptom reduction that he or she is able to function in daily life even though he or she may have to live with a certain amount of pain or disability.

As to the view of symptomatic change by society or the mental health professional, we must repeat our point: The amount of change—in this case, symptom reduction—necessary to be considered clinically meaningful depends on the perspective. Clients may want enough symptom reduction to be content and satisfied; society, on the other hand, may expect normative amounts of symptomatic change; practitioners may expect nonpathology, normality, or health from a theoretical perspective. We have just discussed the client's point of view, but to get a clear picture of clinical significance from societies' or the practitioners' point of view, read on.

Social Validity

From the traditions of applied behavior analysis, practical or clinical significance is known by another name—social validity. *Social validity* refers to the "social acceptability of intervention programs" (Kazdin, 1977, p. 430) and applies to several facets of the intervention: the social significance of the goals of treatment, the social appropriateness of the procedures, and the social importance of the effects (Wolf, 1978). For the purposes of this chapter, we are most concerned with the social importance of the *effects* of treatment—in other words, the importance of the behavior change achieved through treatment. But how does one determine the social importance of individual change?

Normative Groups

Kendall and Grove (1988) suggest taking the perspective of the "skeptical potential consumer" of psychological treatments to better understand the concept of clinical meaningfulness. In order to convince the skeptic, an intervention must be of practical value and should lead to "changes that materially improve the client's functioning" (p. 148). They go on to suggest that the most convincing demonstrations of treatment efficacy provide evidence that once troubled clients are now "not distinguishable from a . . . representative nondisturbed reference group" (p. 148). In other words, if one can demonstrate that clients are easily distinguished from a group of peers before treatment yet after treatment their behavior is indistinguishable from peers, one has demonstrated a clinically meaningful change. There are, of course, instances where it is preferable to change the behavior of the masses (i.e., compliance with seat belt ordinances or recycling programs) rather than change an individual to reflect the norm. However, many circumstances requiring psychological interventions involve the reduction of symptoms or an increase in behavioral skills to levels that are consistent with those evidenced by peers (i.e., attentiveness in the classroom, depressive symptoms, etc.). In these instances, a return to the norm represents a significant and meaningful change.

The original investigations of social validity were primarily concerned with the frequency of observable behaviors in treated patients and their peers. Later, Jacobson and colleagues (Jacobson, 1988; Jacobson, Follete, & Revenstorf, 1984; Jacobson & Revenstorf, 1988; Jacobson & Truax, 1991) extended the methods of small *n* studies by proposing a standardized statistical method for determining clinical significance using outcome measures more common to clinical trials. This method is based on the assumption that clinically significant change involves a return to normal functioning. Jacobson and Truax (1991) propose two criteria for assessing clinical significance.

First, clients receiving psychological interventions should move from a theoretical dysfunctional population to a functional population as a result of treatment. In other words, if the distributions of individuals in need of treatment and "healthy individuals" are represented graphically, the *treated* client should be more likely to be identified as a member of the healthy distribution. For example, a depressed client receiving cognitive therapy must have a BDI score after treatment that is more similar to the scores for the general population than to the results of untreated depressed individuals. This follows the work of Kendall and Grove (1988), who developed statistical methods for comparing treated clients with normative groups.

Second, the change for a client must be reliable—the pre- to posttreatment change must be large enough while considering the reliability of the instrument and the variability of the normative group that differences can be attributed to "real" change and not to measurement error. Jacobson and Truax (1991) calculate a reliable change index (RCI) based on the pretreatment score (X_{pre}), the posttreatment score (X_{post}) and the standard error of the difference between two test scores (S_{diff}):

$$RCI = \frac{X_{post} - X_{pre}}{S_{diff}}$$

The change is considered reliable, or unlikely to be the product of measurement error, if the change index (RCI) is greater than 1.96. If the client meets both criteria, movement from one distribution to the other, and an RCI greater than 1.96, then the change is considered "clinically significant." While the ideas are fairly simple, several additional issues and difficulties with this method must be addressed.

When the functional and dysfunctional distributions are overlapping, several different cutoff points may be used to determine criterion 1. Jacobson and Truax (1991) suggest three possible cutoff points—the posttreatment score is considered part of the functional distribution when it falls within 2 standard deviations of the mean of the functional group, at least 2 standard deviations away from the mean of the dysfunctional group, or at least halfway between these two points. This is not a complicated task if one knows the distributions for both the dysfunctional and functional groups. However, most psychological instruments are not developed to this point. Fortunately, several instruments have been used frequently and have decent normative data available. Interested readers can refer to Jacobson and Truax (1991) for an example of their method using the Dyadic Adjustment Scale as a measure of outcome for marital therapy or Ogles, Lambert, and Sawyer (1995) for an example of clinical significance using the National Institute for Mental Health treatment for depression collaborative research program data. Here, we present an example using the Beck Depression Inventory (BDI) along with data necessary to evaluate clinical significance using the Fear Questionnaire (FQ), the Symptom Checklist-90-Revised (SCL-90-R), the Hamilton Rating Scale for Depression (HRSD), the Child Behavior Checklist (CBCL), the Dyadic Adjustment Scale (DAS), and the Outcome Questionnaire (OQ). Each of these instruments were reviewed in earlier chapters.

Beck Depression Inventory

Nietzel, Russell, Hemmings, and Gretter (1987) located 28 studies involving 20 locations and surveying over 4,000 individuals in order to obtain normative data for the BDI. They then classified the studies into three categories and calculated composite norms for each category by averaging the weighted values (by n) for each study. Category 1, labeled special groups, consisted of studies including people who were undergoing situational stress or experiencing a physical disorder. Category 2, labeled general population, included studies where a large number of college students were sampled. Category 3, a nondistressed group, included subjects who had served as normal controls. These samples may be used to calculate the cutoff scores for criterion 1 and the standard deviations necessary for calculation of the standard error of measurement. Obviously, the cutoff scores will depend on the normative sample selected for comparison. For each of the following calculations, we selected normative samples that might be the most useful comparison groups for clinicians conducting outpatient counseling or psychotherapy.

In order to calculate the standard error, one must also have an estimate of the reliability of the instrument. Beck, Steer, and Garbin (1988) reviewed studies completed during a 25-year period that evaluated the psychometric properties of the BDI. They located 11 studies using a test-retest strategy for investigating the stability of the BDI. The reliabilities for psychiatric samples ranged from .48 to .86. These numbers most likely underestimate the actual reliability, since the patients were involved in treatment and thus changes in scores may reflect real treatment effects. Nevertheless, these estimates give some lower boundaries to use in estimating change scores for clinical significance. Using a combination of Nietzel and associates' samples and Beck, Steer, and Garbin's (1988) reliability estimates, one can calculate the change scores and cutoffs necessary for clinical significance using Jacobson's criteria. In addition, Nietzel and Trull (1988) suggest that in some cases, a 1 standard deviation criterion may be used rather than 2 standard deviations when determining if the client is a member in the functional population, so this cutoff score is included as well.

As you can see in Table 8–1, determining the cutoff point for membership in the functional population and the magnitude of change necessary for an RCI greater than 1.96 depend on the sample and the reliability estimate. If one takes the most conservative estimate of reliability ($r = .48$) and uses the largest variability estimate of a nondepressed sample (general population $\sigma = 6.47$), a client would need at least a 13-point change on the BDI from pretreatment to posttreatment in order for the change to be considered reliable (i.e., RCI ≥ 1.96). In addition, the client would need a posttreatment BDI score less than or equal to 9 to be considered a member of the nondistressed sample when using the most stringent criteria. Using more realistic criteria, a client must make 9 points of change and fall below a score of 13 to be considered part of the nondistressed sample. (This is calculated using .65 as the reliability and using the nondistressed sample for comparison rather than the general population.) We suggest these numbers represent a change score (9) and cutoff point (13) that would be the most useful to clinicians in general outpatient practice. Site-specific norms may be more useful in some locations.

In addition to determining if the client made a clinically significant change or not, these data could be used more appropriately to describe the client's pre- and post-treatment status. For example, "Sigmund entered treatment with a BDI of 25, indicating a moderate level of depression based on the average BDI scores of depressed patients entering treatment (Beck, 1967; Nietzel, Russell, Hemmings, & Gretter, 1987). After treatment, he had a BDI of 10, which can be reasonably considered part of the general population (within 1 standard deviation of the general population mean). The magnitude of change (15 points) also indicates that he made a reliable change for the better." If needed, one more step could be taken to indicate how Sigmund's posttreatment score compared to individuals in the general population, distressed individuals, and nondistressed individuals by calculating percentile scores for each of the distributions. In addition, the BDI could be administered on a weekly or biweekly basis to monitor changes in the level of depression as a result of treatment. The point is that when using the BDI, enough current information is available for clinicians to make clear statements regarding the clinical meaningfulness of the change as operationalized by Jacobson and Truax (1991).

Another way of utilizing the Jacobson method involves the graphic depiction of pre- to posttreatment change. In Figure 8–1, a graph with the pretreatment score on

TABLE 8–1   Means, Standard Deviations, Change Scores, and Cutoff Points for the Beck Depression Inventory Using Four Samples

Sample	$\bar{X}$	s	Change 1[a]	Change 2[b]	Cutoff 1[c]	Cutoff 2[d]
Special group[e]	8.05	5.78	12	6	20	14
General population[e]	7.18	6.47	13	7	20	14
Nondistressed group[e]	4.54	4.46	9	5	13	9
Minimal depression[f]	10.90	8.10	16	8	27	19

[a] Pre/posttest change score necessary for an RCI = 1.96 using .48 as the BDI reliability and the row standard deviation.
[b] Pre/posttest change score necessary for an RCI = 1.96 using .86 as the BDI reliability and the row standard deviation.
[c] High cutoff for membership in the functional population based on 2 standard deviations above the row mean.
[d] High cutoff for membership in the functional population based on 1 standard deviation above the row mean.
[e] Nietzel, Russel, Hemmings, & Gretter (1987).
[f] Beck (1967).

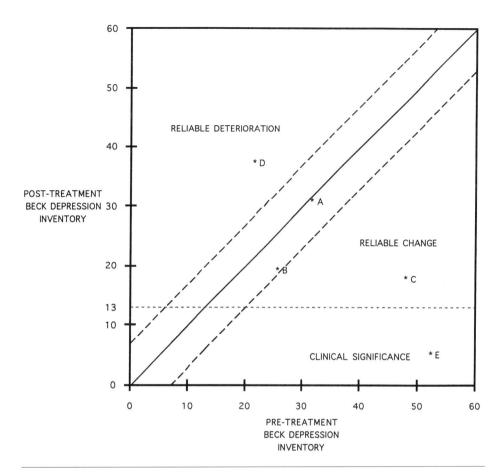

FIGURE 8–1   Clinical Significance on the Beck Depression Inventory

the Beck Depression Inventory on the x-axis and the posttreatment score on the y-axis is presented. The horizontal line represents the posttreatment cutoff score necessary to be considered part of the functional distribution. The center diagonal line running from corner to corner is the line of no change. Clients who have the same pretreatment and posttreatment scores will be plotted on this line (Client A). The dashed diagonal lines on either side of the "line of no change" represent the change scores necessary to result in an RCI greater than 1.96. Clients between the dashed diagonal lines (Client B) did not improve sufficiently to rule out random fluctuations or test unreliability as the source of the change. Clients plotted outside the lines (above the top line or below the bottom line) can be considered to have made reliable changes for the better (below the bottom line; Client C) or for the worse (above the top line; Client D). Individuals who made reliable changes for the better and had end of treatment scores similar to the functional population are plotted below the diagonal and the cutoff score (Client E). Figures for the remaining instruments presented in this section are reproduced in Appendix D.

Fear Questionnaire

Trull, Nietzel, and Main (1988) collected similar information for the Fear Questionnaire. However, they encountered two problems: (1) normative data were less frequently available for the Fear Questionnaire and (2) despite being the most frequently used measure of outcome for treatments of agoraphobia, fewer outcome studies used the Fear Questionnaire (31 percent). As a result, the authors collected their own normative data using college students and community telephone surveys. Based on their samples and including the samples obtained by Mizes and Crawford (1986), we have again calculated the pre- to posttreatment change scores necessary to equal an RCI of 1.96 and cutoff scores to determine membership in the functional population (see Table 8.2). Again picking the numbers most useful in typical outpatient practice, a male suffering from agoraphobia would need to make a 6-point change (7 for women) on the agoraphobia scale (Ag) of the Fear Questionnaire for

TABLE 8–2 Means, Standard Deviations, Reliabilities, Change Scores, and Cutoff Points for the Fear Questionnaire (Agoraphobia Scale), Symptom Checklist-90-Revised (GSI), Hamilton Rating Scale for Depression, Child Behavior Checklist (Total Problem), Dyadic Adjustment Scale, and Outcome Questionnaire

Sample	$\bar{X}$	SD	Reliability	Change[a]	Cutoff
Fear Questionnaire (agoraphobia scale) (men)[b]	4.85	5.09	.82	6	10
Fear Questionnaire (agoraphobia scale) (women)[b]	4.99	6.00	.82	7	11
SCL-90-R (GSI) Community Sample[c]	.31	.31	.84	.32	.62
Child Behavior Checklist (Total Problem)[d]	24.96	17.52	.97	9	60
Hamilton Rating Scale for Depression[e]	6.25	4.24	.81	5	11
DAS functional group[f]	114.70	17.8	.96	9	97[f]
OQ community[g]	48.16	18.23	.84	20	66
State-Trait Anxiety Inventory	38.81	10.20	.84	13	49

[a] Pre/posttest change score necessary for an RCI = 1.96 using the standard deviation and reliability from the given row. Cutoffs represent 1 standard deviation above (below on the DAS) the functional group.
[b] Trull, Nietzel, & Main (1988).
[c] Derogatis (1983).
[d] Sandberg, Meyer-Bahlberg, & Yager (1991).
[e] Carroll, Fielding, & Blashki (1973); Mowbray (1972); Riskind, Beck, Brown, & Steer (1987).
[f] Jacobson & Truax (1991); Spanier (1976).
[g] Lambert, Lunnen, Umphres, Hansen, & Burlingame (1994).

the change to be considered reliable. In addition, the posttreatment score would need to be lower than 10 (11 for women) to be considered a member in the functional population.

Symptom Checklist-90-Revised (SCL-90-R), Child Behavior Checklist (CBCL), Hamilton Rating Scale for Depression (HRSD); Dyadic Adjustment Scale (DAS), Outcome Questionnaire (OQ), and State-Trait Anxiety Inventory (STAI)

Using the same techniques as just mentioned, we present six additional sets of cut-off points and change scores necessary for clinical significance on the SCL-90-R, CBCL, HRSD, DAS, OQ, and STAI. Although multiple comparison samples are available for some of the instruments, the functional groups that appear to be most relevant for assessing the clinical significance of outpatient client change were selected for presentation here. Table 8–2 details the cutoff points and amount of change needed for clinical significance using the SCL-90-R, CBCL, HRSD, DAS, OQ, and STAI. As can be seen, .32 points of change on the GSI are necessary for an RCI of 1.96 and the final GSI must fall below .62 for the posttest score to be considered part of the asymptomatic group. Again we have chosen the conservative yet reasonable numbers to assess clinical significance. Similarly, a change of 9 T-score points is necessary for reliable change on the total score of the CBCL, whereas the lower cutoff between functional and dysfunctional distributions is 60. Change scores necessary for reliable change on the HRSD, DAS, OQ, and STAI are, respectively, 5, 9, 12, and 13, whereas the cutoff scores are, respectively, 11, 97, 66, and 49. Higher scores represent greater distress on all of the measures except the DAS, on which higher scores represent better functioning.

Problems with the Method

Although the methods presented here provide a novel and practical approach to demonstrating both reliable and clinically meaningful change, problems also exist in terms of the validity of the instruments used, potential rater bias, regression to the mean, and the limits of a functional distribution.

The first problem has to do with the validity of the instruments used to assess the clinical change. The SCL-90-R may be an adequate indicator of the number and intensity of symptoms endorsed by a person, but a decrease in reported symptoms may or may not correspond to behavioral changes. In addition, clients entering treatment do not always appear dysfunctional on outcome measures either because of lack of sensitivity of the measures, measurement error, or perhaps temporary fluctuations in the symptoms (Saunders, Howard, & Newman, 1988). Similarly, most instruments are unidimensional, whereas people in treatment present with multidimensional clinical problems. Should one then require that a client show clinically significant change on several measures of the problem to be considered meaningfully improved? And what then does one do in cases of desynchrony (e.g., agoraphobia—where we might observe behavioral change with no accompanying physiological change)?

Another problem with Jacobson's method for assessing clinically meaningful change involves the problem of rater bias. Perhaps self-report instruments are too "reactive" to be used for judging clinical meaningfulness, particularly when social validity implies that someone other than the client can observe the utility of the change that has occurred. Blanchard and Schwarz (1988) suggest that clinical meaningfulness involves objective observable criteria. Perhaps the original investigations of social validity in which clients were observed with peers or videotaped doing role-played scenarios would be preferred methods of determining clinical utility.

A third problem with Jacobson's method involves regression to the mean. Speer (1992) argues that the methods used to calculate the RCI could be biased by regression to the mean. That is, those individuals who have high pretreatment scores on the given outcome measure may be the most likely to make large improvements. Speer (1992) recommends an alternative method for calculating clinical significance when regression to the mean is identified empirically. This method may be particularly useful to administrators who are summarizing evaluation data for a clinic or center. In these circumstances, no comparison group is used and data collected by the clinic that indicate positive change for many clients may be a function of regression to the mean. Interested readers can refer to Speer (1992) for details of his suggested method.

Finally, Tingey, Burlingame, Lambert, and Barlow (1991) argue that Jacobson's method is too conservative, since a client who was severely decompensated and then improved to the level of a mild disturbance would not be considered clinically improved. Although it may be accurate to conclude that the person is not part of the functional distribution, a person with chronic illness may be "meaningfully" improved at a mild level of dysfunction, even from a social validity point of view. Similar problems occur in medical treatment where return to normal functioning is impossible (e.g., lost limbs, chronic illness, etc.). No one would argue that a prosthesis functions exactly like a lost limb. Yet, a prosthesis may facilitate numerous tasks in a meaningful way. The ultimate question then becomes: How many capabilities or functions must be added by the prosthesis before it can be considered to create a clinically relevant and meaningful change? Similarly, if a person with a psychological dysfunction reliably changes yet never falls within the boundaries of a functional distribution, should one rule out clinically meaningful change? And if not, how much change should the person make before the change may be called clinically meaningful?

Tingey and associates (1991) suggest identifying multiple distributions that can then be used to describe a continuum of dysfunction. Specifically, they identified four populations using the GSI: an asymptomatic group, a normal population, a mild disturbance group, and a severely disturbed group. In this case, clinical significance does not require movement into the "functional" distribution, but rather movement into the next or adjacent distribution regardless of where they start. This extension of the method seems particularly relevant for the treatment of people with chronic disturbance where clinical significance may be measured in terms of rehospitalization rates rather than by comparisons to a "normal" reference group. However, few instruments have identifiable distributions along a continuum of severity. Certainly much more work needs to be done before one can easily identify clinically meaningful change in this way. Nevertheless, interested readers can attempt to develop multiple distributions as needed.

Other Calculation Methods

Jacobson is not the only researcher to develop a statistical method of investigating clinical significance. For example, when examining the effectiveness of psychological interventions for headaches, investigators calculate the percent improvement based on the frequency and severity of headaches per week (obtained from headache diaries) at pretreatment and posttreatment (Blanchard & Schwarz, 1988).

$$\text{Percent improvement} = 100 \times \frac{\text{Headache index}_{\text{pretreatment}} - \text{Headache index}_{\text{posttreatment}}}{\text{Headache index}_{\text{pretreatment}}}$$

Using the percent improvement, a 50 percent reduction in headache activity, in the absence of increased medication, is defined as clinically significant change (Blanchard & Schwarz, 1988).

Similarly, agoraphobia researchers have developed criteria for identifying "end-state functioning" and "improvement" based on the combined posttreatment ratings of several outcome measures (Michelson, Mavissakalian, & Marchione, 1985). Clients are given one point each for specified ratings on several outcome measures: (1) < 3 on the Global Assessment of Severity; (2) < 3 on the Self-Rating of Severity; (3) < 4 on the Phobic Anxiety and Avoidance Scales; and (4) 20 on a Behavioral Avoidance course with < 4 on the Subjective Units of Discomfort during the approach test. High endstate functioning is defined as a score of 3 or 4, medium endstate functioning is defined as a score of 1 or 2, and low endstate functioning is defined as a score of 0. A similar method is used for defining improvement by assigning a score of 1 to a change > 1 on each of the instruments listed above. Clients are then classified as low, medium, or high improvement following treatment. In this way, the investigators have evidence of high endstate functioning and improvement based on a combination of a priori cutoffs based on self-report, judge rated, therapist rated, and behavioral approach measures of outcome.

Other disorder specific methods are available. Our hope is that practicing clinicians can find those methods for assessing clinical relevance that match the populations they are treating. The Jacobson method has the advantage of being easily adapted to any instrument that has adequate normative data. Other methods such as percent headache improvement may be available for specific disorders being treated with psychological interventions. It is important to develop explicit, replicable definitions of improvement that can be readily understood by others.

The Therapist's Point of View

Strupp and Hadley (1977) refer to the mental health professional's view of meaningful changes as grounded "within the framework of some theory of personality structure" (p. 189). Although clinical judgments of functioning are often influenced by the client's feelings of contentment or general rules of social conduct, the professional's theoretical definition of health may "transcend social adaptation and subjective well-being" (Strupp & Hadley, 1977, p. 189). Psychoanalytic theory, in particular, is concerned with change that extends beyond symptomatic improvement and client satisfaction even though ratings of dynamic change have been found to correlate with symptomatic change (Mintz, Luborsky, & Christoph, 1979).

For example, after treatment, a previously anxious and shy male asks a young woman for a date and expresses contentment with treatment. Yet, the extent to which the "quality of experience" or the "generalized disposition to deal differently with women" has changed may be another important dimension to consider (Strupp & Hadley, 1977, p. 189). Thus, to the professional, meaningful change can occur within the confines of a theoretical model of psychological structures that may require a degree of inference in observations. Obviously, some models of psychological structures focus on the overt behaviors of the client and require no additional methods of assessment requiring greater amounts of inference. Two relatively atheoretical (theoretical meaning influenced by therapeutic orientation) methods for investigating the clinical meaningfulness of treatment outcomes from the mental health professional's perspective include diagnostic categorization and quality of life.

The Healthy Person

Perhaps one of the most convincing methods of demonstrating that a child is no longer reacting to poison ivy exposure is the absence of red, swollen, itchy skin. Similarly, a cancer patient would be elated with the lab result indicating no cancer cells are present. Even though the patient may feel better, believe that he or she has received high-quality service, and has fewer symptoms, the presence of remaining cancer cells may indicate to the doctor that the individual is still sick and in need of treatment. When considering psychological problems and treatments, many consumers and therapists alike consider the absence of the problem or disorder the best indicator of meaningful change. A suicidal client is clinically changed when he is no longer suicidal. A client with a fear of flying is meaningfully changed when she can fly without fear. The logic of this medical model-based perspective is straightforward: A person is meaningfully changed when he or she no longer has the sickness. However, emotional and behavioral problems are more difficult to identify as either present or absent. Diagnostic formulations are perhaps the most relevant methods available.

To demonstrate the presence of a problem before treatment and the absence of the problem following treatment, clinicians could conduct standardized diagnostic interviews. A number of interviews are available for both children and adults, with shortened versions targeting certain disorders (e.g., affective disorders); several of these methods were described in Chapter 4. Structured interviews could be easily developed and used by clinicians conducting intake and exit interviews. Similarly, the absence of symptoms might be inferred using self-report instruments where normative data have been collected using "normal," "healthy," or asymptomatic subjects. Although the medical model of disease presence or absence is not always applicable in mental health settings, there are methods for attempting to make measurement of therapy outcome similar and relevant.

Quality of Life

In the past two decades, changes in daily life functioning have become increasingly important indicators of "real" change. Particularly in health care and service to people with chronic mental illness, symptomatic change is only part of the expected result of treatment. Unless changes occur in the client's ability to function at work, play, home, and in social situations, symptomatic change is not "meaningful." In fact, Kaplan (1985, 1990) suggests that the only important dependent variables in health psychology research are quality of life and mortality. He argues convincingly that other measures—such as cholesterol, blood pressure, stress, coping, and so on—have little utility unless the quality of life for the person is improved or the risk of mortality decreases. Similarly, quality of life is an important indicator of current mental health or outcome of therapy (Kazdin, 1993). Certainly, contentment and subjective well-being are the most important indicators of outcome from a client's perspective (Strupp & Hadley, 1977). Determining the definitions of and methods for assessing quality of life, however, are more difficult than asserting their importance.

Historically, quality of life was measured by objective observable standards (e.g., in economic research by monetary indicators, or in health care by patient mobility, etc.) without taking into account the perspective of the people who are living the lives. Researchers are, however, increasingly relying on subjective evaluations of well-being, life functioning, or quality of life. Although most quality of life measures are judge or clinician rated, self-report measures of quality of life are being developed and used frequently, and promise to be more easily administered and scored as well as more cost effective.

Quality of Life Inventory (QOLI™)

The most promising quality of life instrument currently available is the Quality of Life Inventory (QOLI; Frisch, 1994; Frisch, Cornell, Villanueva, & Retzlaff, 1992), which measures 16 areas of life satisfaction. According to Frisch and colleagues (1992), life satisfaction or quality of life refers to how well one feels one's most important needs, goals, and wishes are being met. Overall life satisfaction is seen as the sum of satisfactions in those areas of life one deems important. The QOLI consists of 16 items selected to include all domains of life that have been empirically associated with overall life satisfaction. The instrument can be administered individually or in groups and was developed for adults (over age 17) with a sixth-grade reading level or above. Respondents rate how important each of the 16 domains is to their overall happiness and satisfaction (0 = not at all important, 1 = important, 2 = very important) followed by rating how satisfied they are in the area (−3 = very dissatisfied to 3 = very satisfied). The importance and satisfaction ratings for each item are multiplied to form weighted satisfaction ratings ranging from −6 to 6. The overall life satisfaction is then computed by averaging all weighted satisfaction ratings with nonzero importance ratings. The total score thus reflects one's satisfaction in only those areas of life one considers important. Respondents can also indicate what problems interfere with their satisfaction in each area on a supplementary section of the QOLI answer sheet. The QOLI takes only five minutes to complete, is easily scored, and does not require an advanced degree to interpret.

The QOLI is a relatively new instrument and as a result has not been validated as extensively as other therapy outcome measures. Adequate evidence of its reliability has been presented (Frisch, 1994; Frisch et al., 1992)—test-retest reliabilities range from .80 to .91 depending on the sample. Evidence for the QOLIs construct validity has also been collected. The QOLI is positively correlated with measures of happiness, life satisfaction, and general self-efficacy; and negatively correlated with measures of anxiety, depression, and general psychopathology (Frisch et al., 1992). In addition, the QOLI shows an ability to discriminate among groups whose quality of life would be expected to differ (general undergraduates scored higher than students seeking counseling, and recovered VA (Veterans' Administration) patients score higher than VA inpatients and inpatients in a private drug and alcohol rehabilitation unit). The QOLI is also unrelated to social desirability. Unfortunately, no pre- to post-treatment studies of outcome have been conducted using the QOLI. A limited amount of data (16 clients) supporting the QOLIs sensitivity to change are presented in the manual (Frisch, 1994). These data support the QOLIs sensitivity to treatment-related change insofar as the QOLI compared favorably to benchmark outcome measures of depression. Nevertheless, more evidence is needed to support the use of the QOLI before it is used routinely as an outcome measure.

The QOLI has a nationwide standardization sample (nonclinical) with racial/ethnic composition comparable to the 1990 census (Frisch, 1994). The fact that this sample is nonclinical makes it possible to evaluate a person's score relative to his or her well-functioning peers. As a result, both degree of psychopathology and clinical significance of changes occurring during treatment can be determined by comparison to the normative sample.

Since it assesses a broad range of areas, the QOLI has the potential to become a treatment outcome measure for a variety of interventions including psychotherapy, drug treatments, physical and occupational therapy, and even communitywide social interventions. This applicability to a wide variety of areas may be its most important advantage over other quality of life instruments that tend to be developed for specific populations and assess the typical disabling aspects of a narrowly defined disorder or disease. Aside from being a useful measure of outcome, the QOLI has been shown to help plan client treatments by identifying areas of life that clients feel they need to work on and problems they believe they face in those areas (Kazdin, 1993). It can also inform therapists of clients' perceived areas of strength. Overall, the QOLI is a promising instrument with many potential uses.

Quality of Life Questionnaire (QLQ)

Quality of life also has become increasingly important in the treatment of chronic mental illness. Bigelow and colleagues (Bigelow, Brodsky, Stewart, & Olson, 1982; Bigelow, Gareau, & Young, 1990; Bigelow, McFarland, & Olson, 1991; Bigelow, McFarland, Gareau, & Young, 1991; Bigelow & Young, 1991) developed a multidimensional Quality of Life Questionnaire (QLQ) that assesses 14 areas of functioning. Two interview versions are available. One is used with verbal clients who can accurately self-report current information, and one is for less verbal clients, where interviewers are asked to rate quality of life.

Administered by a trained interviewer, the self-report version consists of 263 items assessing how well clients get their needs met and fulfill social role requirements in 14 areas of living, such as work, leisure, interpersonal relations, emotional well-being, and basic needs satisfaction. Interviews are typically conducted at intake and following treatment or, for chronic cases, at regular intervals (usually 90 days). Of the 14 scales, 4 have reported low internal consistency (Cronbach's alpha < .36), 2 scales have moderate internal consistency (.67 to .68), and the remaining scales have high internal consistency (.82 to .98). Evidence for the QLQ's discriminant validity comes from a study comparing clients from four community mental health programs with nonclients from rural, urban, and economically depressed counties. The quality of life for nonclients in the impoverished county was rated lower than for all other nonclients in 9 areas of functioning. In addition, the client sample differed from nonclients on most scales, and nonclient quality of life was higher than posttreatment quality of life for clients, which was in turn higher than pretreatment quality of life ratings for clients. Finally, clients' retrospective assessment of improvement correlated with pretest/posttest differences for 9 scales.

Many clients with chronic mental disorders have trouble giving accurate responses to the self-report form. As a result, the authors constructed a second version of the questionnaire that relies more heavily on the interviewer's observation and judgment of the client during a semi-structured interview. The interviewer may also use information from family, landlords, and other clinicians in his or her ratings. The interviewer version also taps special problems experienced by clients with chronic mental disorders (e.g., medications). To test interrater reliability, six experienced raters rated six clients; all six raters participated in each interview. Over half the items had better than 90 percent interrater agreement, and of the 86 items with at least ordinal scales, 56 had Cronbach's alpha greater than .7 (more than half above .8). The rater version has been used to assess the effectiveness of a bed reduction intervention that was implemented as a result of a legislative mandate. Clients who received more and better community services did show improved quality of life (Bigelow, McFarland, Gareau, & Young, 1991).

In summary, the self-report version appears to be a useful measure of how well community mental health programs improve their clients' quality of life. It taps a broad range of functioning and shows adequate predictive validity and sensitivity to treatment effects. Its use is limited, however, to clients who can self-report fairly accurately. For clients who have verbal difficulties, the interviewer rating form may be useful when further evidence of validity is available. Materials can be obtained by contacting the Western Mental Health Research Center, Gaines Hall, Oregon Health Sciences University, Portland, Oregon, 97201-2985.

Others

A myriad of specialized quality of life instruments are also available in health psychology. Instruments have been developed for geriatric patients, cancer patients, and several other specific populations. Although a complete review of these instruments is beyond the purview of this book, those clinicians practicing in health psychology can access other sources (Karoly, 1985).

Summary

Assessing clients' quality of life is potentially an important contributor to the evaluation of clinically significant treatment affects. Relatively little research has been conducted to assess the complete spectrum of quality of life in psychotherapy outcome research. Many of the dimensions of quality of life or areas of functioning have been assessed, however. For example, social relationships have long been considered an important focus of psychological treatments and an indicator of positive outcome in therapy. Measures such as the Social Adjustment Scale and the Katz Adjustment Scale (discussed in Chapter 4) assess the quality of functioning in these areas. Similarly, symptom-based measures such as the BDI partially assess the level of functioning related to the emotional well-being area of quality of life. Some outcome measures used in psychotherapy research match other areas of life functioning identified in global quality of life measures. Still, overall quality of life ratings generated from instruments created specifically to assess the level and quality of functioning in theoretically important areas of living provide an additional outcome perspective that may enhance the meaningfulness of outcome data. In addition, measures of quality of life, positive mental health, or subjective well-being are somewhat independent of measures of negative affect and symptoms (Frisch, 1994). As a result, the inclusion of quality of life assessment measured separately may be necessary to include a complete picture of a client's mental health status.

Practical Applications of Clinical Significance

Now that we have reviewed much of the thinking concerning the clinical significance of psychotherapy and counseling outcomes, what are the practical applications for the clinician? How can these methods be incorporated in clinical practice?

1. *Obtain client satisfaction ratings.* Many clinics routinely ask clients to rate their satisfaction with services received, and those clinics neglecting to collect this information can easily implement the procedures for collecting such ratings. Similarly, private practitioners can easily obtain posttherapy client satisfaction ratings. Client satisfaction gives a clear indication of the clinical meaningfulness of treatment from the client's perspective and may be useful to the service provider. For example, Azim and Joyce (1986) report the effects of changing implementation methods in a walk-in clinic that were the result of information gained from client satisfaction ratings. In a previous study, they discovered that clients participating in group psychotherapy were less satisfied with treatment than clients receiving other services. As a result, a series of meetings involving supervisors, therapists, and researchers examined potential methods for improving services. The group identified six specific areas of improvement: greater rigor in patient selection, appropriate timing of the group referral, more extensive preparation of patients for group therapy, moving beyond treating the groups as a whole to also treating the individual in the group, greater therapist activity and transparency, and increased quantity and quality of group supervision. Upon examination of client satisfaction ratings a year later, they discovered

across-the-board increases in satisfaction, although not all differences were significant. Client satisfaction ratings are an easily obtained measure of outcome with clear
ramifications for clinical meaningfulness from the client's point of view.

2. *Use standard instruments with normative data when available.* Collecting pretreatment and posttreatment data for clients using instruments with adequate normative data will allow one to make better informed statements regarding the efficacy
of treatments. We recommend selecting the most commonly used outcome instruments for specific disorders, as they will be most likely to provide information regarding the distributions of treated clients and normative samples. Since an instrument's reliability has an impact on clinical significance, it is important to select
reliable instruments. When providing services to depressed clients, the Beck Depression Inventory would be an obvious choice. The Fear Questionnaire would be
appropriate for people being treated for agoraphobia. The SCL-90-R or the Outcome
Questionnaire would be a useful global measure of outpatient client change. And the
Quality of Life Inventory is a useful and versatile measure of overall life satisfaction
with a national comparison sample. A client who makes a 13-point change on the BDI
and has a posttreatment score of 9 or lower would be a likely example of meaningful change.

Despite the problems with this method, clinicians who take advantage of these
frequently used measures to document effective treatment will be a generation
ahead of those who do not. Unfortunately, not all clients will fit this methodology.
Some clients may enter treatment with already low scores; even a portion of the carefully screened clients in the NIMH collaborative depression study had pretreatment
BDI scores below 10 (Ogles, Lambert, & Sawyer, 1995). Others may appear to improve markedly yet report only a 5-point change on the BDI. Still, in a large percentage of the cases, better data with quality comparison groups will add credibility
and improved accountability on insurance claims, in posttreatment summaries, and
when discussing improvement with clients. In cases where the data do not fit, informed statements can be made about why or why not (e.g., perhaps the depressive
symptoms tapped by the BDI are not relevant to the current client, perhaps the client
had a temporary reprieve from symptoms, etc.). Saunders, Howard, and Newman
(1988) suggest that one possible way to combat the problem of clients appearing
functional at pretreatment is to administer several instruments and then select the
instrument that identifies the client as dysfunctional to administer at posttreatment.
The point is that an outcome assessment can be adapted to the unique characteristics of the client in an effort to reflect clinically meaningful change.

3. *Diagnostic interviews pre and post when possible.* A convenient way of demonstrating clinical improvement is through the administration of a standardized diagnostic interview before and after treatment. When clients meet the criteria for a *DSM-
III-R* diagnosis before treatment but not following treatment, one has convincing
evidence of the clinical utility of the treatment. In many circumstances, the time and
cost of a standardized diagnostic interview may be prohibitive; a less formal interview
regarding the specific diagnostic symptoms may yield equally useful information.

4. *For health-related problems and chronic mental illness, it seems imperative to include an assessment of quality of life. Quality of life is also becoming an important supplement to symptom change in other mental health services.* With the recent emphasis on changes in functioning that extend beyond symptomatic improvement, it is important to include an assessment of changes in the client's quality of life whenever possible. Particularly when assessing the affects of psychological interventions on medical conditions, improvements in quality of life may be the only indicator of "real" or "meaningful" change (Kaplan, 1990). Similarly, several interview methods of assessing life functioning changes in chronic mental illness promise to increase the ability to describe the benefits of psychological interventions. Certainly, quality of life assessment in other areas could be useful as well, although there is an implicit assumption that many clients meet a minimum standard of quality living despite problems that require intervention.

5. *Develop site-specific norms for instruments.* Certain clinical settings provide services to narrow target populations. As a result, specific instruments can be selected to assess relevant areas of functioning and institutional normative data can be gathered. With data regarding the history of treatment successes and failures, initial client severity levels, and corresponding quality of life changes in the target group, informed descriptions and decisions can be generated for improved clinical service. Nevertheless, nonclinical norms remain important for comparing clients' functioning with peers (Kazdin, 1992).

6. *Gather nonreactive data.* Many times nonreactive measures of outcome may be particularly telling indices of clinical relevance. Out-of-home placements or days in school may be useful measures of clinical change for disturbed youth. Recidivism or relapse rates should be routinely evaluated when providing treatments in the prison system or in drug and alcohol rehabilitation facilities. Days on the job may be a useful measure of change for individuals with chronic disturbances such as agoraphobia or schizophrenia. Other inconspicuous means may be used to collect a variety of useful and available indirect measures of clinical change. When attempting to influence public policy or obtain state or federal funds, simple nonreactive measures provide quick information that is easily understood by elected officials, administrators, and other laypersons. For example, demonstrating that the number of adolescent suicide attempts have decreased in a catchment area after implementing a new peer support program will be immediately recognized as a positive outcome. Certainly, a number of nonreactive data sources are available with immediate relevance.

Chapter 9

Ethical Issues

When implementing an ongoing service evaluation system, it is necessary to consider the ethical issues involved in assessing clients. Of course, the ethical guidelines concerning informed consent, confidentiality, client feedback regarding assessment, and so on, that typically guide clinical practice are equally applicable when conducting assessment for treatment evaluation purposes. For example, most mental health clinics and many practitioners routinely provide information regarding the usual impact of treatments and obtain written consent to provide services. In addition, many organizations provide information regarding client rights and procedures for filing grievances if the client feels unfairly treated. The same principles that govern informed consent for routine treatment and assessment govern the use of outcome evaluation instruments used solely for treatment-related purposes. However, the implementation of an evaluation system also presents ethical issues that must be separately considered. If outcome evaluation instruments are being used for research purposes other than archival data collection, clients should be informed concerning the research procedures in addition to the treatment procedures. Clients can then be given the option to participate in the research and have the right to discontinue their participation in the research at any time.

The nature of the information provided to properly inform patients will, of course, vary with the purposes of collecting data. To the extent that assessments are actually integrated into treatment and used in decisions about how to proceed with therapy and when to quit, little need be said, as one is merely following a set clinical routine aimed at helping. As clinicians deviate more from this procedure, and begin using assessments solely for measuring change without intending to affect the welfare of a specific client, more information needs to be provided to the patient so that the patient can decide if he or she wants to cooperate. The more elaborate an assessment procedure (e.g., it involves ratings by significant others, employment and school records, etc.), the more potential information must be disclosed. Guidelines for consent are available through a number of professional organizations, including the American Psychological Association (1992).

Generally, subjects in research will sign a consent form that includes in the title the words *research subject.* It will include (1) what is being studied, (2) how participants are being chosen, (3) how treatment may differ from normal, (4) the names of the investigators, (5) risks or disadvantages that are involved, (6) possible benefits, (7) alternatives if applicable, (8) assurance of confidentiality, and (9) acknowledgment that participation is voluntary. Research subjects should know they have the right to refuse participation and to withdraw from participation at anytime.

We suggest the information contained in Figure 9–1 be disclosed to clients who take assessments that are used for tracking clinical progress but that may also be used with data from other clients to provide and report evidence of efficacy. The consent form in Figure 9–2 would be appropriate in a situation that calls for a more specific research study in which the nature of the research is more formal and could involve experimental manipulation.

Another issue that is of primary concern to clinicians will be the contradictory demands of doing research while offering clinical services. For example, most psychotherapy outcome studies guarantee participants that their posttherapy ratings will not be shared with their therapist nor be used "against" their therapist. This

---

FIGURE 9–1   Sample Consent Form

Consent to Be a Research Subject

As part of receiving treatment at this time I will be asking you to complete some questionnaires. These questionnaires have several purposes. First, they will be used as part of your treatment to track the progress you are making. As we review our work together we will use the questionnaires to help us decide when our work is complete. I view the questionnaires as part of your treatment, but I would like to request your permission to use your questionnaire data in research. This research involves (state purpose of research).

I believe that you will generally benefit from this research as it will help me improve as a therapist. There are no known risks to you for participating as I will not modify my treatment from the usual standard. I want your permission to combine your questionnaire data with data from other persons in order to better understand treatment. I will keep your questionnaire data in your file. When it is combined with data from other persons, your name and other identifying information will be removed and replaced with numbers. If for any reason, you don't want me to use this data in research your request that it not be used will be honored.

I have understood and received a copy of the above consent and desire of my own free choice to participate in this study.

_____   _____
Research Subject   Date

_____
Witness

FIGURE 9–2   Sample Consent Form

Consent to Be a Research Subject

The purpose of this study is to better understand how much therapy is needed to help clients overcome their distressing symptoms and behaviors. Results from the study will show how many clients have improved on various symptoms and problems in relation to the number of sessions they have attended. This type of information will be very helpful to therapists preparing their treatment plans, to clients who want an idea of how long their treatment will last, and to insurance companies trying to determine how much therapy they can be expected to pay for.

Participation in the study will require you to complete a questionnaire provided by the receptionist *before each of your therapy sessions.* The questionnaire is short and completion should take no more than five minutes. Information from the questionnaire will not be shown to your therapist. Completed questionnaires will be coded by number and your name will be removed to protect your confidentiality.

There are no known risks or discomfort for participation in this study. Benefits gained from this study include the chance to see the type of questionnaire used by psychologists to measure the progress and outcome of their clients as well as the opportunity to help further our scientific knowledge of client responses to psychotherapy.

This study is being conducted with the usual type of treatment offered by clinicians, which is the reason you have been asked to participate. Participation is voluntary and you have the right to refuse to participate if you desire. Should you agree to participate, you may withdraw at a later time with no penalty to yourself or your therapy. However, we would be grateful for your assistance in this study.

If you have any questions concerning this research you may contact _____ at _____.

I have read the above document and give my consent to be a participant in this research study. I understand that my participation is voluntary and that I may withdraw without consequence at anytime.

Name _____   Date _____

---

instruction presumably encourages patients to report forthrightly their status without concern for the impact such a report could have on their therapist. In clinical settings, however, the assessment data may be collected, in part, to give feedback to the therapist regarding his or her effectiveness. As a result, posttherapy ratings may be obtained without such guarantees, raising both ethical and methodological issues, as it can be argued that the therapist as well as the patient is the "subject" in some research settings. Some measures, particularly satisfaction ratings and process ratings of therapist behavior, can be especially susceptible to the presence or absence of anonymity. Clinicians need to be sensitive to these methodological issues and circumspect in reporting data that have not been provided by clients anonymously.

Practical Guidelines for Assessing Outcome in Practice

In keeping with the previous chapters, a brief set of practical guidelines or general principles may be useful for making ethical decisions regarding outcome assessment in practice.

1. *Be familiar with ethical guidelines applicable to your profession.* There is no substitute for knowing the ethical guidelines concerning assessment and research for your profession. These guidelines will provide principles that will help to guide appropriate behavior concerning the assessment of outcome in practice. Ethical guidelines, however, do not provide situation specific information. As a result, consultation with other professionals will help to identify reasonable and usual methods of practice.

2. *Know the laws and rules specific to your state and organization.* Each state and each organization has different laws or rules governing appropriate use of assessment devices or use of human subjects in research. For example, most community mental health centers have a board that must approve any research project that is conducted using employees or clients of the facility. Of course, the degree to which your data collection represents research versus assessment to inform treatment must be determined beforehand. If in doubt, however, it is best to obtain approval to collect outcome data.

3. *Obtain consent from the client.* Whether the collection of outcome data are considered research or part of ongoing treatment, consent is needed. Many organizations already obtain consent for treatment and evaluation that will cover assessment that is considered part of the treatment process. For research, a second consent form is required.

Many of the more general ethical issues related to assessment and research are not included in this chapter because it is assumed professionals will be familiar with guidelines specific to their area of practice. Nevertheless, the forms and ideas presented here may be useful for those who wish to begin collecting outcome data on a routine basis.

C h a p t e r *10*

Methodological Issues

In writing about assessment as applied to psychotherapy outcome, it is desirable to briefly discuss issues of method. Assessment of outcome typically occurs within the context of a particular therapy research strategy designed to answer specific questions such as: Does the treatment work? Which treatment is best? What are the effective elements in the treatment? Do these treatments work better in combination or alone? In what follows, we will briefly review the history of psychotherapy outcome research. This discussion will include an examination of the difficulties extant in the application of research findings to clinical practice. It will also analyze recent declarations that advocate methodological diversity and highlight the possible contribution of qualitative research methods. We will conclude with some practical suggestions for the conduct of clinical research.

History of Psychotherapy Outcome Research

As a scientific endeavor, the evaluation of psychological interventions is rather young. In what was perhaps the first published outcome study, Fenichel (1930) attempted to evaluate the effectiveness of psychoanalysis by means of analyst-rated outcomes at the Berlin Psychoanalytic Institute. Since then, investigators of treatment outcome have dramatically changed both their research questions and methods. As we review the past 60 plus years of outcome research, we will emphasize these changes. For a more detailed review of this information, the reader is referred to several previously published works (Bergin, 1971; Bergin & Lambert, 1978; Lambert & Bergin, 1994; Lambert, Shapiro, & Bergin, 1986; Kazdin, 1986; Lambert, Masters, & Ogles, 1991; Meltzoff & Kornreich, 1970).

Initial efforts to evaluate psychotherapy were largely concerned with the question: Is psychotherapy effective? These studies typically assessed clients prior to and immediately after treatment to determine if they evidenced improvement. The studies often indicated that indeed the treatment had worked. However, the treatments in vogue at the time were often very lengthy, sometimes continuing for years. The design of these studies made it impossible for them to account for changes that may have occurred simply because of the passage of time or because of other factors extraneous to the treatment. Dramatically illustrating this point, Hans Eysenck (1952) published a report in which he purported to show that the "spontaneous remission rate" in untreated individuals was identical (i.e., at least 67 percent) to the improvement rates often cited for treated patients. Thus, Eysenck maintained that psychotherapy had not yet been proven to be effective.

To answer this challenge, another wave of studies was undertaken that utilized no-treatment or "wait-list" control groups. Included in these wait-list groups were individuals who had sought therapy but were denied it for a period of time, ostensibly because the clinic was full. While the wait-list group was not being treated, the treatment group received services and both groups were assessed in a pre/posttest manner. The design was potentially an effective one for answering Eysenck's challenge; however, many of the early studies had a critical flaw. Rather than randomly assigning all clients to treatment or no-treatment (wait-list), some were assigned to the wait-list condition because their problems were not as great as those in the treated group. Because the two groups were not likely to be equivalent at the outset of treatment, it was difficult to unambiguously attribute differences in outcome to treatment effects. This problem was eliminated in subsequent investigations by randomly assigning patients to treatment and no-treatment groups.

Hundreds of studies have investigated the effectiveness of psychotherapy by use of the pre/posttest, treatment versus no treatment design. The conclusion reached by numerous reviewers (Lambert & Bergin, 1994; Smith, Glass, & Miller, 1980) of this literature is that psychotherapy is generally effective with clients, achieving outcomes superior to those that result from natural healing processes or "spontaneous remission." Logically, however, one must remember that this conclusion applies only to those therapies that have been subjected to investigation. Consequently, the effectiveness of many types of therapy remains an empirical mystery.

Although it was gratifying to learn that many treatments were effective, psychologists soon noted that the available literature did not allow clinicians to know whether the factors believed to be responsible for client improvement were actually the potent elements in the treatment. Subsequently, the focus of investigation changed to answer the question of what, specifically, causes improvement.

There were several related approaches that addressed this fairly complex research question. One theory held that clients were improving simply because they were receiving attention or because they had high expectations of being helped by the therapist. To rule out these possibilities, investigators borrowed a technique from medical research and conducted studies utilizing placebo control groups. The placebo (sometimes called attention) control was designed to provide clients with nonspecific elements of therapy that are common to all treatments (such as attention and the expectation of improvement) without actually exposing the clients to the "theoretically" potent elements of the treatment being tested.

Studies utilizing placebo groups have proven to be more difficult to conduct than was originally anticipated, for two reasons. First, their design actually calls for a double-blind strategy wherein therapists as well as clients believe they are in-volved in treatment regardless of which condition they are actually in. Otherwise, there are likely to be differences in the nonspecifics between groups (e.g., thera-pists in the placebo condition may demonstrate less enthusiasm for the treatment). But how does one keep therapists blind as to whether they are administering a "real" treatment or merely a placebo? This has proven to be perplexing, although Wojciechowski (1984) provides an interesting illustration of some of the possibili-ties. Second, in the context of psychotherapy, defining a placebo control is prob-lematic (Wilkins, 1979a,b). One school's placebo is another school's treatment. Other authors, from several perspectives, questioned the usefulness of the placebo concept in psychotherapy outcome research (Bloch & Lambert, 1985; Prileau, Mur-dock, & Brody, 1983).

In spite of these problems, however, it is generally agreed that this research has demonstrated that placebo treatments are more effective than no treatment but that specific treatments are superior to both (Lambert & Bergin, 1994). Based on the pre-ceding issues and considering methodological, and perhaps ethical, difficulties of conducting placebo studies, investigators decided that a better strategy might be to compare different therapies. The question in the 1970s became: Given that certain treatments are effective, which treatment is more effective? Many of these compara-tive outcome studies were sophisticated in their design and outcome assessments and the results have been extensively reviewed elsewhere (Bergin & Lambert, 1978; Miller & Berman, 1983; Shapiro & Shapiro, 1982). The general conclusion reached by these reviewers has been the now well-known DoDo Bird verdict proclaimed by Luborsky, Singer, and Luborsky (1975): "Everyone has won and so all must have prizes." In other words, therapy works, but, except in a few instances, no one type works better than the others.

The results of these comparative studies are probably to some extent responsi-ble for the current trend toward eclecticism in psychotherapy practice. Since no one therapy was proven to be superior to the others, the choice of therapies may, con-sequently, be made on the basis of other factors, including the particular likes of the client and therapist. Paradoxically, however, these results are somewhat irrelevant to eclectic therapists; therapists who are not invested in any one particular approach to therapy are not likely to be extremely interested in the Grand Prix (Gottman & Mark-man, 1978) question raised by comparative outcome studies.

The DoDo Bird verdict has also led to an increasing interest in studies focusing more closely on the actual processes thought to be responsible for change. Unlike the comparative questions that are addressed by operationalizing psychotherapy as a whole (e.g., "Is psychodynamic therapy better than behavioral therapy?"), process studies focus on specific in-therapy events. These events, once operationalized, are categorized, coded, counted, and then correlated with outcomes. For example, some studies have looked at empathy, warmth, and genuineness as predictors of outcome and have found that they tend to be important predictors (see Beutler, Crago, & Ariz-mendi, 1986). Although this evidence is only correlational, it suggests that training of new psychotherapists should include specific training in empathic skills. This illus-trates one of the chief advantages of process research (i.e., its clear implications for both training and practice).

A final strategy for attempting to ascertain the effective ingredients of therapy is the "dismantling" approach. This method, which has been used often in studies of cognitive and behavioral therapies, pays little attention to the therapist but instead focuses on particular techniques. Researchers using this strategy think of treatment as a package made up of component parts. Once it has been determined that the package as a whole is effective, the investigators dismantle the treatment by comparing some parts of it with other parts and with the whole package (or various combinations of parts). The dismantling approach has produced some surprising conclusions (e.g., Rehm, Kornblith, O'Hara, & Lamparski, 1981), indicating that when it comes to at least some forms of psychotherapy, less may be more.

Other investigators have attempted to make treatments more powerful. One of these enhancement strategies is essentially the opposite of the dismantling design. With this approach, new components are added to an existing and demonstrably effective treatment package in order to enhance its effects. This strategy has been used with many different types of therapies and provides a rigorous test for new techniques.

Another enhancement strategy has been to match clients with treatments based on the idea that although therapy is generally effective and different treatments typically fail to produce disparate results, not all clients benefit to the same degree in a given treatment or do equally well in every treatment. Although this approach has appeal, it has proven difficult to determine the important variables to use as the basis for matching client to therapy type, and at present no firm conclusions can be drawn.

But Not All Is Well

Given this history of empirical examination, including support for the efficacy of psychotherapy, one might expect that practicing clinicians would be grateful to their scientist colleagues for developing the empirical foundation of their work and to use research to guide their practice. Instead, however, many clinicians say that outcome research is oversimplified and irrelevant to clinical practice (Cohen, Sargent, & Sechrest, 1986; Goldfried, Greenberg, & Marmar, 1990). Cohen (1979) found that clinical psychologists are infrequent consumers of the empirical research literature and demonstrated (Cohen et al., 1986) that research books and articles on clinical practice ranked at the bottom of a list of useful information sources. At the top of the list were workshops on clinical practice and discussions with colleagues. Even well-known scientists who also conduct clinical practice have noted that empirical findings are often uninformative. Matarazzo, for example, several years ago stated, "Even after 15 years, few of my research findings affect my practice. Psychological science per se doesn't guide me one bit. I still read avidly, but this is of little direct practical help. My clinical experience is the only thing that has helped me in my practice to date" (Bergin & Strupp, 1972, p. 340). Although this quote is dated, we believe that many clinicians would still agree with it.

Other investigators have noted that clinicians tend to be biased by their theoretical (and probably personal) orientation when considering therapy outcome studies. Cohen and Suchy (1979), for example, found that psychodynamic therapists negatively evaluated the methodology of outcome research that demonstrated superior results for behavior therapy and likewise the behaviorally oriented clinicians tended to do the same regarding psychoanalytic treatments. Interestingly, eclectic respondents were not influenced by the results of a study when making ratings of methodology.

Morrow-Bradley and Elliot (1986) surveyed 279 members of APA Division 29 (Psychotherapy). They found that although psychotherapy research is utilized in some manner by many clinical psychologists, the general pattern of utilization is discouragingly low. These findings were supported by Cohen and colleagues (1986). Consequently, Morrow-Bradley and Elliot concluded that, overwhelmingly, therapists learn about therapy from their practical experience with clients.

Why is this the case? There are no doubt many reasons. Strupp (1981) has suggested the existence of basic temperament and philosophic differences between researchers and practitioners that will probably always limit the degree of interaction between them. One of the places where this may be most obvious has to do with statistical and computer analyses. Barlow and colleagues (Barlow, 1981; Barlow, Hayes, & Nelson, 1984) have highlighted the overemphasis on statistical significance in research studies—an overemphasis that corresponds to an underemphasis on clinical significance. Clinicians, understandably, are not interested in obtaining reliable but meaningless changes in their patients. Fortunately, as noted in Chapter 8, this problem is being addressed, with Neil Jacobson and colleagues leading the way (e.g., Jacobson, 1988; Jacobson et al., 1984; Jacobson, Follette, & Revenstorf, 1984, 1986; Jacobson & Truax, 1991).

A slightly different but related issue is the use of statistics (Cohen et al., 1986). Clinicians want to read about clearly observable change and are generally not interested in wading through complicated statistical analyses. However, with the advent of comprehensive statistical packages for use on powerful computers, it has become commonplace, perhaps even mandatory, for researchers to conduct multivariate and other sophisticated analyses. Although these statistics allow the investigator to consider the effects of several variables simultaneously and are therefore more likely to accurately describe realworld situations, they require advanced training to understand. Most practitioners have little interest in pursuing quantification to this degree. Consequently, the research literature may be becoming more alien to them. Paradoxically, the use of powerful statistical techniques may be undermining the practical implementation of research findings. In addressing similar issues, Cohen (1990) concluded that, in terms of research and analysis, less is more and simple is better.

Often, problems between researchers and practitioners concern the generalizability of research findings. For example, it is generally good research practice to randomly assign clients to treatments (or to no treatment), yet in what clinic would this occur? Further, researchers have too often used samples (e.g., college students) and/or therapists (e.g., graduate students in training) of convenience who were, at best, only analogous to the patients and therapists who actually engage in clinical practice. This has led to considerable debate over the relevance of findings produced using analog samples (Kazdin, 1978, 1980; Rakover, 1980).

A basic and very important problem stemming from methodological issues is the nomothetic versus idiographic dilemma. Nomothetic or group-based research results are believed to produce effects that are reliable and generalizable beyond the particular sample of subjects employed. They have, therefore, been favored by researchers. However, within any one group of treated research participants, there may be vast differences in individual outcomes. While, on the average, the group may have demonstrated improvement, some subjects probably improved a great deal, some stayed the same, and others perhaps deteriorated (Bergin, 1966, 1971). This is problematic for practitioners. Nomothetic data do not tell them how any individual client will respond to treatment.

This problem also applies to therapists. Group-based statistics do not convey information regarding the effectiveness of any individual therapist. Furthermore, there is evidence to suggest that there are bigger differences between therapists offering the same treatment than between the average of two treatments (Luborsky, McLellan, Woody, O'Brien, & Auerbach, 1985; Crits-Cristoph & Mintz, 1991). In other words, some therapists may be highly effective and others may be relatively ineffective. The use of outcome measures in clinical practice, however, can help to provide individually based evaluations of both client improvement and therapist effectiveness. As health care reform progresses, it is becoming obvious that individual practitioners must be able to verify their efficacy with the patients they treat.

A final significant problem encountered by practitioners who attempt to use clinical research in their practice pertains to determining exactly what the clinicians and clients in the study did. Bednar, Burlingame, and Masters (1988) highlighted one example of this problem when they reviewed marital and family therapies. They noted that, based on the published reports, it was very difficult to determine what constituted systemic therapy and how this therapy had been implemented. This represents a problem not only for practitioners but also for researchers who attempt to replicate a study. In some cases, researchers do cite previous sources that provide more detailed accounts of the intended therapy. This is helpful and, given space limitations in journals, probably the best that can be done. The implementation of treatment manuals may also help. These manuals were originally intended to confirm treatment integrity in research studies but they are also being used in training and practice settings (Goldfried et al., 1990; Lambert & Ogles, 1989). Although treatment manuals clarify, to some extent, what the therapists did, because information pertaining to particular client behaviors is not obtained, it is difficult to determine how individual therapists and clients interacted to produce an effect.

The Search for Meaning and the Rising Popularity of Qualitative Methods

In the last decade or so, a group of research strategies generally referred to as "qualitative methods" have been advanced as a means of better connecting research results with practice. Several authors have called for methodological diversity (Barlow, 1981; Gelso, 1979; Gelso et al., 1988; Howard, 1984; Kazdin, 1981; Polkinghorne, 1984, 1991; Russell, 1994) or even epistemological eclecticism (Borgen, 1984; Patton, 1991; Polkinghorne, 1991), and for some (e.g., Polkinghorne, 1984, 1991) this has amounted to a ringing endorsement of qualitative methods in psychotherapy research. Defining qualitative methods and differentiating them from quantitative methods has proven to be difficult (Whitt, 1991), possibly because the qualitative approach draws from many different disciplines, each having its own unique perspective. A precise definition is elusive, yet there is general agreement that qualitative research includes an emphasis on holistic perspectives, understanding and meaning (rather than frequency) in natural settings, naturalistic and participant observation, and human beings as instruments of data collection. The qualitative methods are becoming increasingly popular among practicing clinicians and some university faculty. Several doctoral programs in clinical and counseling psychology that we are familiar with now not only accept, but encourage, qualitatively based dissertations and theses.

In psychotherapy outcome research, the qualitative approach is best illustrated by the case study. Case studies have always had considerable appeal because of their ability to richly describe the process of therapy, but they often lack both internal and external validity and tend to be subject to the personal perspective of the reporting therapist. However, there are many ways to conduct what could be called a case study, some being more obviously qualitative than others.

In the purest qualitative sense, a case study consists of observations made about a particular client that are analyzed and presented to the scholarly community. These observations may initially take many forms (e.g., video or audio recordings, handwritten notes) and are subsequently subjected to linguistic or hermeneutic analysis. As a final step, the investigator searches for contradictions within the data and between the data and his or her developing theory. It is quite evident that basic differences exist between the qualitative and positivist camps regarding the nature of data (and even reality) and the meaning, desirability, and possibility of objectivity.

Nevertheless, current authors who endorse qualitative techniques call for meticulous data collection and for public scrutiny of each phase of the process (Kuh & Andreas, 1991; Polkinghorne, 1991; Scott, 1991). These authors also suggest that investigators keep their original recordings and notes, including information regarding why they progressed and thought as they did. That is, the investigator must not only describe what happened in the sessions but should also account for the actions taken and explain why he or she concluded that the case was either successful or unsuccessful. Because of the public nature of the process, claims regarding reliability, objectivity, and replicability may then be made. One can readily see that this does not amount to taking the easy way out.

Unfortunately, most case studies in psychology have not followed the precise and elaborate course described here. Furthermore, even in those cases where qualitative procedures are followed fastidiously, we believe there are clear limits to the utility of "pure" qualitative research in answering the questions posed by psychotherapy outcome investigations. The history of psychotherapy is filled with exaggerated claims made by both sincere and insincere individuals regarding the effectiveness, supported by case studies, of their particular form of treatment. By what method can one distinguish good qualitative research from poor qualitative research? Although in principle one may retrieve original records and carefully examine both the data and the investigator's reasoning, this would easily prove to be an overwhelming undertaking. An alternative would be for authors to publish the original material with their manuscripts. This would certainly facilitate examination by the scholarly community but would require the reintroduction of monographs to the field, and there is no telling how many different types of treatment would be presented.

Must one therefore conclude that the case study belongs to the Museum of Ancient Methods and that it has no relevance to psychotherapy outcome research? Absolutely not. Although the lack of quantitative information makes it difficult to document that changes have in fact occurred, this problem can be overcome. Kazdin (1981, 1986) has authored several works detailing how case study methods may be used while preserving internal validity. In what follows, we will use Kazdin's work as an outline and provide practical suggestions for how clinicians may actually conduct this research.

Like other forms of experimentation, case study experiments may be divided according to the criteria proposed by Campbell and Stanley (1963). These evaluate the extent to which internal validity is preserved and threats to internal validity are controlled or eliminated. Essentially all research can be divided into the pre-experimental, in which causation cannot be determined; quasi-experimental, in which some control over threats to internal validity is exerted; and true experiments, which are the most stringent and in which control is maximized. These classifications, particularly the last two, differ along a continuum. True experimental case studies would be characterized by the following: use of standardized, objective measures that are pertinent to the areas expected to change; repeated measurements over time; delineation of a baseline that does not depict improvement in the condition; delineation of treatment phases; prediction of how the patient will progress given both treatment and no treatment; and immediate and large changes. Obviously, while a single study of a single individual is of interest, it is also possible to aggregate the data obtained from studies of many individuals assessed and treated one at a time. This kind of report offers enhanced external validity over the singular case study. Quasi-experimental case studies differ from true experiments in that they may not have an adequate baseline, the number of measurements are limited, or the magnitude and immediacy of change is relatively small.

Resulting from the characteristics of true and quasi-experiments are several practical suggestions for clinicians desiring to conduct case study research. First, standardized assessment is critical to the unambiguous demonstration of change. By applying the scheme depicted earlier in this book, clinicians can make informed decisions regarding which instruments suit the purposes of their particular investigation. Obviously, clinicians could vary their choice of instruments with different cases. In this way, valuable knowledge could be gained regarding differential improvement and the impact of assessment on outcome conclusions. In an ideal (though probably unrealistic) scenario, a clinician treating, say depression, would over time collect data from numerous patients utilizing measures from different areas of the conceptual scheme and would reach the same conclusion!

A second implication is that clinicians need to be continuously measuring the object of change (behavior, affect, cognitions, etc.) while at the same time maintaining copious notes regarding the treatment. This is important for a couple of reasons. First, change may occur in a dramatic and unexpected manner. By being able to correlate in time the precise intervention that immediately preceded the change, some suggestion regarding the relationship between the two can be made. Second, the mere use of pre/posttest measurement does not control for a host of potentially confounding variables. However, more continuous assessment allows for the determination of trends as well as discontinuous change, and thereby reduces some of these threats. Third, continuous assessment is an important factor in establishing a baseline or no-treatment condition. Finally, continuous assessment offers numerous practical or clinical benefits. For example, it allows for precise determination of the client's current condition, may alert the clinician to potentially harmful results, and could, thereby, inform the treatment plan in numerous ways.

From a practical point of view, continuous assessment may seem time consuming and expensive. Yet, once it has become a regular part of a clinic's functioning it can be really quite routine. This means that support staff are often going to be included in collecting the data and must therefore be trained in the proper methods. But once this is established, the collection can run smoothly. Consider your last visit to a physician. Did he or she simply take a guess at your blood pressure, temperature, and so forth, or were these measurements collected in a routine, expected, and relatively unobtrusive manner? Many of the instruments discussed in this book are cost effective and other instruments are introduced regularly. David Burns, for instance, has developed a set of measures that assess anxiety and depression in a brief, inexpensive, and useful manner. (For information, contact: David D. Burns, M.D., and Associates, c/o Presbyterian Medical Center of Philadelphia, 39th and Market Streets, Philadelphia, PA 19104.) Obviously, the scope of measurement must be narrow since the collection is continuous, but again, by varying what is measured across patients and making wise choices of measures, valuable information can be gained.

Although the individual clinician may regard the collection of continuous assessment data a paperwork nightmare, several software programs are in the final stages of development to assist in this task. It is now possible for the clinician to continuously record outcome data as part of the clinical record. These data, once entered in an electronic record, are aggregated to display patient progress on specific treatment targets and on standardized rating scales across treatment episodes. The software also includes billing procedures and computes cost/benefit ratios. Computer software will allow for immediate clinician feedback regarding patient progress without increased time expenditures by the clinician. The computer-based collection of outcome data may soon become a requirement of doing business with some managed care companies.

Assumed in the preceding discussion is that the treating clinician is clear on what it is that he or she expects to change in the patient as a result of therapy. The choice of instruments will be highly influenced and largely based on this consideration. Clearly, one will want to include instruments specific to the particular area of change being addressed. However, in some cases it may also be desirable to measure areas that are deemed irrelevant to the treatment, and therefore not expected to change. This will allow for some determination of the specificity of both treatment and measurement. Practically, by having to consciously make decisions regarding assessment instruments, clinicians may be forced to think more clearly in terms of their goals of treatment, expected outcomes, and treatment plan. This should improve the quality of treatment rendered.

A third major implication drawn from the characteristics of case study research is that clinicians need to be aware of the natural history of disorders and can thus make predictions regarding their expectations for particular cases. If we know, for example, that untreated cases do not improve but find demonstrated improvement in our cases, then we have reasonably good evidence that the treatment is effective. Of course, this is based on the assumption that the natural history of the disorder is known—an assumption that may not always be true. These predictions may also be made on the basis of baseline observations or the patient's personal history. For example, if a chronic pain patient is being treated in your pain center and the history indicates that she has been treated in three other similar and reputable centers with minimal improvement, you would not be expecting immediate or substantial changes. In fact, in this case, if you did see dramatic initial improvement, you may be somewhat skeptical of its duration and would therefore want to continue assessment for some time.

It is important to realize that there is much the clinician can do to improve the quality of research. Nevertheless, in some instances limitations inherent in the nature of the problem, patient, or setting may stifle even the best efforts. Baselines, for example, may be difficult to establish due to a number of factors including ethical concerns, practical considerations, and patient characteristics. Additionally, the nature of some disorders is that the symptoms tend to fluctuate. Thus, even if it were possible to measure continuously prior to treatment, it may prove difficult to find stability. A documented history that includes previous measurements can be helpful in these instances but does not replace the baseline.

Other problems may arise due to the population being served. It is obviously more difficult to demonstrate that therapy was responsible for improvement in patients who have an acute, rapid onset, condition. Another problem is that it is impossible to know what magnitude of change will occur. Although larger and more immediate changes are generally more informative regarding treatment effects, these may not always be obtained and, even when they are, may not be lasting (as discussed earlier). Finally, some patients may simply refuse to complete the measures. This resistance can be minimized by structuring the measurements as a necessary part of the treatment process, informing the patient as to their use, not overburdening the patient with excessive measures, and having an office environment where assessments are routinely collected in a professional and efficient manner.

We believe that the case study can be a valuable source of information regarding the effectiveness of therapy and is a viable candidate to bridge the gap between scientist and clinician. The requirements for conducting quality case studies are not onerous and the results can be intensely gratifying. When one's practice is improved as result of research, the research is no longer extraneous but instead becomes vital. Further, Barlow (1981) has called for the "accumulation of case studies using well-described procedures and realistic and practical measures of change" (p. 153). He goes on to note that "rather than relying on inferential statistical techniques for large scale factorial studies to establish generality of findings and higher order interactions, clinical procedures developed or elaborated in clinical research centers could be turned over to clinicians. Clinicians could then collect data on hundreds or thousands of cases over several years, noting both degree of improvement, percentage of improvement, and most importantly, those who failed (i.e., intense local observation). This information could then be fed back to the large clinical research centers, which, taking hints from innovations in the clinical series, could test out variations of currently effective therapeutic procedures with those specific groups of individuals who do not benefit from treatment" (pp. 153–154). This scenario is well within the reach of currently developed software programs that will be relatively inexpensive to implement and maintain. In this manner, clinicians and researchers could begin to work together in an effort to better evaluate current psychotherapy interventions. In fact, the recent formation of the Consortium of Counseling Centers by several major universities may be a positive step in this direction.

Although we have provided many practical suggestions, we have not spelled out in detail how to conduct these case studies. Interested readers are referred to the work of Kazdin and others who have written on this topic. Neither have we discussed the various single-case experimental designs (Hayes, 1981; Hersen & Barlow, 1976) or time-series methodologies (Barlow, Hayes, & Nelson, 1984) that may be useful to the practicing clinician. But our point is this: We have available a variety of techniques and methods for investigating the effectiveness of psychotherapy, all of which need to be employed. Furthermore, the practitioner can and should be involved in this investigation. As Gelso (1979) so vividly demonstrated with the "bubble hypothesis," all research and assessment methods are limited. None by itself can, once and for all, answer the questions we all face. Rather, what is needed is an accumulation nomothetic and idiographic research that is carefully conducted so as to rule out competing hypotheses and enhance the generality of conclusions. This research must be designed to enable practitioners to apply the findings readily to their work. Not only will universities and training centers need to invest their time in traditional group-based experimental designs but they should also teach and place value on the other methods described here. Correspondingly, journals must be willing to consider case studies. As Kazdin noted (1981), the important issue is whether the study has ruled out threats to internal and external validity.

By relying on a combination of research designs that offer vivid descriptions of the therapy process, we are optimistic that the gap between research and practice can be spanned and that the scientist-practitioner will be taken off the endangered species list. With this book, we hope to increase full-time clinicians' consumption of and participation in therapy research. It is becoming more clear everyday that in the near future, health care reform is going to require that outcomes be measured by all health care providers. Further, it seems very likely that simply citing published studies to support one's clinical practice will be inadequate. Third-party payers, government agencies, patients, and other stakeholders will demand to know the success rates and general outcomes of specific practices and practitioners. In fact, at this writing, these ideas have already been proposed in a number of areas by several different authors. Certainly, it will be to the benefit of all of us to take the initiative and begin this important work immediately.

Despite our idealism regarding the potential wealth of clinical data and resultant empirical evidence that could be discovered via cooperation between research and clinical centers, we are realistic about the potential applications of outcome assessment in practice. Most clinicians will use outcome assessment methods if there are genuine, day-to-day, practical advantages to doing so, and if the costs of time, effort, and money to implement these procedures are kept to a minimum. We believe this can be accomplished with a limited amount of organizational change and personal effort. The extent to which clinicians participate in the distribution of their efforts to other professionals or for the advancement of science will be determined by their own personal goals, time demands, and job descriptions. Adequate outcome measurement provides the core component to be able to make these communications of the highest value.

C h a p t e r *11*

Final Comment

The dedicated reader who has made it to this point in the book has endured a history of outcome assessment in psychotherapy research; a critique of the diversity among measures; the presentation of an organizational and conceptual scheme to guide the selection of outcome assessment devices; the presentation of several global, specific, idiographic, and process measures; a commentary and illustration on the potential use of these measures to assess statistical as well as practical change; and two brief excursions regarding ethics and methodology. Hopefully, amid the numerous descriptions, explanations, and commentaries, as well as some diversions, clinicians will find useful material to help them begin evaluating the effectiveness of therapy in their ongoing practices. Several reasonable measures often used in research with well-established psychometric properties have been presented that can be accessed immediately for clinical use. Several appendices have been included with many of the important details necessary to obtain these measures. In addition, the organizational and conceptual scheme can be used to guide the selection of other relevant instruments. The final act, however, remains in the hands of the reader. The practical and meaningful outcome evaluation of your practice can be conducted or permitted only by you.

Appendix A

Characteristics of the Instruments

Measure	Chapter	Item Content	Rater	Population	Norms
ASI (structured interview)	5	Addiction severity	Interviewer	Substance abuse; individual; certain important limitations	Not cited
BDI	5	Depression	Self-report	Clinical/institutional, individual	Available
BLRI (several versions available)	7	Therapy process/ Relationship	Client	General clinical; individual	Not available
Brief Symptom Inventory	4	Symptomatology	Client	Clinical/institutional; individual	Not cited
CALPAS (client and therapist versions)	7	Therapy process Relationship	Client or therapist	General clinical; individual	Not cited
CALTARS	7	Therapy.process/ Relationship	Rater	General clinical; individual	Not cited
CBCL (self-report and teacher-rated versions also available)	5	Behavioral problems	Parent or surrogate	Child, adolescent; ages 4 to 16	Available
CCRT	7	Therapy relationship	Rater or therapist	General clinical; individual	Not applicable
CGAS	4	Functioning	Therapist or interviewer	Child, adolescent; ages 4 to 16	Available
COMPASS	5	Well-being, symptoms, functioning, therapeutic bond	Self-report and therapist	Adult outpatient	Available
CSQ-8	8	Post-Tx satisfaction	Self-report	General clinical; individual	Not cited
DAS	5	Relationship satisfaction	Self-report	General clinical; couples	Available
ES	7	Therapy process	Rater	General clinical; individual, group, couples	Not applicable
FQ	5	Tx outcome: Phobias	Self-report	Clinical/institutional; individual	Available
GAS	4	Level of functioning	Therapist or interviewer	Clinical/institutional; individual,	Not cited

# Items/ Time	Administration Ease	Scoring/Rating Ease	Reliability	Validity
180-item interview/ 40 min.	Moderate difficulty	Relatively easy	Good	Good
21 items/5 min.	Easy	Easy	Adequate	Adequate
64 items/15 min.	Easy	Relatively easy	Adequate	Adequate
53 items/10 min.	Easy	Relatively easy	Questionable	Questionable
Patient: 48 items; therapist: 25 items/ 5 min.	Easy	Easy	Adequate	Adequate
41 items/time consuming	Moderate difficulty	Relatively easy	Questionable	Questionable
138 items/25–45 min.	Relatively easy	Moderate difficulty	Very good	Very good
Time consuming	Moderate difficulty	Relatively easy	Adequate	Adequate
1 item/2–10 minutes	Moderate difficulty	Easy	Good	Adequate
Client 141 items/ 15 min.; therapist 7 items/ 3 min.	Easy	Scored by COMPASS	Adequate	Good where reported
8 items/5 min.	Easy	Easy	Adequate	Adequate
32 items/10 min.	Easy	Relatively easy	Adequate	Adequate
1 item/time consuming	Moderate difficulty	Easy	Adequate	Fair
21 items/5 min.	Easy	Relatively easy	Good	Good
1 item/2–10 minutes	Moderate difficulty	Easy	Adequate	Fair

Continued

Measure	Chapter	Item Content	Rater	Population	Norms
Goal Attainment Scaling	6	Level of functioning	Rater	Clinical/institutional; individual, couples, family	Not applicable
HAcs (counting signs) (client and therapist versions)	7	Therapy process/ Relationship	Rater	General clinical; individual	Not cited
HAr (rating) (client and therapist versions)	7	Therapy process/ Relationship	Rater	General clinical; individual	Not cited
HAq (questionnaire)	7	Therapy process/ Relationship	Self-report/ Therapist	General clinical; individual	Not cited
HARS	5	Anxiety	Therapist/ Rater	Clinical/institutional; individual	Not cited
Health Sickness Rating	4	Degree of pathology	Therapist/ Rater	Clinical/institutional; individual	Not cited
HVRM (client and counselor versions)	7	Therapy process/ Relationship	Rater	General clinical; individual	Not available
IIP	5	Interpersonal problems	Self-report	General clinical; individual	Available
Katz Adjustment Scale (client and relative versions)	4	Level of function-ing/Degree of psycho-pathology	Self-report	Clinical/institutional; individual	Available
Marital Satisfaction Inventory	4	Marital satisfaction	Self-report	General clinical; couples	Not cited
PES (child, adolescent, adult, & D.D. versions)	6	Tx goal attainment	Self-report/ Therapist	Clinical/institutional; individual; child, adolescent, adult, devel. disabled	Not cited
OQ	4	Symptoms, social adjustment, inter-personal problems	Self-report	General clinical	Available
QLQ (self-report and inter-viewer-rated versions available	8	Quality of life	Self-report or Interviewer	Clinical/institutional; individual; chronic mental illness	Not cited
QOLI	8	Quality of life	Self-report	Clinical/institutional; individual; adult	Available

# Items/ Time	Administration Ease	Scoring/Rating Ease	Reliability	Validity
Variable	Difficult	Relatively easy	Questionable	Questionable
7 subscales/variable	Difficult	Easy	Questionable	Questionable
10 subscales/variable	Difficult	Easy	Adequate	Adequate
17 items/5 min.	Easy	Easy	Adequate	Adequate
14 items/variable	Relatively easy	Relatively easy	Not cited	Questionable
7 ratings plus global	Moderate difficulty	Relatively easy	Adequate	Adequate
Variable	Moderate difficulty	Moderate difficulty	Adequate	Adequate
127 items/ 15–30 min.	Easy	Easy	Good	Questionable
205 items (5 forms) per version 25–45 min.	Easy	Relatively easy	Relative version: adequate; client version: not reported	Relative version: adequate; client version: not reported
280 items/30–60 min.;	Easy	Relatively easy	Very good	Very good
45 items/5–7 min.	Easy	Easy	Very good	Very good
7 ratings/5–8 min.	Relatively easy	Relatively easy	Adequate	Adequate
263 items/interview format	Moderate difficulty	Not cited	Adequate	Adequate
17 items/10 min.	Easy	Relatively easy	Good	Preliminary

Continued

Measure	Chapter	Item Content	Rater	Population	Norms
SADS-C	4	Recent global functioning	Therapist	Clinical/institutional; individual; affective disorder and schizophrenia	Not cited
SCID (also specific versions for psychiatric and nonpsychiatric patients)	4	Diagnosis	Therapist	Clinical/institutional; individual, adult	Not available
SCL-90 (and SCL-90-R)	4	Symptomatology	Self-report	Clinical/institutional, individual	Not available
SCL-90-Analog	4	Symptomatology	Therapist/ Rater	Clinical/institutional, individual	Not cited
SEQ	7	Therapy process/ Relationship	Self-report/ Therapist	General clinical; individual	Not available
Social Adjustment Scales (self-report and schizophrenia versions also available)	4	Social adjustment/ Functioning	Therapist/ Rater	General clinical; individual	Not cited
STAI	5	Anxiety	Self-report	General clinical; individual	Not cited
SUDS	4	Distress	Self-report	General clinical; individual	Not available
TSR	7	Therapy process/ Relationship	Client and therapist	General clinical; individual, couples, groups	Available
VNIS	7	Therapy process/ Relationship	Therapist/ Rater	General clinical; individual	Not cited
VPPS:	7	Therapy process/ Relationship	Rater	General clinical; individual	Not cited
WAI (observer-rated version also available)	7	Therapy process/ Relationship	Client/ Therapist	General clinical; individual	Not cited

# Items/ Time	Administration Ease	Scoring/Rating Ease	Reliability	Validity
45 items/variable	Moderate difficulty	Relatively easy	Adequate	Adequate
Semi-structured interview/60–90 min.	Moderate difficulty	Relatively easy	Adequate	Questionable
90 items/10–20 min.	Easy	Relatively easy	Adequate	Adequate
9 items/1–2 min.	Relatively easy	Relatively easy	Adequate	Adequate
24 items/5 min.	Easy	Relatively easy	Adequate	Questionable
Semi-structured interview/45–90 min.	Moderate difficulty	Relatively easy	Good	Adequate
40 items/10 min.	Easy	Easy	Adequate	Adequate
Variable	Easy	Easy	Lacking	Lacking
167 items/10–20 min.	Easy	Not cited	Not cited	Not cited
42 items/time consuming	Difficult	Not cited	Adequate	Adequate
80 items per segment/ time consuming	Moderate difficulty	Not cited	Good	Adequate
36 items/10 min.	Easy	Relatively easy	Good	Adequate

Appendix *B*

=====

Instruments or Example Items

Example Items from the Addiction Severity Index

Drug/Alcohol Use

17. How many times have you:
    had alcohol d.t.'s   _____
    Overdosed on drugs   _____

Legal Status

How many times in your life have you been charged with the following:

17. Driving while intoxicated   _____

Family/Social Relationships

9. How many close friends do you have?_____

Example Items from the Barrett-Lennard
Relationship Inventory:
Form OS-64

Below are listed various ways that one person might feel or behave in relation to another person. Please consider each numbered statement with reference to your present relationship with _____ , mentally adding his or her name in the space provided. For example, if the other person's name was John, you would read statement #1, as "<u>John</u> respects me as a person." Mark each statement in the answer column on the right, according to how strongly you feel that it is true, or not true, in this relationship. *Please be sure to mark every one.* Write in a plus number (+3, +2, or +1) for each "yes" answer, and minus numbers (−1, −2, or −3) to stand for "no" answers. Here is the exact meaning of each answer number:

+3: Yes (!), I strongly feel that it is true.   −1: (No) I feel that it is probably untrue, or
+2: Yes, I feel it is true.   more untrue than true.
+1: (Yes) I feel that it is probably true,   −2: No, I feel it is not true.
    or more true than untrue.   −3: No (!), I feel strongly that it is not true.

_____ ANSWER

1. _____ respects me as a person. . . . . _____
5. _____ feels a true liking for me. . . . . _____
36. _____ expresses his/her true impressions and feelings with me. . . . . _____
41. I feel that _____ really values me. . . . . _____
58. _____'s response to me is usually so fixed and automatic that I don't
    really get through to him or her. . . . . _____

Example Items from the Beck Depression Inventory

Instructions:

This questionnaire consists of 21 groups of statements. After reading each group of statements carefully, circle the number (0, 1, 2, or 3) next to the one statement in each group which best describes the way you have been feeling the past week, including today. If several statements within a group seem to apply equally well, circle each one. Be sure to read all the statements in each group before making your choice.

5. 0 I don't feel particulary guilty.
    1 I feel guilty a good part of the time.
    2 I feel quite guilty most of the time.
    3 I feel guilty all of the time.

12. 0 I have not lost interest in other people.
    1 I am less interested in other people than I used to be.
    2 I have lost most of my interest in other people.
    3 I have lost all of my interest in other people.

From the Beck Depression Inventory. Copyright © 1987 by Aaron T. Beck. Reproduced by permission of Publisher, The Psychological Corporation, San Antonio, Texas. All rights reserved.

Example Items from the
Brief Symptom Inventory™ (BSI®)

Instructions to the Rater

Listed below are nine specific dimensions of psychopathology. Definitions of each dimension appear on the reverse side of this form. The rating continuum for each dimension ranges from "Not At All" to "Extremely." Rate the patient on each dimension by placing a vertical mark on the continuum to represent the level of the dimension the patient is now manifesting.

Item	Not at all	A little bit	Moderately	Quite a bit	Extremely
16. Feeling lonely	0	1	2	3	4
30. Hot or cold spells	0	1	2	3	4
36. Trouble concentrating	0	1	2	3	4

Example Items from the California Psychotherapy Alliance Scales Patient Version

DIRECTIONS: Below is a list of questions that describe attitudes people might have about their therapy or therapist. Think about the session you just completed and decide which category best describes your attitude for each question. Make a check on the line under that category. Please answer each question.

Item	Not at all	A little bit	Moderately	Quite a bit	Very much
10. Did your therapist's comments help you to see your difficulties in a new light?	_____	_____	_____	_____	_____
23. Did you feel that it was important for you to come to this session?	_____	_____	_____	_____	_____
36. During this session, how committed was your therapist to understanding your difficulties?	_____	_____	_____	_____	_____

Example Items from the California Psychotherapy Alliance Scales Therapist Version

DIRECTIONS: There are four CALPAS-T dimensions to be rated for this session. The rating proceeds in two steps yielding separate ratings.

1 = not at all, 2 = a little bit, 3 = somewhat, 4 = moderately, 5 = quite a bit, 6 = quite a lot, 7 = very much so.

Item							
10. Patient views therapy as important.	1	2	3	4	5	6	7
18. Patient and therapist agree on salient themes.	1	2	3	4	5	6	7
25. Therapist facilitates work on salient themes.	1	2	3	4	5	6	7

Example Items from the Child Behavior Checklist

Below is a list of items that describe children and youth. For each item that describes your child *now or within the past six months,* please circle the <u>2</u> if the item is <u>very</u> <u>true</u> or <u>often</u> <u>true</u> of your child. Circle the <u>1</u> if the item is <u>somewhat</u> or <u>sometimes</u> <u>true</u> of your child. If the item is <u>not</u> <u>true</u> of your child, circle the <u>0</u>. Please answer all the items as well as you can, even if some do not seem to apply to your child.

0 = Not True (as far as you know)   1 = Somewhat or Sometimes True   2 = Very True or Often True

0	1	2	1. Acts too young for his/her age
0	1	2	31. Fears he/she might think or do something bad
0	1	2	51. Feels dizzy

Children's Global Assessment Scale

Rate the subject's most impaired level of general functioning during the past six months by selecting the lowest level which describes his or her functioning on a hypothetical continuum of health-illness. Use the intermediary levels (e.g., 35, 58, 62). Rate actual functioning regardless of treatment or prognosis. The examples of behavior provided are only illustrative and are not required for a particular rating. Place your rating in the space provided in the upper left hand corner of the form.

100–91   Superior functioning in all areas (at home, at school, and with peers); involved in a wide range of activities and has many interests (e.g., has hobbies or participates in extracurricular activities or belongs to an organized group such as Scouts, etc.); likable, confident; "everyday" worries never get out of hand; doing well in school; no symptoms.

90–81   Good functioning in all areas; secure in family, school, and with peers; there may be transient difficulties and "everyday" worries that occasionally get out of hand (e.g., mild anxiety associated with an important exam, occasional "blow-ups" with siblings, parents, or peers).

80–71   No more than slight impairment in functioning at home, at school, or with peers; some disturbance of behavior or emotional distress may be present in response to life stresses (e.g., parental separation, deaths, birth of a sib), but these are brief and interference with functioning is transient; such children are only minimally disturbing to others and are not considered deviant by those who know them.

70–61   Some difficulty in a single area, but generally functioning pretty well (e.g., sporadic or isolated antisocial acts, such as occasionally playing hooky or petty theft; consistent minor difficulties with school work; mood changes of brief duration; fears and anxieties which do not lead to gross avoidance behavior; self-doubts); has some meaningful interpersonal relationships; most people who do not know the child well would not consider him/her deviant but those who do know him/her well might express concern.

60–51   Variable functioning with sporadic difficulties or symptoms in several but not all social areas; disturbance would be apparent to those who encounter the child in a dysfunctional setting or time but not to those who see the child in other settings.

50–41   Moderate degree of interference in functioning in most social areas or severe impairment of functioning in one area, such as might result from, for example, suicidal preoccupations and ruminations, school refusal and other forms of anxiety, obsessive rituals, major conversion symptoms, frequent anxiety attacks, poor or inappropriate social skills, frequent episodes of aggressive or other antisocial behavior with some preservation of meaningful social relationships.

40–31   Major impairment in functioning in several areas and unable to function in one of these areas, i.e., disturbed at home, at school, with peers, or in society at large, e.g., persistent aggression without clear instigation; markedly withdrawn and isolated behavior

Continued

due to either mood or thought disturbance, suicidal attempts with clear lethal intent; such children are likely to require special schooling and/or hospitalization or withdrawal from school (but this is not a sufficient criterion for inclusion in this category).

30–21   Unable to function in almost all areas, e.g., stays at home, in ward, or in bed all day without taking part in social activities or severe impairment in reality testing or serious impairment in communications (e.g., sometimes incoherent or inappropriate).

20–11   Needs considerable supervision to prevent hurting others or self (e.g., frequently violent, repeated suicide attempts) or to maintain personal hygiene or gross impairment in all forms of communication, e.g., severe abnormalities in verbal and gestural communication, marked social aloofness, stupor; etc.

10–1   Needs constant supervision (24-hr care) due to severely aggressive or self-destructive behavior or gross impairment in reality testing, communication, cognition, affect, or personal hygiene.

Reprinted by permission of David Shaffer.

Client Satisfaction Questionnaire (CSQ-8)

Please help us improve our program by answering some questions about the services you have received. We are interested in your honest opinions, whether they are positive or negative. Please answer all of the questions. We also welcome your comments and suggestions. Thank you very much, we really appreciate your help.

1. How would you rate the quality of service you have received?

4	3	2	1
Excellent	Good	Fair	Poor

2. Did you get the kind of service you wanted?

1	2	3	4
No, definitely	No, not really	Yes, generally	Yes, definitely

3. To what extent has our program met your needs?

4	3	2	1
Almost all of my needs have been met	Most of my needs have been met	Only a few of my needs have been met	None of my needs have been met

4. If a friend were in need of similar help, would you recommend our program to him or her?

1	2	3	4
No, definitely not	No, I don't think so	Yes, I think so	Yes, definitely

5. How satisfied are you with the amount of help you have received?

1	2	3	4
Quite dissatisfied	Indifferent or mildly dissatisfied	Mostly satisfied	Very satisfied

Continued

6. Have the services you received helped you to deal more effectively with your problems?

4	3	2	1
_____	_____	_____	_____
Yes, they helped a great deal	Yes, they helped somewhat	No, they really didn't help	No, they seemed to make things worse

7. In an overall, general sense, how satisfied are you with the service you have received?

4	3	2	1
_____	_____	_____	_____
Very satisfied	Mostly satisfied	Indifferent or mildly dissatisfied	Quite dissatisfied

8. If you were to seek help again, would you come back to our program?

1	2	3	4
_____	_____	_____	_____
No, definitely not	No, I don't think so	Yes, I think so	Yes, definitely

Example Items from the COMPASS Outpatient Tracking System

CURRENT WELL-BEING

	Not at All Satisfied	Slightly Satisfied	Pretty Satisfied	Very Satisfied	Extremely Satisfied
4. At the present time, how satisfied have you been feeling with your life?	1	2	3	4	5

CURRENT LIFE FUNCTIONING

My Emotional/Psychological Problems interfere with my:

	Not Applicable	Not at All	Little Bit	Moderately	Quite a Bit	Extremely
7. Interaction with my brothers and sisters	0	1	2	3	4	5
12. Participation in social activities	0	1	2	3	4	5

CURRENT SYMPTOMS

During the past month how often have you experienced . . .

	Not at All	Once or Twice	Several Times	Often	Most of the Time	All of the Time
5. Headaches	0	1	2	3	4	5
20. Trouble falling asleep	0	1	2	3	4	5

Core Conflictual Relationship Theme

Basic Steps for Scoring the Core Conflictual Relationship Theme (CCRT)

Phase A: Locate relationship episodes using a transcript of the session. A relationship episode is characterized as a "discrete episode of explicit narration about relationships with others or with the self" (pgs. 15–16).

Phase B: Extract the Core Conflictual Relationship Theme
Step 1. Identify thought units within the relationship episode
Step 2. Score each thought unit using either tailor-made or standard category scoring. Scoring consists of identifying the Wish or Need, the Response from Other, and Response of Self.
Step 3. Count the scores and formulate the Core Conflictual Relationship Theme.
Step 4. Repeat steps 2 and 3 making additions or revisions.

Summarized from Luborsky, L. (1990). A guide to the CCRT Method. In L. Luborsky & P. Crits-Cristoph, *Understanding Transference.* New York: Basic Books. Reprinted by permission of Lester Luborsky. Permission to use the material is to be obtained by writing to the author of the assessment measure, Lester Luborsky, 514 Spruce Street, Philadelphia, PA 19106.

Example Items from the Dyadic Adjustment Scale

Most persons have disagreements in their relationships. Please indicate below the approximate extent of agreement or disagreement between you and your partner for each item on the following list.

1	2	3	4	5	6
always agree	almost always agree	occasionally disagree	frequently disagree	almost always disagree	always disagree

___ 1. Handling family finances
___ 2. Matters of recreation
___ 3. Religious matters
___ 4. Demonstrations of affection
___ 5. Friends

1	2	3	4	5	6
All the time	Most of the time	More often than not	Occasionally	Rarely	Never

___ 16. How often do you discuss or have you considered divorce, separation, or terminating your relationship?
___ 17. How often do you or your mate leave the house after a fight?
___ 18. In general, how often do you think that things between you and your partner are going well?

Graham B. Spanier, "Measuring Dyadic Adjustment: New Scales for Assessing the Quality of Marriage and Similar Dyads," *Journal of Marriage and the Family, 38,* 15–28, 1976. Reprinted by permission of Graham B. Spanier.

Short-Form of the Experiencing Scale

	Stage Content	Treatment
1	External events; refusal to participate	Impersonal, detached
2	External events; behavioral or intellectual self-description	Interested, personal, self-participation
3	Personal reactions to external events; limited self-descriptions; behavioral descriptions of feelings	Reactive, emotionally involved
4	Descriptions of feelings and personal experiences	Self-descriptive; associative
5	Problems or propositions about feelings and personal experiences	Exploratory, elaborative, hypothetical
6	Felt sense of an inner referent	Focused on there being more about "it"
7	A series of felt senses connecting the content	Evolving, emergent

Reprinted by permission of Marjorie H. Klein, Philippa L. Mathieu, Eugene T. Gendlin, and Donald J. Kiesler.

Fear Questionnaire

Choose a number from the scale below to show how much you would avoid each of the situations listed below because of fear or other unpleasant feelings. Then write the number you chose in the blank opposite each situation.

0	**1**	**2**	**3**	**4**	**5**	**6**	**7**	**8**
would not avoid it		slightly avoid it		definitely avoid it		markedly avoid it		always avoid it

_____   1. Main phobia you want treated (describe in your own words).

_____   2. Injections or minor surgery.
_____   3. Eating or drinking with other people.
_____   4. Hospitals.
_____   5. Traveling alone by bus or coach.
_____   6. Walking alone in busy streets.
_____   7. Being watched or stared at.
_____   8. Going into crowded shops.
_____   9. Talking to people in authority.
_____   10. Sight of blood.
_____   11. Being criticized.
_____   12. Going alone far from home.
_____   13. Thought of injury or illness.
_____   14. Speaking or acting to an audience.
_____   15. Large open spaces.
_____   16. Going to the dentist.
_____   17. Other situations (describe).

Now choose a number from the scale below to show how much you are troubled by each problem listed, and write the number in the blank.

0	**1**	**2**	**3**	**4**	**5**	**6**	**7**	**8**
Hardly at all		Slightly troublesome		Definitely troublesome		Markedly troublesome		Very severely troublesome

_____   18. Feeling miserable or depressed.
_____   19. Feeling irritable or angry.
_____   20. Feeling tense or panicky.
_____   21. Upsetting thoughts coming into your mind.
_____   22. Feeling you or your surroundings are strange or unreal.
_____   23. Other feelings (describe).

Continued

24. How would you rate the present state of your phobic symptoms on the scale below? Please circle one number between 0 and 8.

0	**1**	**2**	**3**	**4**	**5**	**6**	**7**	**8**
No phobias present		Slightly disturbing/ not really disturbing		Definitely disturbing/ disabling		Markedly disturbing/ disabling		Very severely disturbing/ disabling

Reprinted by permission of I. M. Marks.

Scoring: Total phobia rating = sum of items 2 through 16. Agoraphobia scale = sum items 5, 6, 8, 12, 15. Blood Injury scale = sum items 2, 4, 10, 13, 16. Social phobia scale = sum items 3, 7, 9, 11, 14. Anxiety and Depression scale = sum items 18 through 22. Global phobic severity scale = item 24.

Global Assessment Scale (GAS)

Rate the subject's lowest level of functioning in the last week by selecting the lowest range which describes his functioning on a hypothetical continuum of mental health-illness. For example, a subject whose "behavior is considerably influenced by delusions" (range 21–30) should be given a rating in that range even though he has "major impairment in several areas" (range 31–40). Use intermediate levels when appropriate (e.g., 35, 58, 63). Rate actual functioning independent of whether or not subject is receiving and may be helped by medication or some other form of treatment.

Name of Patient _____ ID # _____ Consec. # _____ Code # _____
Admission Date _____ Date of Rating _____ Rater _____ Rating _____

91–100   No symptoms, superior functioning in a wide range of activities, life's problems never seem to get out of hand, is sought out by others because of his warmth and integrity.

81–90   Transient symptoms may occur, but good functioning in all areas, interested and involved in a wide range of activities, socially effective, generally satisfied with life, "everyday" worries that only occasionally get out of hand.

71–80   Minimal symptoms may be present but no more than slight impairment in functioning, varying degrees of "everyday" worries and problems that sometimes get out of hand.

61–70   Some mild symptoms (e.g., depressive mood and mild insomnia) OR some difficulty in several areas of functioning, but generally functioning pretty well, has some meaningful interpersonal relationships, and most untrained people would not consider him "sick."

51–60   Moderate symptoms or generally functioning with some difficulty (e.g., few friends and flat affect, depressed mood and pathological self-doubt, euphoric mood and pressure of speech, moderately severe antisocial behavior).

41–50   Any serious symptomatology or impairment in functioning that most clinicians would think obviously requires treatment or attention (e.g., suicidal preoccupation or gesture, severe obsessional rituals, frequent anxiety attacks, serious antisocial behavior, compulsive drinking).

31–40   Major impairment in several areas, such as work, family relations, judgment, thinking, or mood (e.g., depressed woman avoids friends, neglects family, unable to do housework), OR some impairment in reality testing or communication (e.g., speech is at times obscure, illogical or irrelevant), OR single serious suicide attempt.

21–30   Unable to function in almost all areas (e.g., stays in bed all day) OR behavior is considerably influenced by either delusions or hallucinations OR serious impairment in communication (e.g., sometimes incoherent or unresponsive) or judgment (e.g., acts grossly inappropriately).

Continued

11–20 Needs some supervision to prevent hurting self or others, or to maintain minimal personal hygiene (e.g., repeated suicide attempts frequently violent, manic excitement, smears feces), OR gross impairment in communication (e.g., largely incoherent or mute).

1–10 Needs constant supervision for several days to prevent hurting self or others, or makes no attempt to maintain minimal personal hygiene.

Reprinted by permission of Jean Endicott, Ph.D.

Goal Attainment Scaling

An example of goal attainment scaling is presented in Table 6–2.

Ten Steps for Scaling Goals

1. Identify the focal issues of treatment.
2. Translate problems into at least three goals.
3. Choose a title for each goal.
4. Select a behavior, skill, affect, or process that can be an indicator for goal attainment.
5. Specify the expected level of outcome for the goal.
6. Review the consistency between the goal and expected outcome.
7. Specify a somewhat more and somewhat less level of goal attainment.
8. Specify a much more and much less level of goal attainment.
9. Repeat the steps for each goal.
10. When complete, each goal will be represented by a five-point scale (–2 = Much less than expected; –1 = somewhat less than expected; 0 = expected level of outcome; 1 = somewhat more than expected; 2 = much more than expected) with specific indicators of goal attainment at each level. Goal attainment is then rated following treatment.

Summarized from Kiresuk, T. J., Smith, A., & Cardillo, J. E., (Eds.). (1994). *Goal Attainment Scaling: Applications, theory, and measurement.* Hillsdale, NJ: Lawrence Erlbaum. Interested readers should obtain this source for more detailed instructions for clinical applications of Goal Attainment Scaling as well as numerous clinical examples and additional consideration of psychometric issues.

Hamilton Anxiety Rating Scale

INSTRUCTIONS: Rate the patient on each of the following items.

Item	Not Present	Mild	Moderate	Severe	Very Severe
1. *Anxious mood* worries, anticipation of the worst, fearful anticipation, irritability	0	1	2	3	4
2. *Tension* Feelings of tension, fatigability, startle response, moved to tears easily, trembling, feelings of restlessness, inability to relax	0	1	2	3	4
3. *Fears* Of dark, of strangers, of being left alone, of animals, of traffic, of crowds	0	1	2	3	4
4. *Insomnia* Difficulty in falling asleep, broken sleep, unsatisfying sleep and fatigue on waking, dreams, nightmares, night terrors	0	1	2	3	4
5. *Intellectual* Difficulty in concentration, poor memory	0	1	2	3	4
6. *Depressed mood* Loss of interest, lack of pleasure in hobbies, depression, early waking, diurnal swing	0	1	2	3	4
7. *Somatic (muscular)* Pains and aches, twitching, stiffness, myoclonic jerks, grinding of teeth, unsteady voice, increased muscular tone	0	1	2	3	4
8. *Somatic (sensory)* Tinnitus, blurring of vision, hot and cold flushes, feelings of weakness, pricking sensation	0	1	2	3	4

Continued

	Not present	Mild	Moderate	Severe	Very Severe
9. *Cardiovascular symptoms* Tachycardia, palpitations, pain in chest, throbbing of vessels, fainting feelings, sighing, dyspnea	0	1	2	3	4
10. *Respiratory symptoms* Pressure or constriction in chest, choking feelings, sighing, dyspnea	0	1	2	3	4
11. *Gastrointestinal symptoms* Difficulty in swallowing, wind, abdominal pain, burning sensations, abdominal fullness, nausea, vomiting, borborygmi, looseness of bowels, loss weight, constipation	0	1	2	3	4
12. *Genitourinary symptoms* Frequency of micturition, urgency of micturition, amenorrhea, menorrhagia, development of frigidity, premature ejaculation, loss of libido, impotence	0	1	2	3	4
12. *Autonomic symptoms* Dry mouth, flushing, pallor, tendency to sweat, giddiness, tension headaches, raising of hair	0	1	2	3	4
12. *Behavior at interview* Fidgeting, restlessness or pacing, tremor of hands, furrowed brow, strained face, sighing or rapid respiration, facial pallor, swallowing, etc.	0	1	2	3	4

Hamilton Rating Scale for Depression

INSTRUCTIONS: Using the key beneath each symptom, please fill in the blank to the far right with the number that best describes that symptom's severity.

1. DEPRESSED MOOD (sadness, hopeless, helpless, worthless) . . . . _____
   - 0 = Absent
   - 1 = These feeling states indicated only on questioning
   - 2 = These feeling states spontaneously reported verbally
   - 3 = Communicates feeling states nonverbally—i.e., through facial expression, posture, voice, and tendency to weep
   - 4 = Patient reports VIRTUALLY ONLY these feeling states in his spontaneous verbal and nonverbal communications

2. FEELING OF GUILT . . . . _____
   - 0 = Absent
   - 1 = Self reproach, feels he has let people down
   - 2 = Ideas of guilt or rumination over past errors or sinful deeds
   - 3 = Present illness is a punishment. Delusions of guilt
   - 4 = Hears accusatory or denunciatory voices and/or experiences threatening visual hallucinations

3. SUICIDE . . . . _____
   - 0 = Absent
   - 1 = Feels life is not worth living
   - 2 = Wishes he were dead or any thoughts of possible death to self
   - 3 = Suicide ideas or gesture
   - 4 = Attempts at suicide (any serious attempt rates 4)

4. INSOMNIA EARLY . . . . _____
   - 0 = No difficulty falling asleep
   - 1 = Complains of occasional difficulty falling asleep—i.e., more than 1/2 hour
   - 2 = Complains of nightly difficulty falling asleep

5. INSOMNIA MIDDLE . . . . _____
   - 0 = No difficulty
   - 1 = Patient complains of being restless and disturbed during the night
   - 2 = Waking during the night—any getting out of bed rates 2 (except for purposes of voiding)

6. INSOMNIA LATE . . . . _____
   - 0 = No difficulty
   - 1 = Waking in early hours of the morning but goes back to sleep
   - 2 = Unable to fall asleep again if he gets out of bed

7. WORK AND ACTIVITIES . . . . _____
   - 0 = No difficulty
   - 1 = Thoughts and feelings of incapacity, fatigue or weakness related to activities: work or hobbies

Continued

2 = Loss of interest in activity: hobbies or work—either directly reported by patient, or indirect in listlessness, indecision and vacillation (feels he/she has to push self to work or activities)

3 = Decrease in actual time spent in activities or decrease in productivity

4 = Stopped working because of present illness

8. RETARDATION (slowness of thought and speech; impaired ability to concentrate; decreased motor activity). . . . . _____

    0 = Normal speech and thought

    1 = Slight retardation at interview

    2 = Obvious retardation at interview

    3 = Interview difficult

    4 = Complete stupor

9. AGITATION . . . . _____

    0 = None

    1 = Fidgetiness

    2 = Playing with hands, hair, etc.

    3 = Moving about, can't sit still

    4 = Hand-wringing, nail-biting, hair-pulling, biting of lips

10. ANXIETY PSYCHIC. . . . . _____

    0 = No difficulty

    1 = Subjective tension and irritability

    2 = Worrying about minor matters

    3 = Apprehensive attitude apparent in face or speech

    4 = Fears expressed without questioning

11. ANXIETY SOMATIC (Physiological concomitants of anxiety such as: Gastrointestinal—dry mouth, wind, indigestion, diarrhea, cramps, belching; Cardiovascular—palpitations, headaches; Respiratory—hyperventilation, sighing; urinary frequency; sweating) . . . . _____

    0 = Absent

    1 = Mild

    2 = Moderate

    3 = Severe

    4 = Incapacitating

12. SOMATIC SYMPTOMS GASTROINTESTINAL. . . . . _____

    0 = None

    1 = Loss of appetite but eating without encouragement. Heavy feeling in abdomen

    2 = Difficulty eating without urging. Requests or requires laxatives or medication for bowels or medication for G.I. symptoms.

13. SOMATIC SYMPTOMS GENERAL. . . . . _____

    0 = None

    1 = Heaviness in limbs, back or head. Backaches, headaches, muscle aches. Loss of energy and fatigability

    2 = Any clear-cut symptom rates 2

14. GENITAL SYMPTOMS (symptoms such as: loss of libido, menstrual disturbances) . . . _____
    0 = Absent
    1 = Mild
    2 = Severe

15. HYPOCHONDRIASIS . . . . _____
    0 = Not present
    1 = Self-absorption (bodily)
    2 = Preoccupation with health
    3 = Frequent complaints, requests for help, etc.
    4 = Hypochondriacal delusions

16. LOSS OF WEIGHT . . . . _____
    0 = No weight loss
    1 = Probable weight loss associated with present illness
    2 = Definite (according to patient) weight loss

17. INSIGHT. . . . . _____
    0 = Acknowledges being depressed and ill (or no longer depressed)
    1 = Acknowledges illness but attributes cause to bad food, climate, overwork, virus, need
        for rest, etc.
    2 = Denies being ill at all

18. DIURNAL VARIATION
    A. Note whether symptoms are worse in morning or evening.
    If NO diurnal variation, record "0". . . . . _____
    0 = No variation
    1 = Worse in A.M.
    2 = Worse in P.M.
    B. When present, mark the severity of the variation.
    Record "0" if NO variation . . . . _____
    0 = None
    1 = Mild
    2 − Severe

19. DEPERSONALIZATION AND DEREALIZATION
(such as: feelings of unreality; nihilistic ideas) . . . . _____
    0 = Absent
    1 = Mild
    2 = Moderate
    3 = Severe
    4 = Incapacitating

20. PARANOID SYMPTOMS . . . . _____
    0 = None
    1 = Suspicious
    2 = Ideas of reference
    3 = Delusions of reference and persecution

Continued

21. OBSESSIONAL AND COMPULSIVE SYMPTOMS. . . . . _____
    0 = Absent
    1 = Mild
    2 = Severe

Scoring for the Hamilton 17 item version consists of the summation of the scores for items one through seventeen.

Example Item from the
Health Sickness Rating Scale

2. The patient's need to be protected and/or supported by the therapist or hospital versus the patient's ability to function autonomously.

The greater the ability to function autonomously, the higher the rating. Attempt to make an objective estimate of this ability rather than considering only the patient's subjective experience.

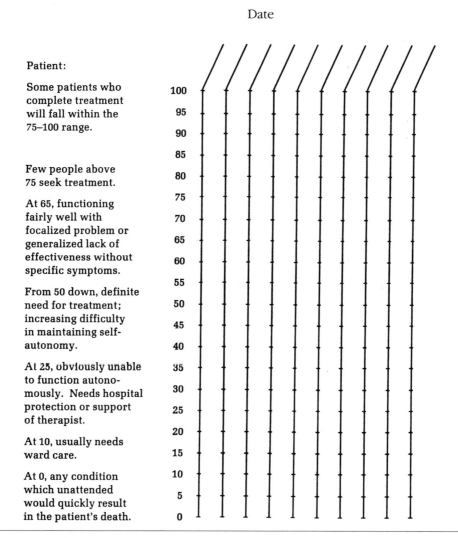

Date

Patient:

Some patients who complete treatment will fall within the 75–100 range.

Few people above 75 seek treatment.

At 65, functioning fairly well with focalized problem or generalized lack of effectiveness without specific symptoms.

From 50 down, definite need for treatment; increasing difficulty in maintaining self-autonomy.

At 25, obviously unable to function autonomously. Needs hospital protection or support of therapist.

At 10, usually needs ward care.

At 0, any condition which unattended would quickly result in the patient's death.

The Helping Alliance Questionnaire:
Patient Version

INSTRUCTIONS: These are ways that a person may feel or behave in relation to another person—their therapist. Consider carefully your relationship with your therapist, and then mark each statement according to how strongly you agree or disagree. *Please mark every one.*

	strongly disagree	disagree	slightly disagree	slightly agree	agree	strongly agree
1. I feel I can depend upon the therapist.	1	2	3	4	5	6
2. I feel the therapist understands me.	1	2	3	4	5	6
3. I feel the therapist wants me to achieve my goals.	1	2	3	4	5	6
4. At times I distrust the therapist's judgment.	1	2	3	4	5	6
5. I feel I am working together with the therapist in a joint effort.	1	2	3	4	5	6
6. I believe we have similar ideas about the nature of my problems.	1	2	3	4	5	6
7. I generally respect the therapist's views about me.	1	2	3	4	5	6
8. The procedures used in my therapy are *not* well suited to my needs.	1	2	3	4	5	6
9. I like the therapist as a person.	1	2	3	4	5	6
10. In most sessions, the therapist and I find a way to work on my problems together.	1	2	3	4	5	6
11. The therapist relates to me in ways that slow up the progress of the therapy.	1	2	3	4	5	6

	strongly disagree	disagree	slightly disagree	slightly agree	agree	strongly agree
12. A good relationship has formed with my therapist.	1	2	3	4	5	6
13. The therapist appears to be experienced in helping people.	1	2	3	4	5	6
14. I want very much to work out my problems.	1	2	3	4	5	6
15. The therapist and I have meaningful exchanges.	1	2	3	4	5	6
16. The therapist and I sometimes have unprofitable exchanges.	1	2	3	4	5	6
17. From time to time, we both talk about the same important events in my past.	1	2	3	4	5	6
18. I believe the therapist likes me as a person.	1	2	3	4	5	6
19. At times the therapist seems distant.	1	2	3	4	5	6

Reprinted by permission of Lester Luborsky. Permission to use the material is to be obtained by writing to the author of the assessment measure, Lester Luborsky, 514 Spruce Street, Philadelphia, PA 19106.

The Helping Alliance Questionnaire:
Therapist Version

INSTRUCTIONS: These are ways that a person may feel or behave in relation to another person—their therapist. Consider carefully your relationship with your patient, and then mark each statement according to how strongly you agree or disagree. *Please mark every one.*

	strongly disagree	disagree	slightly disagree	slightly agree	agree	strongly agree
1. The patient feels he/she can depend upon me.	1	2	3	4	5	6
2. He/she feels I understand him/her.	1	2	3	4	5	6
3. The patient feels I want him/her to achieve the goals.	1	2	3	4	5	6
4. At times the patient distrusts my judgment.	1	2	3	4	5	6
5. The patient feels he/she is working together with me in a joint effort.	1	2	3	4	5	6
6. I believe we have similar ideas about the nature of his/her problems.	1	2	3	4	5	6
7. The patient generally respects my views about him/her.	1	2	3	4	5	6
8. The patient believes the procedures used in his/her therapy are *not* well suited to his/her needs.	1	2	3	4	5	6
9. The patient likes me as a person.	1	2	3	4	5	6
10. In most sessions, we find a way to work on his/her problems together.	1	2	3	4	5	6

	strongly disagree	disagree	slightly disagree	slightly agree	agree	strongly agree
11. The patient believes I relate to him/her in ways that *slow up* the progress of the therapy.	1	2	3	4	5	6
12. The patient believes a good relationship has formed between us.	1	2	3	4	5	6
13. The patient believes I am experienced in helping people.	1	2	3	4	5	6
14. I want very much for the patient to work out his/her problems.	1	2	3	4	5	6
15. The patient and I have meaningful exchanges.	1	2	3	4	5	6
16. The patient and I sometimes have unprofitable exchanges.	1	2	3	4	5	6
17. From time to time, we both talk about the same important events in his/her past.	1	2	3	4	5	6
18. The patient believes I like him/her as a person.	1	2	3	4	5	6
19. At times the patient sees me as distant.	1	2	3	4	5	6

Example Items from the
Inventory of Interpersonal Problems

Here is a list of problems that people report in relating to other people. Please read the list below, and for each item, consider whether that problem has been a problem for you with respect to *any* significant person in your life. Then select the number that describes how distressing that problem has been, and circle that number.

Part I. The following are things you find hard to do with other people.
It is hard for me to:

	Not at all	A little bit	Moderately	Quite a bit	Extremely
3. join in on groups	0	1	2	3	4

Part II. The following are things that you do too much.

	Not at all	A little bit	Moderately	Quite a bit	Extremely
80. I am too sensitive to criticism	0	1	2	3	4

Example Item from the
Katz Adjustment Scales—Form R1

Item	Almost never	Sometimes	Often	Almost always
11. Feelings get hurt easily	1	2	3	4
21. Jittery	1	2	3	4
31. Laughs or cries at strange times	1	2	3	4
51. Deliberately upsets routine	1	2	3	4

Source: Katz & Lyerly, 1963.

Example Items from the Marital Satisfaction Inventory

Directions: This inventory consists of numbered statements. Read each statement and decide whether it is true as applied to you or false as applied to you. Mark your answer on the special answer sheet provided. . . .

1. I believe our marriage is reasonably happy.
52. At times I have very much wanted to leave my spouse.
91. My spouse keeps most of his (her) feelings inside.

Example Items from the Outcome Questionnaire

Instructions: Looking back over the last week, including today, help us understand how you have been feeling. Read each item and circle the number that best describes your current situation. If you are not employed, consider "housework" as "work."

	Never	Rarely	Sometimes	Frequently	Almost Always
1. I get along well with others.	0	1	2	3	4
2. I tire easily.	0	1	2	3	4
11. After heavy drinking, I need a drink the next morning to get going. (If you do not drink, mark "Never.")	0	1	2	3	4
12. I find my work/school satisfying.	0	1	2	3	4
28. I am not working/studying as well as I used to.	0	1	2	3	4
29. My heart pounds too much.	0	1	2	3	4
39. I have too many disagreements at work/school.	0	1	2	3	4
40. I feel something is wrong with my mind.	0	1	2	3	4
41. I have trouble falling asleep or staying asleep.	0	1	2	3	4
42. I feel blue.	0	1	2	3	4
43. I am satisfied with my relationships with others.	0	1	2	3	4
44. I feel angry enough at work/school to do something I might regret.	0	1	2	3	4
45. I have headaches.	0	1	2	3	4

Reprinted by Permission of IHC Center for Behavioral Healthcare Efficacy.

Progress Evaluation Scales—Adult Form

Instructions: Please circle *one* statement in each column that describes best how you were in the last two weeks.

Family interaction	Occupation (school, job or homemaking)	Getting along with others	Feelings and mood	Use of free time	Problems	Attitude toward self
Often must have help with basic needs (for example, feeding, dressing, toilet).	Does not hold job or care for home or go to school.	Always fighting or destructive; or always alone.	Almost always feels nervous, or depressed, or angry and bitter, or no emotions at all.	Almost no recreational activities or hobbies.	Severe problems most of the time.	Negative attitude toward self most of the time.
Takes care of own basic needs but must have help with everyday plans and activities.	Seldom holds job, or attends classes, or cares for home.	Seldom able to get along with others without quarreling or being destructive; or is often alone.	Often feels nervous, or depressed, or angry and bitter, or hardly shows any emotion for weeks at a time.	Only occasional recreational activities or repeats the same activity over and over again.	Severe problems more of the time or moderate problems continuously.	Negative attitude toward self much of the time.
Makes own plans but without considering the needs of other family members.	Sometimes holds job, or attends some classes, or does limited housework.	Sometimes quarreling, but seldom destructive; difficulties in making friends.	Frequently in a good mood but occasionally feels nervous, or depressed, or angry for days at a time.	Participates in some recreational activities or hobbies.	Moderate problems most of the time, or mild problems almost continuously.	Almost equal in positive and negative attitude toward self.
Tries to consider every one's needs but somehow decisions and actions do not work well for every body in the family.	Holds regular job, or classes, or does housework (or some combination of these), but with difficulty.	Gets along with others most of the time; has occasional friends.	Usually in a good mood, but occasionally feels nervous, or depressed, or angry all day.	Often participates in recreational activities and hobbies.	Occasional moderate problems.	Positive attitude toward self much of the time.
Usually plans and acts so that own needs as well as needs of others in the family are considered.	Holds regular job, or attends classes, or does housework (or some combination of these) with little difficulty.	Gets along with others most of the time; has regular close friends.	In a good mood most of the time, and usually able to be as happy, or sad, or angry as the situation calls for.	Participates in, as well as creates, variety of own recreational activities and hobbies for self and others.	Occasional mild problems.	Positive attitude toward self most of the time.

Progress Evaluation Scales—Adolescent Form

Instructions: Please circle *one* statement in each column that describes best how you were in the last two weeks.

Family interaction	Occupation (school, job or homemaking)	Getting along with others	Feelings and mood	Use of free time	Problems	Attitude toward self
Often must have help with basic needs (for example, feeding, dressing, toilet).	Expelled from school, or dropped out of school, and holds no job.	Always fighting or destructive; or always alone.	Almost always feels nervous, or depressed, or angry and bitter, or no emotions at all.	Almost no recreational activities or hobbies.	Severe problems most of the time.	Negative attitude toward self most of the time.
Takes care of own basic needs but must have help with everyday plans and activities.	Often skips school, or fails most subjects, or seldom holds job.	Seldom able to get along with others without quarreling or being destructive; or is often alone.	Often feels nervous, or depressed, or angry and bitter, or hardly shows any emotion for weeks at a time.	Only occasional recreational activities or repeats the same activity over and over again.	Severe problems more of the time or moderate problems continuously.	Negative attitude toward self much of the time.
Makes own plans but without considering the needs of other family members.	Some school skipping, but passes most subjects, or sometimes holds job.	Sometimes quarreling, but seldom destructive; difficulties in making friends.	Frequently in a good mood but occasionally feels nervous, or depressed, or angry for days at a time.	Participates in some recreational activities or hobbies.	Moderate problems most of the time, or mild problems almost continuously.	Almost equal in positive and negative attitude toward self.
Tries to consider every one's needs but somehow decisions and actions do not work well for every body in the family.	Regular school attendance and passes all subjects, or holds regular job (or some combination of these), but with difficulty.	Gets along with others most of the time; has occasional friends.	Usually in a good mood, but occasionally feels nervous, or depressed, or angry all day.	Often participates in recreational activities and hobbies.	Occasional moderate problems.	Positive attitude toward self much of the time.
Usually plans and acts so that own needs as well as needs of others in the family are considered.	Holds regular job, or attends classes, or does housework (or some combination of these) with little difficulty.	Gets along with others most of the time; has regular close friends.	In a good mood most of the time, and usually able to be as happy, or sad, or angry as the situation calls for.	Participates in, as well as creates, variety of own recreational activities and hobbies.	Occasional mild problems.	Positive attitude toward self most of the time.

Progress Evaluation Scales—Child Form

Instructions: Please circle *one* statement in each column that describes best how you were in the last two weeks.

Family interaction	Occupation (school, job or homemaking)	Getting along with others	Feelings and mood	Use of free time	Problems	Attitude toward self
Often must have help with basic needs (for example, feeding, dressing, toilet).	Failed all school subjects.	Always fighting or destructive; or always alone.	Almost always feels nervous, or depressed, or angry and bitter, or no emotions at all.	Almost no recreational activities or hobbies.	Severe problems most of the time.	Negative attitude toward self most of the time.
Occasionally needs some help with dressing or feeding.	Failed more than half school subjects.	Seldom able to get along with others without quarreling or being destructive; or is often alone.	Often feels nervous, or depressed, or angry and bitter, or hardly shows any emotion for weeks at a time.	Only occasional recreational activities or repeats the same activity over and over again.	Severe problems more of the time or moderate problems continuously.	Negative attitude toward self much of the time.
Seldom needs help with dressing or feeding. Sometimes helps with family chores when asked.	Passed more than half school subjects, but not all.	Sometimes quarreling, but seldom destructive; difficulties in making friends.	Frequently in a good mood but occasionally feels nervous, or depressed, or angry for days at a time.	Participates in some recreational activities or hobbies.	Moderate problems most of the time, or mild problems almost continuously.	Almost equal in positive and negative attitude toward self.
Takes care of self and usually helps with family chores when asked.	Passed all school subjects, but with difficulty.	Gets along with others most of the time; has occasional friends.	Usually in a good mood, but occasionally feels nervous, or depressed, or angry all day.	Often participates in recreational activities and hobbies.	Occasional moderate problems.	Positive attitude toward self much of the time.
Takes care of self and willingly helps with family chores.	Passed all school subjects with no or little difficulty.	Gets along with others most of the time; has regular close friends.	In a good mood most of the time, and able to be as happy, or sad, or angry as the situation calls for.	Participates in, as well as creates, variety of own recreational activities and hobbies.	Occasional mild problems.	Positive attitude toward self most of the time.

Example Items from the
Quality of Life Inventory

<u>HEALTH</u> is being physically fit, not sick, and without pain or disability.

1. How *important* is HEALTH to your overall happiness?

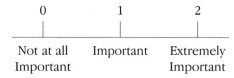

2. How *satisfied* are you with your "health?"

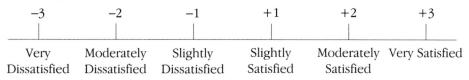

<u>PLAY</u> is what you do in your free time to relax, have fun, or improve yourself. This could include watching movies, visiting friends, or pursuing a hobby like sports or gardening.

11. How *important* is PLAY to your overall happiness?

12. How *satisfied* are you with your the PLAY in your life?

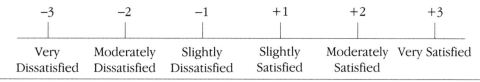

Example Item from the Schedule for Affective Disorders and Schizophrenia

Dysphoric Mood and Related Symptoms

Subjective feelings of depression based on verbal complaints of feeling depressed, sad, blue, gloomy, down in the dumps, empty, "don't care." Do not include such ideational aspects as discouragement, pessimism or worthlessness; suicide attempts or depressed appearance (all of which are to be rated separately).

How have you been feeling? Describe your mood?

Have you felt depressed (sad, blue, moody, down, empty, as if you didn't care)? (Have you cried or been tearful?) (How often? Does it come and go?) (How long does it last?)

(How bad is the feeling? Can you stand it?)

0   No information

1   Not at all

2   Slight, e.g., only occasionally feels "sad" or "down"

3   Mild, e.g., often feels somewhat "depressed," "blue" or "downhearted"

4   Moderate, e.g., most of the time feels "depressed"

5   Severe, e.g., most of the time feels "wretched"

6   Extreme, e.g., most of the time feels extreme depression which "I can't stand"

7   Very extreme, e.g., constant unrelieved extremely painful feelings of depression

Reprinted by permission of Jean Endicott, Ph.D.

Example Items from the
Social Adjustment Self-Report Questionnaire

We are interested in finding out how you have been doing in the last 2 *weeks*. We would like you to answer some questions about your work, spare time, and your family life. There are no right or wrong answers to these questions. Check the answers that best describe how you have been in the last 2 *weeks*.

WORK OUTSIDE THE HOME

Check the answer that best describes how you have been in the last 2 weeks.

2. Have you been able to do your work in the last 2 weeks?

1 _____ I did my work very well.

2 _____ I did my work well but had some minor problems.

3 _____ I needed help with work and did not do well about half the time.

4 _____ I did my work poorly most of the time.

5 _____ I did my work poorly all the time.

SPARE TIME

19. How many friends have you seen or spoken to on the telephone in the last 2 weeks?

1 _____ Nine or more friends.

2 _____ Five to eight friends.

3 _____ Two to four friends.

4 _____ One friend.

5 _____ No friends.

FAMILY

30. Have you had open arguments with your relatives in the last 2 weeks?

1 _____ We always got along very well.

2 _____ We usually got along very well, but had some minor arguments.

3 _____ I had more than one argument with at least one relative.

4 _____ I had many arguments.

5 _____ I was constantly in arguments.

FINANCIAL

54. Have you had enough money to take care of your own and your family's financial needs during the last 2 weeks?

1 _____ I had enough money for needs.

2 _____ I usually had enough money with minor problems.

Continued

3 _____ About half the time I did not have enough money but did not have to borrow money.

4 _____ I usually did not have enough money and had to borrow from others.

5 _____ I had great financial difficulty.

Example items reprinted by permission of Myrna M. Weissman.

Example Items from the
State-Trait Anxiety Inventory

Form Y-1 (State)

A number of statements which people have used to describe themselves are given below. Read each statement and then circle the appropriate number to the right of the statement to indicate how you feel right now, that is, at this moment. There are no right or wrong answers. Do not spend too much time on any one statement but give the answer which seems to describe your present feelings best.

Anxiety Present	**not at all**	**somewhat**	**moderately so**	**very much so**
I am tense.	1	2	3	4
Anxiety Absent	1	2	3	4
I feel calm.	1	2	3	4
I feel secure.	1	2	3	4

Form Y-2 (Trait)

A number of statements which people have used to describe themselves are given below. Read each statement and then circle the appropriate number to the right of the statement to indicate how you generally feel There are no right or wrong answers. Do not spend too much time on any one statement but give the answer which seems to describe how you generally feel

Anxiety Present	**not at all**	**somewhat**	**moderately so**	**very much so**
I feel nervous and restless.	1	2	3	4
Anxiety Absent	1	2	3	4
I feel pleasant.	1	2	3	4
I feel satisfied with myself	1	2	3	4

Example Items from the
Structured Clinical Interview for DSM-IIIR

F. Anxiety Disorders

Panic Disorder

? = inadequate information   1 = absent or false   2 = subthreshold   3 = threshold or true

	?	1	2	3

Have you ever had a panic attack, when you *suddenly* felt frightened, anxious or extremely uncomfortable?

If YES: Tell me about it. When does that happen? (Have you ever had one that just seemed to come on out of the blue?)

IF PANIC ATTACKS IN EXPECTED SITUATIONS: Did you ever have one of these attacks when you weren't in (EXPECTED SITUATION)

A. At some time during the disturbance, one or more panic attacks (discrete periods of intense fear or discomfort) have occurred that were (1) unexpected, i.e., did not occur immediately before or on exposure to a situation that almost always causes anxiety, and (2) not triggered by situation in which the person was the focus of others' attention   ? 1 2 3

Have you ever had four attacks like that in a four week period?

IF NO: Did you worry a lot about having another one? (How long did you worry?)

When was the last bad one (EXPECTED OR UNEXPECTED)?

B. Either four attacks, as defined in criterion A, have occurred within a four-week period, or one or more attacks have been followed by a period of at least a month of persistent fear of having another attack.   ? 1 2 3

Now I am going to ask you about that attack. What was the first thing you noticed? Then what?

During that attack . . .

C. At least four of the following symptoms developed during at least one of the attacks   ? 1 2 3

. . were you short of breath? (Have trouble catching your breath?)

(1) shortness of breath (dyspnea or smothering sensations   ? 1 2 3

. . did you feel dizzy, unsteady, or like you might faint?

(2) dizziness, unsteady feelings, or faintness

. . did your heart race, pound or skip?

(3) palpitations or accelerated heart rate (tachycardia)   ? 1 2 3

. . did you tremble or shake?

(4) trembling or shaking   ? 1 2 3

. . did you sweat?

(5) sweating   ? 1 2 3

. . did you feel as if you were choking?

(6) choking   ? 1 2 3

. . did you have nausea or upset stomach or the feeling that you were going to have diarrhea?	(7) nausea or abdominal distress	?	1	2	3
. . did things around you seem un-real or did you feel detached from things around you or detached from part of your body?	(8) depersonalization or derealization	?	1	2	3
. . did you have tingling or numb-ness in parts of you body?	(9) numbness or tingling sensations (paresthesias)	?	1	2	3
. . did you have flushes (hot flashes) or chills?	(10) flushes (hot flashes) or chills	?	1	2	3
. . did you have chest pain or pressure?	(11) chest pain or discomfort	?	1	2	3
. . were you afraid that you might die?	(12) fear of dying	?	1	2	3
. . were you afraid you were going crazy or might lose control?	(13) fear of going crazy or of doing something uncontrolled	?	1	2	3

? = inadequate information   1 = absent or false   2 = subthreshold   3 = threshold or true

Reprinted by permission of Robert L. Spitzer, M. D.

Example Items from the
Symptom Checklist-90 Analogue

Instructions to the Rater

Listed below are nine specific dimensions of psychopathology. Definitions of each dimension appear on the reverse side of this form. The rating continuum for each dimension ranges from "Not At All" to "Extremely." Rate the patient on each dimension by placing a vertical mark on the continuum to represent the level of the dimension the patient is now manifesting.

	Not At All	**Extremely**
Somatization	– –	
Depression	– –	
Global Psychopathology	– –	

Example Definition

Depression—Depression reflects a broad range of signs and symptoms of the clinical depressive syndrome. Dysphoric affect and mood, loss of interest in activities, lack of motivation, and loss of vital energy are all depressive symptoms. Feelings of hopelessness, helplessness, and futility are also key signs.

Example Items from the
Symptom Checklist-90-Revised (SCL-90-R)

Instructions: Below is a list of problems people sometimes have. Please read each one carefully, and blacken the circle that best describes HOW MUCH THAT PROBLEM HAS DISTRESSED OR BOTHERED YOU DURING THE PAST 7 DAYS INCLUDING TODAY. . . .

Item	Not at all	A little bit	moderately	Quite a bit	Extremely
1. Headaches	0	1	2	3	4
30. Feeling Blue	0	1	2	3	4
33. Feeling fearful	0	1	2	3	4

Target Complaints

Client Name _____   Date _____

Therapist _____

Target Symptom #1 _____

_____

_____

_____

Judged Severity _____|_____|_____|_____|_____
               Absent   Trivial   Mild   Moderate   Severe

Target Symptom #2 _____

_____

_____

_____

Judged Severity _____|_____|_____|_____|_____
               Absent   Trivial   Mild   Moderate   Severe

Target Symptom #3

_____

_____

_____

Judged Severity _____|_____|_____|_____|_____
               Absent   Trivial   Mild   Moderate   Severe

Example Items from the Therapy Session Report (Patient)

Session Content Area Themes

What subjects did you talk about during this session?

During this session, I talked about:

	No	Some	A lot
8. Work, career or education	1	2	3
19. Attitudes or feelings toward my therapist	1	2	3

Feelings in Therapy Session

During this session I felt:

	No	Some	A lot
_____ 3. relaxed	1	2	3
_____ 9. tearful	1	2	3

Satisfactions in Therapy Session

What do you feel that you got out of this session?

I feel that I got:

	No	Some	A lot
4. Relief from tensions or unpleasant feelings	1	2	3
9. Ideas for better ways of dealing with people and problems	1	2	3

Reproduced by permission of Kenneth I. Howard.

Example Items from the
Therapy Session Report (Therapist)

Patient's Aims in Therapy Session

What did your patient seem to want this session?

This session my patient seemed to want:

	No	Some	A lot
28. A chance to let go and express feelings	1	2	3
19. To explore emerging feelings and experiences	1	2	3

Feelings in Therapy Session

How did your patient seem to feel during this session?

	No	Some	A lot
1. confident	1	2	3
9. tearful	1	2	3

Goals in Therapy Session

In what direction were you working with your patient during this session?

I was working toward:

	No	Some	A lot
4. Helping my patient get relief from tensions or un-happy feelings	1	2	3
11. Helping my patient get better self control over feelings and impulses	1	2	3

Reproduced by permission of Kenneth I. Howard.

Example Items from the
Vanderbilt Psychotherapy Process Scale

Characterize the Patient's Behavior During the Hour:

	Not at all		Fair amount		Great deal
1. He actively participated in the interaction	1	2	3	4	5
4. He sought advice on how to deal more effectively with the self or others.	1	2	3	4	5
8. He tried to learn more about what to do in therapy and what to expect from it.	1	2	3	4	5

Characterize the Therapist's Behavior During this Hour:

	Not at all		Fair amount		Great deal
32. He showed warmth and friendliness towards the patient.	1	2	3	4	5
38. He helped the patient recognize his feelings.	1	2	3	4	5
42. He actively participated in the interaction.	1	2	3	4	5

Reprinted by Permission of Hans H. Strupp.

Example Items from the
Vanderbilt Negative Indicators Scale

Section	Category	Item	Segment 1	2	3	4	5	6	Overall
I. Patient Qualities*	A. Motivation	1.1 Distress							
		1.4 Ambivalence							
	F. Unrealistic Expectations	1.11 Inappropriate expectations							
III. Errors in Technique	A. Necessary Interventions	3.1 Structure							
		3.4 Resistance							
	C. Harmful Interventions	3.8 Destructive							

* For each item a brief definition is given in the manual to aid the rater. Two examples of definitions are included here.

PATIENT QUALITIES

A.   LACK OF MOTIVATION

Lack of MOTIVATION for psychotherapy which may include:

1.1 Lack of Distress

The patient does not express the concern, discomfort, or pain about his situation that can reasonably be expected from a person in psychotherapy. This item should be rated on the basis of the patient's perception and presentation of his problem, rather than on whether you as a clinical judge feel that he needs help.

ERRORS IN TECHNIQUE

A.   FAILURE TO MAKE NECESSARY INTERVENTIONS

3.1 Failure to *structure* or *focus* the session

The session seems aimless or lacks coherence. The therapist fails to make interventions that would help to organize the content and/or process of the therapy session. Evidence for this item includes:

  a. Therapist fails to identify focal therapeutic issues in the material presented by the patient.
  b. Therapist fails to integrate the material presented by the patient. The therapist does not identify themes or patterns in the patient's communications, reported behaviors, or manner of interacting with the therapist.
  c. Therapist lets the patient flounder, ramble, and/or repeatedly pursue tangents.

Categories from the
Verbal Response Modes Category System (Counselor)

Category	Definition
Minimal Encourager	A *short* phrase indicating agreement or acknowledgment.
Silence	A pause of 5 seconds (if after a client's statement and before a counselor statement.
Approval-Reassurance	Provides support or approval.
Information	Supplies information about facts, resources, etc.
Direct Guidance	Advice suggested by the counselor (within or outside of counseling).
Closed Question	Inquiry requiring a one or two word answer.
Open Question	A probe that does not purposefully limit the response.
Restatement	Simple repeating or rephrasing of the client statement.
Reflection	Rephrasing the includes or implies a reference to feelings.
Interpretation	Goes beyond client material (e.g., establishes connections, indicates themes, gives alternatives, etc.).
Confrontation	A restatement followed by a "but" clause that points out a contradiction or discrepancy in the client's statement(s), or behavior(s).
Nonverbal Referent	Directs attention to some aspect of the client's nonverbal behavior.
Self-Disclosure	Counselor shares a personal experience or feelings with the client.
Other	Unrelated statements (e.g., small talk, salutations), criticism, or statements that do not fit any category.

Summarized from: Hill, C. E. (1986). An overview of the Hill Counselor and client verbal response modes category systems. In L. Greenberg & W. Pinsof (Eds.), *The psychotherapeutic process: A research handbook* (pp. 131–160). New York: Guilford.

Example Items from the
Working Alliance Inventory

On the following pages there are sentences that describe some of the different ways a person might think or feel about his or her therapist (counselor). As you read the sentences mentally insert the name of your therapist (counselor) in place of _____ in the text. Below each statement inside there is a seven point scale. If the statement describes the way you always feel (or think) circle the number 7; if it never applies to you circle the number 1. Use the numbers in between to describe the variations between these extremes. This questionnaire is CONFIDENTIAL: neither your therapist nor the agency will see your answers. Work fast, your first impressions are the ones we would like to see. (PLEASE DON'T FORGET TO RESPOND TO EVERY ITEM.)

1. I feel comfortable with _____ .

1	2	3	4	5	6	7
Never	Rarely	Occasionally	Sometimes	Often	Very Often	Always

2. _____ and I agree about the things I will need to do in therapy to help improve my situation.

1	2	3	4	5	6	7
Never	Rarely	Occasionally	Sometimes	Often	Very Often	Always

22. _____ and I are working towards mutually agreed upon goals.

1	2	3	4	5	6	7
Never	Rarely	Occasionally	Sometimes	Often	Very Often	Always

31. I am frustrated by the things I am doing in therapy.

1	2	3	4	5	6	7
Never	Rarely	Occasionally	Sometimes	Often	Very Often	Always

Reprinted by permission of Adam Horvath, Working Alliance Inventory, 1982. Simon Fraser University.

Information about How to Obtain the Instruments

Addiction Severity Index

The Addiction Severity Index (ASI) is in the public domain. The instrument, along with manuals and other information including a User's Guide, publications list, and the companion Treatment Services Review instrument, can be obtained for a modest fee (to cover postage and photocopying) by writing to Deltametrics, ASI Materials, 1 Commerce Square, 2005 Market Street, Suite 1020, Philadelphia, PA 19103. Phone: (800) 238–2433.

Barrett-Lennard Relationship Inventory

The basic Relationship Inventory (RI) forms (OS and MO) and scoring sheet can be obtained for $10. Permission to recopy the RI forms, up to 150 copies: $15. A resource bibliography (approximately 50 pages with 300 sources) is also available for $20. Two articles (which amount to a manual) are available for $25. Additional articles regarding empathy and congruence or details concerning other special purpose uses of the RI (e.g., schools, couples, with groups) are also available. Contact Godfrey T. Barrett-Lennard, Ph.D., 6 Dover Crescent, Wembley Downs, Western Australia 6019. Phone: International 61–9–245–1700.

Beck Depression Inventory

The Beck Depression Inventory (BDI) and related materials are available from The Psychological Corporation, 555 Academic Court, San Antonio, TX 78204-2498. Phone: (800) 634–0424.

Brief Symptom Inventory

See Symptom Checklist-90-Revised.

California Therapeutic Alliance Rating Scales; California Psychotherapy Alliance Scales (Therapist and Patient Versions)

A manual for all versions of the California Therapeutic Alliance scales, along with additional materials, can be obtained by writing to Alliance Scales, Langley Porter Institute, Box F-0984, 401 Parnassus Avenue, San Francisco, CA 94143-0984. Phone: (415) 221–4810.

Child Behavior Checklist

Various manuals, computer scoring programs, bibliographies, and testing materials for the different versions of the Child Behavior Checklist (CBCL) (e.g., parent rated, teacher rated, youth self-report, structured interview, etc.) are available. Machine-readable answer forms will also be available in the future. For ordering information, write to University Associates in Psychiatry, 1 South Prospect Street, Burlington, VT 05401–3456. Phone: (802) 656–2602. Fax: (802) 656–8313.

Children's Global Assessment Scale

The Children's Global Assessment Scale (CGAS) is readily available and can be used without permission. The details of rating are available in journal articles concerning the scale:

> Shaffer, D., Gould, M. S., Brasic, J., Ambrosini, P., Fisher, P., Bird, H., & Aluwahlia, S. (1983). A Children's Global Assessment Scale (CGAS). *Archives of General Psychiatry, 40,* 1228–1231.
> Bird, H. R., Canino, G. J., Rubio-Stipec, M., & Ribera, J. C. (1987). Further measures of the psychometric properties of the Children's Global Assessment Scale. *Archives of General Psychiatry, 44,* 821–824.
> Bird, H. R., Yager, T. J., Staghezza, B., Gould, M. S., et al. (1990). Impairment in the epidemiological measurement of childhood psychopathology in the community. *Journal of the American Academy of Child & Adolescent Psychiatry, 29,* 796–803.

Client Satisfaction Questionnaire

Permission to use the Client Satisfaction Questionnaire (CSQ-8) or other versions can be obtained by writing to Clifford Attkisson, Ph.D., Professor of Medical Psychology, Millberry Union, 200 West, San Francisco, CA 94143-0244. Cost for 500 uses—$250 and 30 cents per use in blocks of 100 for uses beyond 500. Phone: (415) 476–9716.

COMPASS Outpatient Tracking

The COMPASS system is currently available to mental health organizations on a fee-per-use basis, but will soon be available for individual practitioners. It is also available via a site license for large volume clients. Information concerning the COMPASS system can be obtained at the following address: COMPASS Information Services, Inc., 1060 First Avenue, Suite 410, King of Prussia, PA 19406. Phone: (610) 992–7060. Fax: (610) 992–7070.

Core Conflictual Relationship Theme Rating

See Health Sickness Rating Scale.

Derogatis Psychiatric Rating Scale

See Symptom Checklist-90-Revised.

Dyadic Adjustment Scale

Testing materials are available through Multi-Health Systems. Costs are: Manual ($19), Nonreusable test forms 20 per package ($20; suitable for 10 couples), computer program with 50 uses ($125; suitable for 25 couples). MHS, 908 Niagara Falls Boulevard, North Tonawanda, NY 14120–2060. Phone: (800) 456–3003. Fax: (416) 424–1736.

Experiencing Scale

A manual, transcripts, and tapes for practice scoring can be purchased from Dr. Marjorie Klein, Department of Psychiatry, University of Wisconsin, Madison, WI 53792. Manual and training transcripts cost $26. Additional training tapes are available for $42.

Fear Questionnaire

The Fear Questionnaire (FQ) instrument is available from the original journal article: Marks, I. M., & Mathews, A. M. (1978). Brief standard self-rating for phobic patients. *Behavior Research and Therapy, 17,* 263–267.

Global Assessment Scale

See Schedule for Affective Disorders and Schizophrenia.

Goal Attainment Scaling

Because Goal Attainment Scaling is individualized, interested users could develop their own scales based on the example presented in the book. In addition, Kiresuk has published a recent book that details the Goal Attainment Scaling method: Kiresuk, T. J., Smith, A., & Cardillo, J. E. (Eds.). (1994). *Goal attainment scaling: Applications, theory, and measurement*. Hillsdale, NJ: Lawrence Erlbaum.

Hamilton Anxiety Rating Scale

The Hamilton Anxiety Rating Scale (HARS) is reproduced in this book. Rating and scoring procedures are also published in: Guy, W. (1976). *ECDEU Assessment Manual for Psychopharmacology*. Washington, DC: U.S. Department of Health, Education, and Welfare. There is no published manual. Information concerning psychometrics and normative data can be obtained through a search of the psychological literature, some of which is summarized in Chapter 5.

Hamilton Rating Scale for Depression

The Hamilton Rating Scale for Depression (HRSD) is reproduced in this book. Rating and scoring procedures are published in: Guy, W. (1976). *ECDEU Assessment Manual for Psychopharmacology*. Washington, DC: U.S. Department of Health, Education, and Welfare. A structured interview version is also available (see Williams, J. B. W. (1988). A structured interview guide for the Hamilton Depression Rating Scale. *Archives of General Psychiatry, 45*, 742–747). There is no published manual. Information concerning psychometrics and normative data can be obtained through a search of the psychological literature, some of which is summarized in Chapter 5.

Health Sickness Rating Scale; Helping Alliance Questionnaire; Core Conflictual Relationship Theme Rating

These instruments, scoring manuals, and literature reviews are available for a modest fee. Contact Lester Luborsky, Ph.D., University of Pennsylvania, Department of Psychiatry, The Science Center, 3600 Market Street, 7th Floor, Room 703, Philadelphia, PA 19104–2648. Phone: (215) 662–2822.

Helping Alliance Questionnaire

See Health Sickness Rating Scale.

Inventory of Interpersonal Problems

Contact Leonard Horowitz, Department of Psychology, Building 420, Stanford University, Stanford, CA 94305–2130. Phone: (415) 725–2407.

Katz Adjustment Scales

The various forms of the Katz Adjustment Scales (KAS), along with administration and scoring instructions and psychometric data, are published in the following source: Katz, M. N., & Lyerly, S. V. (1963). Methods for measuring adjustment and social behavior in the community: I. Rationale, description, discriminative validity and scale development. *Psychological Reports, 13*, 503–535.

Marital Satisfaction Inventory

A manual and scoring and test materials of the MSI can be purchased through Western Psychological Services, 12031 Wilshire Blvd., Los Angeles, CA 90025. Computerized scoring programs are also available to purchase. Phone: (800) 648–8857.

Outcome Questionnaire

The Outcome Questionnaire (OQ) and manual can be obtained through applying for a licensing agreement. A one-time licensing fee is required, after which the licensee can make copies of the instrument as needed. The fee depends on the size of the organization (independent practitioner—$10; group practice—$50; Institution, Group Practice—$50, Hospital, College—$100; One state Healthcare Network, Association, group of hospitals or clinics—$250; Multistate Network, Association, Regional, National Health Care Hospital Corp., etc.—$500). For more information or to become a licensee user of the instrument, write to Center for Behavioral Health Care Efficacy, 36 South State, Suite 2100, Salt Lake City, UT 84111. Phone: (801) 442–3493. Or contact Michael J. Lambert, Dept. of Psychology, Brigham Young University, Provo, UT 84602. Phone: (801) 378–6480.

Progress Evaluation Scales

The Progress Evaluation Scales (PES) are in the public domain. They are printed in this book and in: Ihilevich, D., & Gleser, G. C. (1982). *Evaluating mental-health programs: The Progress Evaluation Scales.* Lexington, MA: D. C. Heath (includes detailed information about the scales including scoring, etc.).

Quality of Life Inventory

Test materials and a detailed test manual are available from National Computer Systems, Inc. (NCS). Prices for scoring manuals, answer sheets, and product sheets are available at the following address: NCS Assessments, P.O. Box 1416, Minneapolis, MN 55440. Phone: (800) 617–7271. Additional materials, including a treatment guide, are available from Michael B. Frisch, QOLI Materials, Psychology Department, P.O. Box 97334, Waco, TX 76798–7334.

Schedule for Affective Disorders and Schizophrenia; Global Assessment Scale

More detailed information regarding the SADS, SADS-C, and other SADS versions, the GAS, and respective training materials, manuals, and so on are available from Department of Research Assessment and Training Unit 123, 722 West 168 Street, New

York, NY 10032. A cost list will be mailed upon request. Phone: (212) 960–2270. Fax: (212) 960–2386.

Social Adjustment Self Report Questionnaire

The manual and instrument are available for $17 from Myrna M. Weissman, Ph.D., New York State Psychiatric Institute, 722 West 168th Street, Unit 14, New York, NY 10032.

State-Trait Anxiety Inventory

The STAI instrument, scoring key, and manual can be purchased through Consulting Psychologist's Press (CPP) (manual—$10, scoring key—$5, package of 25 nonreusable answer sheets—$9) at the following address: CPP, P.O. Box 10096, Palo Alto, CA 94303-0979. Phone: (800) 624–1765. Fax: (415) 969–8608.

Structured Clinical Interview for DSM-IIIR

The patient version (other versions are available as well) of the structured interview is available from American Psychiatric Press, 1400 K St. N.W., Washington, DC 20005. The user's guide, plus a package of 10 instruments, costs $75. Phone: (800) 368–5777. (The *DSM-IV* version of this interview will also be available in the future at the same address.)

Symptom Checklist Analogue Scale

See Symptom Checklist-90-Revised.

Symptom Checklist-90-Revised, Brief Symptom Inventory, Symptom Checklist Analogue Scale

These instruments are available through National Computer Systems, Inc. (NCS). Prices for scoring manuals, answer sheets, and product sheets are available at the following address: NCS Assessments, P.O. Box 1416, Minneapolis, MN 55440. Phone: (800) 617–7271.

Target Complaints

The form presented in this book can be used to produce Target Complaint rating forms for clinical use. Check the references in Chapter 6 for more detailed instructions concerning the scoring and use of the Target Complaints.

Therapy Session Report

The Therapy Session Report (TSR) is printed in: Orlinsky, D. E., & Howard, K. I. (1975). *Varieties of psychotherapeutic experience.* New York: Teacher's College

Press. For information regarding the Therapy Session Report, write to Kenneth Howard, Ph.D., Dept. of Psychology, Northeastern University, Evanston, IL 60201.

Vanderbilt Negative Indicators Scale; Vanderbilt Psychotherapy Process Scale

A manual and rating forms are available from Hans H. Strupp, Ph.D., Department of Psychology, Vanderbilt University, 301 A&S Psychology Building, Nashville, TN 37240. Phone: (615) 322–0058. Cost is $25 for both instruments with manuals.

Vanderbilt Psychotherapy Process Scale

See Vanderbilt Negative Indicators Scale.

Verbal Response Modes

The manual and information regarding the rating of therapist utterances can be obtained by writing to Clara Hill, Ph.D., Department of Psychology, University of Maryland, College Park, MD 20742. Phone: (301) 405–5791.

Working Alliance Inventory

The WAI rating scale is available from Adam Horvath, Faculty of Education, Simon Fraser University, Burnaby, British Columbia V5A 1S6, Canada. Phone: (604) 291–3624.

Clinical Significance Figures

Beck Depression Inventory, Fear Questionnaire, Symptom Checklist-90-Revised, Child Behavior Checklist, Hamilton Rating Scale for Depression, Dyadic Adjustment Scale, Outcome Questionnaire, and State-Trait Anxiety Scale

FIGURE D–1   Clinical Significance on the Beck Depression Inventory

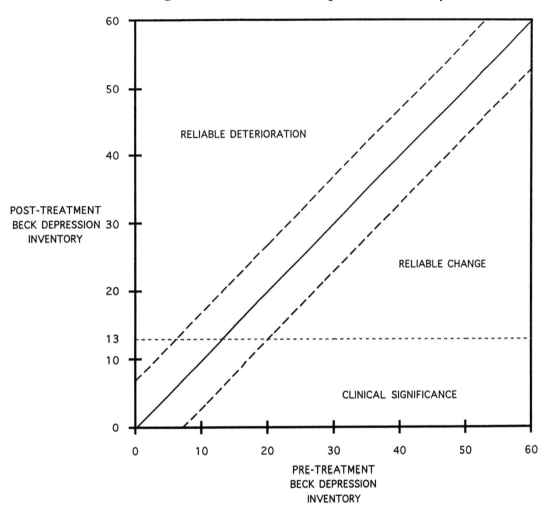

FIGURE D–2 **Clinical Significance on the Agoraphobia Scale of the Fear Questionnaire**

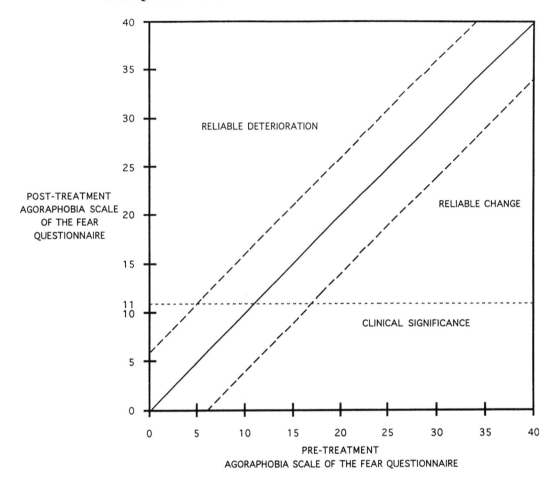

FIGURE D–3   Clinical Significance on the SCL-90R (GSI)

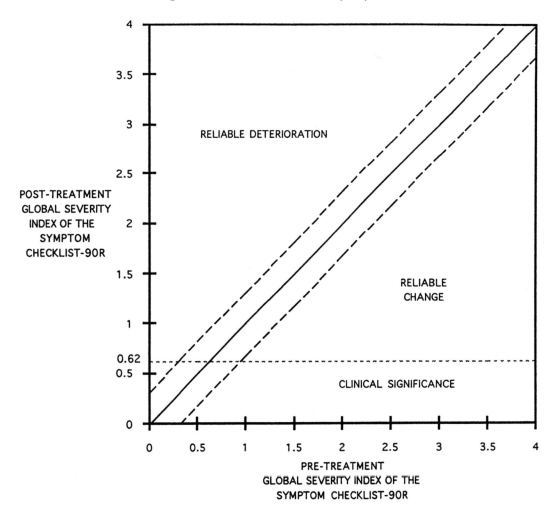

FIGURE D–4   Clinical Significance on the CBCL

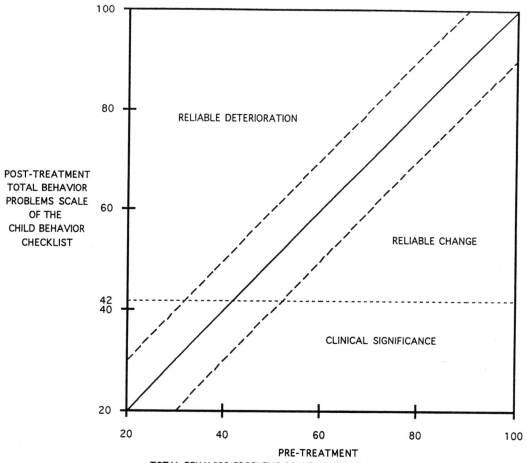

FIGURE D–5   Clinical Significance on the HRSD

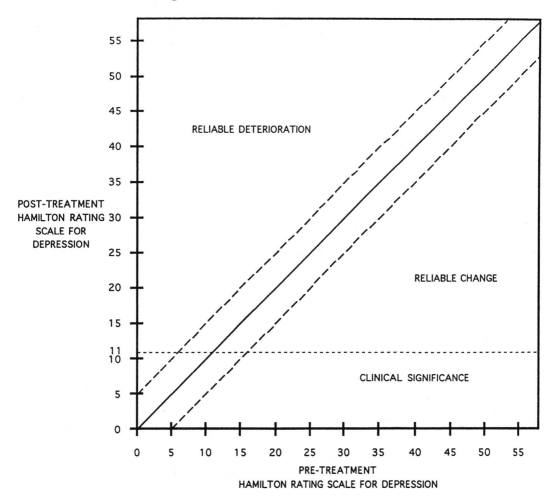

FIGURE D–6   Clinical Significance on the DAS

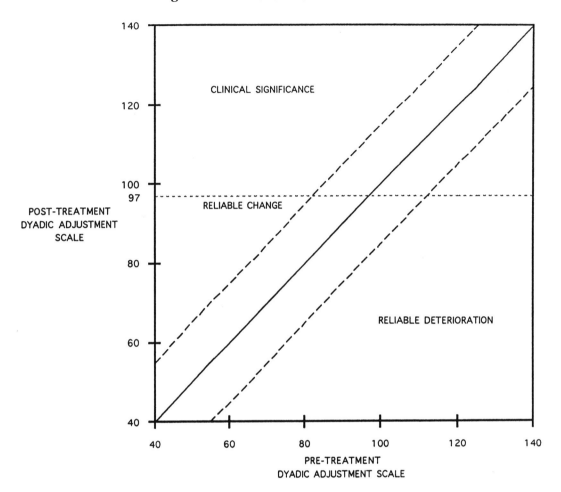

FIGURE D–7   Clinical Significance on the OQ

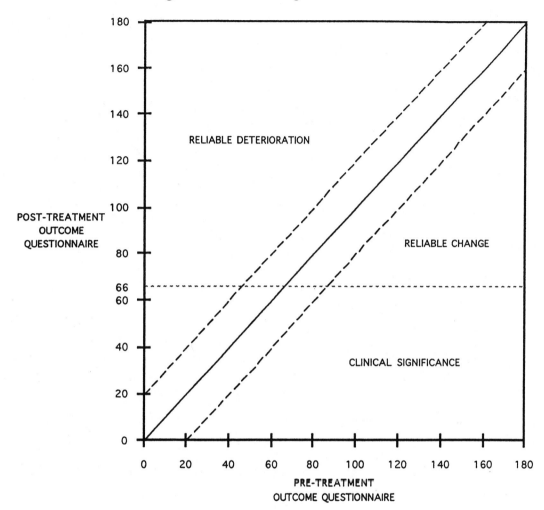

FIGURE D–8   Clinical Significance on the STAI

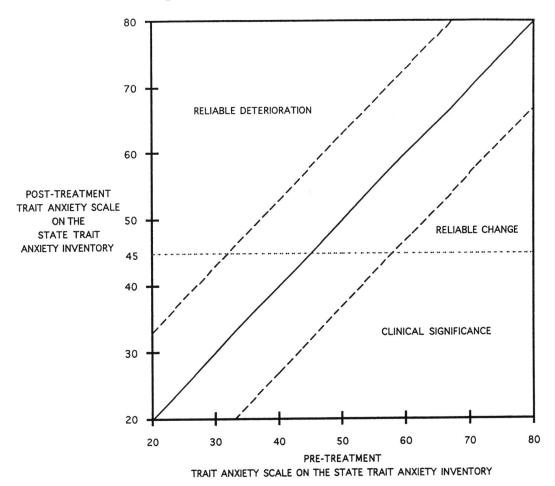

Detailed Normative Data for the Calculation of Clinical Significance

Beck Depression Inventory, Fear Questionnaire, Symptom Checklist-90-Revised, Child Behavior Checklist, Hamilton Rating Scale for Depression, Dyadic Adjustment Scale, Outcome Questionnaire, and State-Trait Anxiety Scale

TABLE E–1 Means, Standard Deviations, Change Scores and Cutoff Points for the Beck Depression Inventory Using Four Samples

Sample	$\overline{X}$	s	Change 1[a]	Change 2[b]	Cutoff 1[c]	Cutoff 2[d]
Special Group[e]	8.05	5.78	12	6	20	14
General Population[e]	7.18	6.47	13	7	20	14
Nondistressed Group[e]	4.54	4.46	9	5	13	9
Minimal Depression[f]	10.90	8.10	16	8	27	19

[a]Pre/posttest change score necessary for an RCI = 1.96 using .48 as the BDI reliability and the row standard deviation.
[b]Pre/posttest change score necessary for an RCI = 1.96 using .86 as the BDI reliability and the row standard deviation.
[c]High cutoff for membership in the functional population based on 2 standard deviations above the row mean.
[d]High cutoff for membership in the functional population based on 1 standard deviation above the row mean.
[e]Nietzel, Russel, Hemmings, & Gretter (1987).
[f]Beck (1967).

TABLE E–2 Means, Standard Deviations, Change Scores, and Cutoff Points for the Agoraphobia Scale of the Fear Questionnaire Using Four Samples

Sample	$\overline{X}$	s	Change 1[a]	Cutoff 1[b]	Cutoff 2[c]
Collegiate Sample 1[d]	5.37	4.72	6	15	10
Community Sample[d]	11.83	8.61	10	29	20
Collegiate Men 2[e]	4.65	4.36	5	13	9
Collegiate Women[e]	7.89	5.44	6	19	13
Fear Questionnaire (agoraphobia subscale) Adult Men[e]	4.85	5.09	6	15	10
Fear Questionnaire (agoraphobia subscale) Adult Women[e]	4.99	6.00	7	17	11

[a]Pre/posttest change score necessary for an RCI = 1.96 using .82 as the Ag scale reliability and the row standard deviation.
[b]High cutoff for membership in the functional population based on 2 standard deviations above the row mean.
[c]High cutoff for membership in the functional population based on 1 standard deviation above the row mean.
[d]Trull, Nietzel, and Main (1988).
[e]Mizes & Crawford (1986).

TABLE E-3 **Means, Standard Deviations, Change Scores, and Cutoff Points for the Global Severity Index of the Symptom Checklist-90 Revised for Two Samples**

Sample	$\overline{X}$	s	Change[a]	Cutoff 1[b]	Cutoff 2[c]
Asymptomatic Sample[d]	.14	.13	.14	.40	.27
Community Sample[e]	.31	.31	.32	.93	.62

[a]Pre/posttest change score necessary for an RCI = 1.96 using .84 as the GSI reliability and the row standard deviation.

[b]High cutoff for membership in the functional population based on 2 standard deviations above the row mean.

[c]High cutoff for membership in the functional population based on 1 standard deviation above the row mean.

[d]Tingey (1990).

[e]Derogatis (1977).

TABLE E-4 **Means, Standard Deviations, Change Scores, and Cutoff Points for the Social Competence Section of the Child Behavior Checklist for Four Samples**

Sample	$\overline{X}$	s	Change[a]	Cutoff 1[b]	Cutoff 2[c]
Asymptomatic[d]	22.24	3.26	4	29	26
Mildly Symptomatic[e]	19.73	3.51	5	27	23
Moderately Symptomatic[f]	15.00	3.70	5	22	19
Severely Symptomatic[g]	13.60	4.40	6	22	18

[a]Pre/posttest change score necessary for an RCI = 1.96 using .76 as the reliability value and the row standard deviation.

[b]High cutoff for membership in the functional population based on 2 standard deviations above the row mean.

[c]High cutoff for membership in the functional population based on 1 standard deviation above the row mean.

[d]Grundy (1994).

[e]Sandberg, Meyer-Bahlburg, & Yager (1991).

[f]Achenbach & Edelbrock (1983).

[g]Jones, Latkowski, Kircher, & McMahon (1988).

TABLE E-5 **Means, Standard Deviations, Change Scores, and Cutoff Points for the Total Behavior Problems of the Child Behavior Checklist for Four Samples**

Sample	$\overline{X}$	s	Change[a]	Cutoff 1[b]	Cutoff 2[c]
Asymptomatic[d]	13.48	8.31	4	30	22
Mildly Symptomatic[e]	24.96	17.52	8	60	42
Moderately Symptomatic[f]	58.90	24.00	12	107	83
Severely Symptomatic[g]	78.60	31.90	15	142	111

[a]Pre/posttest change score necessary for an RCI = 1.96 using .97 as the reliability value and the row standard deviation.

[b]High cutoff for membership in the functional population based on 2 standard deviations above the row mean.

[c]High cutoff for membership in the functional population based on 1 standard deviation above the row mean.

[d]Grundy (1994).

[e]Sandberg, Meyer-Bahlburg, & Yager (1991).

[f]Achenbach & Edlebrock (1983).

[g]Jones, Latkowski, Kircher, & McMahon (1988).

TABLE E-6 **Means, Standard Deviations, Change Scores, and Cutoff Points for the Hamilton Rating Scale for Depression (17 items) for Three Samples**

Sample	$\overline{X}$	s	Change[a]	Cutoff 1[b]	Cutoff 2[c]
Asymptomatic[d]	2.66	2.44	3	8	5
Mildly Symptomatic[e]	6.25	4.24	5	15	11
Clinically Symptomatic[f]	22.03	7.19	9	36	29

[a]Pre/posttest change score necessary for an RCI = 1.96 using .81 as the HRSD reliability and the row standard deviation.

[b]High cutoff for membership in the functional population based on 2 standard deviations above the row mean.

[c]High cutoff for membership in the functional population based on 1 standard deviation above the row mean.

[d]Grundy (1994).

[e]Carroll, Fielding, & Blashki (1973); Mowbray (1972); Riskind, Beck, Brown, & Steer (1987).

[f]Zimmerman, Coryell, Pfohl, & Stangl (1986); Pfohl, Stangl, & Zimmerman (1984); Reynolds, Perel, Kupfer, Zimmer, Stack, & Hoch (1987); Mulsant, Rosen, Thorton, & Zubenko (1991); Mowbray (1972); Carroll, Fielding, & Blashki (1973).

TABLE E-7 Means, Standard Deviations, Change Scores, and Cutoff Points for the Dyadic Adjustment Scale for Two Samples

Sample	$\overline{X}$	s	Change[a]	Cutoff 1[b]	Cutoff 2[c]
Functional Group[d]	114.7	17.8	10	150	133
Dysfunctional Group[e]	81.6	11.8	7	105	93

[a]Pre/posttest change score necessary for an RCI = 1.96 using .96 as the DAS reliability and the row standard deviation.

[b]High cutoff for membership in the functional population based on 2 standard deviations above the row mean.

[c]High cutoff for membership in the functional population based on 1 standard deviation above the row mean.

[d]Spanier (1976).

[e]Jacobson & Truax (1991).

TABLE E-8 Means, Standard Deviations, Change Scores, and Cutoff Points for the Outcome Questionnaire for Five Samples[a]

Sample	$\overline{X}$	s	Change[b]	Cutoff 1[c]	Cutoff 2[d]
College	42.33	16.60	18	76	59
Community	48.16	18.23	20	85	66
Employee Assistance Program	73.02	21.05	23	115	94
Outpatient Clinic	78.01	25.71	28	129	104
Community Mental Health Center	86.07	19.33	21	125	105

[a]Lambert, Lunnen, Umphres, Hansen, & Burlingame (1994).

[b]Pre/posttest change score necessary for an RCI = 1.96 using .84 as the OQ reliability and the row standard deviation.

[c]High cutoff for membership in the functional population based on 2 standard deviations above the row mean.

[d]High cutoff for membership in the functional population based on 1 standard deviation above the row mean.

TABLE E-9 **Means, Standard Deviations, Change Scores, and Cutoff Points for the State-Trait Anxiety Inventory[a]**

Sample	$\overline{X}$	s	Change[b]	Cutoff 1[c]	Cutoff 2[d]
Asymptomatic	26.43	4.61	6	31	36
Community	38.81	10.20	13	49	59
Clinical	51.80	10.16	13	62	72

[a]From Condon, K. M. (1994). *Assessing Clinical Significance: Application to the State-Trait Anxiety Inventory.* Unpublished Doctoral Dissertation Brigham Young University.

[b]Pre/posttest change score necessary for an RCI = 1.96 using .84 as the reliability and the row standard deviation.

[c]High cutoff for membership in the functional population based on 2 standard deviations above the row mean.

[d]High cutoff for membership in the functional population based on 1 standard deviation above the row mean.

References

Achenbach, T. M. (1978). The child behavior profile: I. Boys aged 6–11. *Journal of Consulting and Clinical Psychology, 46*, 478–488.

Achenbach, T. M., & Edelbrock, C. S. (1979). The child behavior profile: II. Boys aged 12–16 and girls aged 6–11 and 12–16. *Journal of Consulting and Clinical Psychology, 47*, 223–233.

Achenbach, T. M., & Edelbrock, C. S. (1983). *Manual for the Child Behavior Checklist and Revised Child Behavior Profile.* Burlington, VT: Department of Psychiatry, University of Vermont.

Alexander, L. B., & Luborsky, L. (1986). The Penn Helping Alliance Scales. In L. S. Greenberg & W. M. Pinsoff (Eds.), *The psychotherapeutic process: A research handbook* (pp. 325–366). New York: Guilford.

American Psychiatric Association. (1987). *Diagnostic and statistical manual of mental disorders* (3rd ed. rev.). Washington, DC: Author.

Andrasik, F., Holroyd, K. A., & Abell, T. (1979). Prevalence of headache within a college student population: A preliminary analysis. *Headache, 20*, 384–387.

Attkisson, C. C., & Zwick, R. (1982). The client satisfaction questionnaire: Psychometric properties and correlations with service utilizations and psychotherapy outcome. *Evaluation and Program Planning, 5*, 233–237.

Auerbach, A. H. (1983). Assessment of psychotherapy outcome from the viewpoint of expert observer. In M. J. Lambert, E. R. Christensen, & S. S. DeJulio (Eds.), *The assessment of psychotherapy outcome* (pp. 537–568). New York: John Wiley.

Azim, H. F. A., & Joyce, A. S. (1986). The impact of data-based program modification on the satisfaction of outpatients in group psychotherapy. *Canadian Journal of Psychiatry, 31*, 119–122.

Baer, D. M. (1988). If you know why you're changing a behavior, you'll know when you've changed it enough. *Behavioral Assessment, 10*, 219–223.

Barlow, D. H. (1981). On the relation of clinical research to clinical practice: Current issues, new directions. *Journal of Consulting and Clinical Psychology, 49*, 147–155.

Barlow, D. H., Hayes, S. C., & Nelson, R. O. (1984). *The scientist-practitioner: Research and accountability in clinical and educational settings.* New York: Pergamon.

Barrett-Lennard, G. T. (1959). *The Relationship Inventory: A technique for measuring therapeutic dimensions of an interpersonal relationship.* Paper presented at the annual meeting of the Southeastern Psychological Association, St. Augustine, Florida.

Battle, C. C., Imber, S. D., Hoehn-Saric, R., Stone, A. R., Nash, E. H., & Frank, J. D. (1966). Target complaints as a criteria of improvement. *American Journal of Psychotherapy, 20*, 184–192.

Bech, P., Gram, L. F., Dein, E., Jacobsen, O., Vitger, J., & Bolwig, T. G. (1975). Quantitative rating of depressive states. *Acta Psychiatrica Scandinavia, 51*, 161–170.

Beck, A. T. (1967). *Depression: Causes and treatment.* Philadelphia: University of Pennsylvania Press.

Beck, A. T., Rush, A. J., Shaw, B. F., & Emery, G. (1979). *Cognitive therapy of depression.* New York: Guilford.

Beck, A. T., Steer, R. A., & Garbin, M. G. (1988). Psychometric properties of the beck depression inventory: Twenty-five years of evaluation. *Clinical Psychology Review, 8*, 77–100.

Beck, A. T., Ward, C. H., Mendelson, M., Mock, J., & Erbaugh, J. (1961). An inventory for measuring depression. *Archives of General Psychiatry, 4*, 561–571.

Bednar, R. L., Burlingame, G. M., & Masters, K. S. (1988). Systems of family treatment: Substance or semantics? *Annual Review of Psychology, 39*, 401–434.

Bellack, A. S., & Hersen, M. (1988). *Behavioral assessment: A practical handbook* (3rd ed.). New York: Pergamon.

Berger, M. (1983). Toward maximizing the utility of consumer satisfaction as an outcome. In M. J. Lambert, E. R. Christensen, & S. S. DeJulio, (Eds.), *The assessment of psychotherapy outcome* (pp. 56–80). New York: John Wiley.

Bergin, A. E. (1966). Some implications of psychotherapy research for therapeutic practice. *Journal of Abnormal Psychology, 71*, 235–246.

Bergin, A. E. (1971). The evaluation of therapeutic outcomes. In S. L. Garfield & A. E. Bergin (Eds.), *Handbook of psychotherapy and behavior change* (pp. 217–270). New York: John Wiley.

Bergin, A. E. (1980). Psychotherapy and religious values. *Journal of Consulting and Clinical Psychology, 48*, 95–105.

Bergin, A. E., & Lambert, M. J. (1978). The evaluation of therapeutic outcomes. In S. L. Garfield & A. E. Bergin (Eds.), *Handbook of psychotherapy and behavior change* (pp. 139–189). New York: John Wiley.

Bergin, A. E., & Strupp, H. (1972). *Changing frontiers in the science of psychotherapy*. Chicago: Aldine-Atherton.

Beutler, L. E., & Crago, M. (1983). Self-report measures of psychotherapy outcome. In M. J. Lambert, E. R. Christensen, & S. S. DeJulio (Eds.), *The assessment of psychotherapy outcome* (pp. 453–497). New York: John Wiley.

Beutler, L. E., Crago, M., & Arizmendi, T. G. (1986). Therapist variables in psychotherapy process and outcome. In S. L. Garfield & A. E. Bergin (Eds.), *Handbook of psychotherapy and behavior change* (3rd ed., pp. 257–310). New York: John Wiley.

Bigelow, D. A., Brodsky, G., Stewart, L., & Olson, M. (1982). The concept and measurement of quality of life as a dependent variable in evaluation of mental health services. In W. Tash & G. Stahler (Eds.), *Innovative approaches to mental health evaluation*. New York: Academic Press.

Bigelow, D. A., Gareau, M. J., & Young, D. J. (1990). A quality of life interview for chronically disabled people. *Psychosocial Rehabilitation Journal, 14*, 94–98.

Bigelow, D. A., McFarland, B. H., Gareau, M. J., & Young, D. J. (1991). Implementation and effectiveness of a bed reduction project. *Community Mental Health Journal, 27*, 125–133.

Bigelow, D. A., McFarland, B. H., & Olson, M. (1991). Quality of life of community mental health program clients: Validating a measure. *Community Mental Health Journal, 27*, 43–55.

Bigelow, D. A., & Young, D. J. (1991). Effectiveness of a case management program. *Community Mental Health Journal, 27*, 115–123.

Blanchard, E. B., & Schwarz, S. P. (1988). Clinically significant changes in behavioral medicine. *Behavioral Assessment, 10*, 171–188.

Bloch, S., & Lambert, M. J. (1985). What price psychotherapy? A rejoinder. *British Journal of Psychiatry, 146*, 96–98.

Bloom, M., & Fischer, J. (1982). *Evaluating practice: Guidelines for the accountable professional*. Englewood Cliffs, NJ: Prentice Hall.

Bordin, E. S. (1976, September). *The working alliance: Basis for a general theory of psychotherapy*. Paper presented at a symposium of the American Psychological Association, Washington, DC.

Borgen, F. H. (1984). Are there necessary linkages between research practices and the philosophy of science? *Journal of Counseling Psychology, 31*, 457–460.

Butcher, J. N., Dahlstrom, W. G., Graham, J. R., Tellegen, A. M., & Kaemmer, B. (1989). *Minnesota Multiphasic Personality Inventory-2 (MMPI-2): Manual for administration and scoring*. Minneapolis: University of Minnesota Press.

Calsyn, R. J., & Davidson, W. S. (1978). Do we really want a program evaluation strategy based on individualized goals? A critique of goal attainment scaling. *Evaluation Studies: Review Annual, 1*, 700–713.

Campbell, D. T., & Stanley, J. C. (1963). *Experimental and quasi-experimental designs for research*. Chicago: Rand McNally.

Carroll, B. J., Fielding, J. M., & Blashki, T. G. (1973). Depression rating scales: A critical review. *Archives of General Psychiatry, 38*, 361–366.

Ciarlo, J. A., with Edwards, D. W., Kiresuk, T. J., Newman, F. L., & Brown, T. R. (1981). *Final re-*

port: The assessment of client/patient outcome techniques for use in mental health programs (Contract No. 278-80-0005 DB). Washington, DC: National Institute of Mental Health.

Ciarlo, J. A., & Reihman, J. (1977). The Denver community mental health questionnaire: Development of a multidimensional program evaluation instrument. In R. D. Coursey (Ed.), *Program evaluation for mental health: Methods, strategies, participants* (pp. 131–168). New York: Grune & Stratton.

Clark, M. S., & Caudrey, D. J. (1986). Evaluation of rehabilitation services: The use of goal attainment scaling. *International Rehabilitation Medicine, 5,* 41–45.

Cohen, J. (1990). Things I have learned (so far). *American Psychologist, 45,* 1304–1312.

Cohen, L. H. (1979). The research readership and information source reliance of clinical psychologists. *Professional Psychology, 10,* 780–785.

Cohen, L. H. (1980). Methodological prerequisites for psychotherapy outcome research. *Knowledge: Creation, Diffusion, Utilization, 2,* 263–272.

Cohen, L. H., Sargent, M. M., & Sechrest, L. B. (1986). Use of psychotherapy research by professional psychologists. *American Psychologist, 41,* 198–206.

Cohen, L. H., & Suchy, K. R. (1979). The bias in psychotherapy research evaluation. *Journal of Clinical Psychology, 35,*

Cone, J. D. (1988). Psychometric considerations and the multiple models of behavioral assessment. In A. S. Bellack & M. Hersen (Eds.), *Behavioral assessment: A practical handbook* (3rd ed.). New York: Pergamon.

Corcoran, K., & Fischer, J. (1987). *Measures for clinical practice.* New York: The Free Press.

Crits-Cristoph, P., & Mintz, J. (1991). Implications of therapist effects for the design and analysis of comparative studies of psychotherapies. *Journal of Consulting and Clinical Psychology, 59,* 20–26.

Derogatis, L. R. (1983). *SCL-90: Administration, Scoring, and Procedures Manual for the Revised Version.* Baltimore: Clinical Psychometric Research.

Derogatis, L. R., Lipman, R. S., Rickels, K., Uhlenhuth, E. H., & Covi, L. (1974). The Hopkins Symptom Checklist (HSCL): A self-report symptom inventory. *Behavioral Science, 19,* 1–15.

Derogatis, L. R., & Melisaratos, N. (1983). The Brief Symptom Inventory: An introductory report. *Psychological Medicine, 13,* 595–605.

Dill, D. L., Eisen, S. V., & Grob, M. C. (1989). Validity of record ratings of the Global Assessment Scale. *Comprehensive Psychiatry, 30,* 320–323.

Elkin, I., Shea, T, Watkins, J. T., Imber, S. D., Sotsky, S. M., Collins, J. F., Glass, D. R., Pilkonis, P. A., Leber, W. R., Docherty, J. P., Fiester, S. J., & Parloff, M. B. (1989). National Institute of Mental Health Treatment of Depression Collaborative Research Program. *Archives of General Psychiatry, 46,* 971–982.

Elliot, R. (1986). Interpersonal process recall (IPR) as a psychotherapy process research method. In L. S. Greenberg & W. M. Pinsof (Eds.), *The psychotherapeutic process: A research handbook* (pp. 503–528). New York: Guilford.

Elliot, R. (1992). A conceptual analysis of Lambert et al.'s conceptual scheme for outcome assessment. *Journal of Counseling and Development, 70,* 535–537.

Elliot, R., Hill, C. E., Stiles, W. B., Friedlander, M. L., Mahrer, A. R., & Margison, F. R. (1987). Primary therapist response modes: Comparison of six rating systems. *Journal of Consulting and Clinical Psychology, 55,* 218–223.

Endicott, J., Cohen, J., Nee, J., Fleiss, J., & Sarantakos, S. (1981). Hamilton Depression Rating Scale. *Archives of General Psychiatry, 38,* 98–103.

Endicott, J., & Spitzer, R. L. (1978). A diagnostic interview: The Schedule for Affective Disorders and Schizophrenia. *Archives of General Psychiatry, 35,* 837–844.

Endicott, J., Spitzer, R. L., Fleiss, J. L., & Cohen, J. (1976). The Global Assessment Scale: A procedure for measuring overall severity of psychiatric disturbance. *Archives of General Psychiatry, 33,* 776–771

Eysenck, H. J. (1952). The effects of psychotherapy: An evaluation. *Journal of Consulting Psychology, 16,* 319–324.

Fenichel, O. (1930). *Ten years of the Berlin Psychoanalytic Institute, 1920–1930.* Berlin: Berlin Psychoanalytic Institute.

Fleuridas, C., Rosenthal, D. M., Leigh, G. K., & Leigh, T. E. (1990). Family goal recording: An adaptation of goal attainment scaling for enhancing family therapy and assessment. *Journal of Marital and Family Therapy, 16,* 389–406.

Frisch, M. B. (1994). *Manual and treatment guide for the Quality of Life Inventory.* Minneapolis, MN: NCS Assessments.

Frisch, M. B., Cornell, J., Villanueva, M., & Retzlaff, P. J. (1992). Clinical validation of the quality of life inventory: A measure of life satisfaction for use in treatment planning and outcome assessment. *Psychological Assessment: A Journal of Consulting and Clinical Psychology, 4*, 92–101.

Froyd, J., & Lambert, M. J. (1989, May). *A 5-year survey of outcome measures in psychotherapy research*. Paper presented at the Western Psychological Association Conference, Reno, NE.

Garfield, S. L. (1991). Psychotherapy models and outcome research. *American Psychologist, 46*, 1350–1351.

Gaston, L. (1991). Reliability and criterion-related validity of the California Psychotherapy Alliance Scales-Patient Version. *Psychological Assessment, 3*, 68–74.

Gelso, C. J. (1979). Research in counseling: Methodological and professional issues. *The Counseling Psychologist, 8*, 7–35.

Gelso, C. J., Betz, N. E., Friedlander, M. L., Helms, J. E., Hill, C. E., Patton, M. J., Super, D. E., & Wampold, B. E. (1988). Research in counseling psychology: Prospects and recommendations. *The Counseling Psychologist, 16*, 385–406.

Goldfried, M. R., Greenberg, L. S., & Marmar, C. (1990). Individual psychotherapy: Process and outcome. In M. R. Rosenzweig & L. W. Porter (Eds.), *Annual review of psychology* (pp. 659–688). Palo Alto: Annual Reviews Inc.

Gomes-Schwartz, B. (1978). Effective ingredients in psychotherapy: Prediction of outcome from process variables. *Journal of Consulting and Clinical Psychology, 46*, 1023–1035.

Gottman, J., & Markman, H. J. (1978). Experimental designs in psychotherapy research. In S. L. Garfield & A. E. Bergin (Eds.), *Handbook of psychotherapy and behavior change* (pp. 23–62). New York: John Wiley.

Greenberg, L. S., & Pinsoff, W. M. (Eds.). (1986). *The psychotherapeutic process: A research handbook*. New York: Guilford.

Greenberg, L. S., & Webster, M. C. (1982). Resolving decisional conflict by gestalt two-chair dialogue: Relating process to outcome. *Journal of Counseling Psychology, 29*, 468–477.

Greenfield, T. K., & Attkisson, C. C. (1989). Steps toward a multifactorial satisfaction scale for primary care and mental health services. *Evaluation and Program Planning, 12*, 271–278.

Grundy, C. T. (1994). Assessing clinical significance: Application to the Hamilton Rating Scale for Depression. (Doctoral dissertation, Brigham Young University, 1994). *Dissertation Abstracts International, 55*, 0592.

Grundy, C. T., Lunnen, K. M., Lambert, M. J., Ashton, J. E, & Tovey, D. R. (1994). The Hamilton Rating Scale for Depression: One scale or many?. *Clinical Psychology: Science and Practice, 1(2)*, 197–205.

Gurman, A. S. (1977). The patient's perception of the therapeutic relationship. In A. S. Gurman & A. M. Razin (Eds.), *Effective psychotherapy: A handbook of research*. New York: Pergamon.

Guy, W. (1976). *ECDEU Assessment Manual for Psychopharmacology*. Washington, DC: U.S. Department of Health, Education, and Welfare.

Hadley, S. W., & Strupp, H. H. (1976). Contemporary views of negative effects in psychotherapy. *Archives of General Psychiatry, 33*, 1291–1302.

Hamilton, M. (1959). The assessment of anxiety states by rating. *British Journal of Medical Psychology, 32*, 50–55.

Hamilton, M. (1960). A rating scale for depression. *Journal of Neurology, Neurosurgery and Psychiatry, 23*, 56–62.

Hamilton, M. (1967). Development of a rating scale for primary depressive illness. *British Journal of Social and Clinical Psychology, 6*, 278–296.

Hammen, C. L. (1980). Depression in college students: Beyond the Beck Depression Inventory. *Journal of Consulting and Clinical Psychology, 48*, 126–128.

Hathaway, S. R., & McKinley, J. C. (1983). *The Minnesota Multiphasic Personality Inventory manual*. New York: Psychological Corporation.

Hayes, S. C. (1981). Single case experimental design and empirical clinical practice. *Journal of Consulting and Clinical Psychology, 49*, 193–211.

Herbert, J. D., & Mueser, K. T. (1991). Proof is in the pudding: A commentary on Persons. *American Psychologist, 46*, 1347–1348.

Hersen, M., & Barlow, D. H. (1976). *Single case experimental designs: Strategies for studying behavior change*. New York: Pergamon.

Hill, C. E. (1986). An overview of the Hill counselor and client verbal response modes category systems. In L. Greenberg & W. Pinsof (Eds.), *The psychotherapeutic process: A research handbook* (pp. 131–160). New York: Guilford.

Hodges, K., McKnew, D., Cytryn, L., Stern, L., & Klien, J. (1982). The Child Assessment Schedule (CAS) diagnostic interview: A report on reliability and validity. *Journal of the American Academy of Child Psychiatry, 21*, 468–473.

Hogarty, G. E. (1975). Informant ratings of community adjustment. In I. E. Waskow & M. B. Parloff (Eds.), *Psychotherapy change measures* (pp. 202–221). Rockville, MD: National Institute of Mental Health.

Horowitz, L. M., Rosenberg, S. E., Baer, B. A., Ureno, G., & Villesenor, V. S. (1988). Inventory of Interpersonal Problems: Psychometric properties and clinical applications. *Journal of Consulting and Clinical Psychology, 56*, 885–892.

Horvath, A. O. (1981). *An exploratory study of the working alliance: Its measurement and relationship to outcome.* Unpublished Doctoral Dissertation, University of British Columbia.

Horvath, A. O., & Greenberg, L. S. (1986). The development of the working alliance inventory. In L. S. Greenberg & W. M. Pinsof (Eds.), *The psychotherapeutic process: A research handbook* (pp. 529–556). New York: Guilford.

Horvath, A. O., & Greenberg, L. S. (1989). Development and validation of the working alliance inventory. *Journal of Counseling Psychology, 36*, 223–233.

Howard, G. S. (1984). A modest proposal for a revision of strategies for counseling research. *Journal of Counseling Psychology, 31*, 430–441.

Howard, K. I., Brill, P. L., Lueger, R. J., O'Mahoney, M. T., & Grissom, G. R. (1993). *Integra outpatient tracking assessment: Psychometric properties.* King of Prussia, PA: Integra, Inc.

Howard, K. I., Lueger, R. J., Maling, M. S., & Martinovich, Z. (1993). A phase model of psychotherapy outcome: Causal mediation of change. *Journal of Consulting and Clinical Psychology, 61*, 678–685.

Ihilevich, D., & Gleser, G. C. (1979). *A manual for the progress evaluation scales.* Shiawasse, MI: Community Mental Health Services Board.

Ihilevich, D., & Gleser, G. C. (1982). *Evaluating mental-health programs: The Progress Evaluation Scales.* Lexington, MA: D. C. Heath.

Jacobson, N. S. (1988). Defining clinically significant change: An introduction. *Behavioral Assessment, 10*, 131–132.

Jacobson, N. S., Follette, W. C., & Revenstorf, D. (1984). Psychotherapy outcome research: Methods for reporting variability and evaluating clinical significance. *Behavior Therapy, 15*, 336–352.

Jacobson, N. S., Follette, W. C., & Revenstorf, D. (1986). Toward a standard definition of clinically significant change. *Behavior Therapy, 17*, 308–311.

Jacobson, N. S., Follette, W. C., Revenstorf, D., Baucom, D. H., Hahlweg, K., & Margolin, G. (1984). Variability in outcome and clinical significance of behavioral marital therapy: A reanalysis of outcome data. *Journal of Consulting and Clinical Psychology, 52*, 497–504.

Jacobson, N. S., & Revenstorf, D. (1988). Statistics for assessing the clinical significance of psychotherapy techniques: Issues, problems, and new developments. *Behavioral Assessment, 10*, 133–145.

Jacobson, N. S., & Truax, P. (1991). Clinical significance: A statistical approach to defining meaningful change in psychotherapy research. *Journal of Consulting and Clinical Psychology, 59*, 12–19.

Kaplan, R. M. (1985). Quality-of-life measurement. In P. Karoly (Ed.), *Measurement strategies in health psychology.* New York: John Wiley.

Kaplan, R. M. (1990). Behavior as the central outcome in health care. *American Psychologist, 45*, 1211–1220.

Karoly, P. (Ed.). (1985). *Measurement strategies in health psychology.* New York: John Wiley.

Katz, M. M., Gudeman, H., & Sanborn, K. O. (1969). Characterizing differences in psychopathology among ethnic groups: A preliminary report on Hawaii-Japanese and Mainland-American schizophrenics. In W. Caudill & T. Lin (Eds.), *Mental health research in Asia and the Pacific.* Honolulu: East-West Center.

Katz, M. M., & Lyerly, S. B. (1963). Methods for measuring adjustment and social behavior in the community: I. Rationale, description, discriminative validity and scale development. *Psychological Reports, 13*, 503–535.

Kazak, A. E., Jarmas, A., & Snitzer, L. (1988). The assessment of marital satisfaction: An evaluation of the Dyadic Adjustment Scale. *Journal of Family Psychology, 2*, 82–91.

Kazdin, A. E. (1977). Assessing the clinical or applied importance of behavior change through social validation. *Behavior Modification, 1*, 427–452.

Kazdin, A. E. (1978). Evaluating the generality of findings in analogue therapy research. *Journal of Consulting and Clinical Psychology, 46*, 673–686.

Kazdin, A. E. (1980). Investigating generality of findings from analogue research: A rejoinder. *Journal of Consulting and Clinical Psychology, 48*, 772–773.

Kazdin, A. E. (1981). Drawing valid inferences from case studies. *Journal of Consulting and Clinical Psychology, 49*, 183–192.

Kazdin, A. E. (1986). The evaluation of psychotherapy: Research design and methodology. In S. L. Garfield & A.E. Bergin (Eds.), *Handbook of psychotherapy and behavior change* (3rd ed., pp. 23–68). New York: Wiley.

Kazdin, A. E. (1992). *Research design in clinical psychology* (2nd ed.). New York: Macmillan.

Kazdin, A. E. (1993). Evaluation in clinical practice: Clinically sensitive and systematic methods of treatment delivery. *Behavior Therapy, 24*, 11–45.

Kendall, P. C., & Grove, W. M. (1988). Normative comparisons in therapy outcome. *Behavioral Assessment, 10*, 147–158.

Kiresuk, T. J., & Sherman, R. E. (1968). Goal Attainment scaling: A general method for evaluating comprehensive community mental health programs. *Community Mental Health Journal, 4*, 443–452.

Kiresuk, T. J., Smith, A., & Cardillo, J. E. (Eds.). (1994). *Goal attainment scaling: Applications, theory, and measurement*. Hillsdale, NJ: Lawrence Erlbaum.

Klein, M. H., Mathieu, P. L., Gendlin, E. T., & Kiesler, D. J. (1969). *The experiencing scale: A research and training manual* (Vol. 1). Madison: University of Wisconsin Extension Bureau of Audiovisual Instruction.

Klein, M. H., Mathieu-Coughlan, P., & Keisler, D. J. (1986). The experiencing scales . In L. S. Greenberg & W. M. Pinsof (Eds.), *The psychotherapeutic process: A research handbook* (pp. 21–72). New York: Guilford.

Klonoff, H., & Cox, B. A. (1975). Problem-oriented approach to analysis of treatment outcome. *American Journal of Psychiatry, 132*, 836–841.

Knesevich, J. W., Biggs, J. T., Clayton, P. J., & Ziegler, V. E. (1977). Validity of the Hamilton Rating Scale for Depression. *British Journal of Psychiatry, 131*, 49–52.

Kobak, K. A., Reynolds, W. M., Rosenfeld, R., & Griest, J. H. (1990). Development and validation of a computer-administered version of the Hamilton Depression Rating Scale. *Psychological Assessment, 2*, 56–63.

Kuh, G. D., & Andreas, R. E. (1991). It's about time: Using qualitative methods in student life studies. *Journal of College Student Development, 32*, 397–404.

Kuhlman, T. L., Sincaban, V. A., & Bernstein, M. J. (1990). Team use of the Global Assessment Scale for inpatient planning and evaluation. *Hospital and Community Psychiatry, 41*, 416–419.

Lambert, M. J. (1983). Introduction to assessment of psychotherapy outcome: Historical perspective and current issues. In M. J. Lambert, E. R. Christensen, & S. S. DeJulio (Eds.), *The assessment of psychotherapy outcome* (pp. 3–32). New York: John Wiley.

Lambert, M. J., & Bergin, A. E. (1994). The effectiveness of psychotherapy. In A. E. Bergin & S. L. Garfield (Eds.), (pp. 143–189) *Handbook of psychotherapy and behavior change* (4th ed., pp. 143–189). New York: John Wiley.

Lambert, M. J., Christensen, E. R., & DeJulio, S. S. (1983). *The assessment of psychotherapy outcome*. New York: John Wiley.

Lambert, M. J., DeJulio, S. S., & Stein, D. M. (1978). Therapist interpersonal skills: Process, outcome, methodological considerations, and recommendations for future research. *Psychological Bulletin, 85*, 467–489.

Lambert, M. J., & Hill, C. E. (1994). Assessing psychotherapy outcomes and processes. In A. E. Bergin & S. L. Garfield (Eds.) *Handbook of psychotherapy and behavior change* (4th ed., pp. 72–113). New York: John Wiley.

Lambert, M. J., Lunnen, K., Umphres, V., Hansen, N. B., & Burlingame, G. (1994). *Administration and Scoring Manual for the Outcome Questionnaire (OQ–45.1)*. Salt Lake City, UT: IHC Center for Behavioral Healthcare Efficacy.

Lambert, M. J., Masters, K. S., & Ogles, B. M. (1991). Outcome research in counseling. In C. E. Watkins, Jr. & L. J. Schneider (Eds.), *Research in counseling* (pp. 51–83). Hillsdale, NJ: Erlbaum.

Lambert, M. J., Masters, K. S., & Ogles, B. M. (1992). Measuring counseling outcome: A rejoinder. *Journal of Counseling and Development, 70*, 538–539.

Lambert, M. J., & Ogles, B. M. (1989). Treatment manuals: Problems or promise. *Journal of Integrative and Eclectic Psychotherapy, 7*, 187–204.

Lambert, M. J., Ogles, B. M., & Masters, K. S. (1992). Choosing outcome assessment devices: An organizational and conceptual scheme. *Journal of Counseling and Development, 70*, 527–532.

Lambert, M. J., Shapiro, D. A., & Bergin, A. E. (1986). The effectiveness of psychotherapy. In S. L. Garfield & A. E. Bergin (Eds.), *Handbook of psychotherapy and behavior change* (3rd ed., pp. 157–211). New York: John Wiley.

Larsen, D. L., Attkisson, C. C., Hargreaves, W. A., & Nguyen, T. D. (1979). Assessment of client/patient satisfaction: Development of a general scale. *Evaluation and Program Planning, 2*, 197–207.

Lewis, A. B., Spencer, J. H., Haas, G. L., & DeVittis,

A. (1987). Goal attainment scaling: Relevance and replicability in follow-up of inpatients. *The Journal of Nervous and Mental Diseases, 175,* 408–418.

Lloyds, M. E. (1983). Selecting systems to measure client outcome in human service agencies. *Behavioral Assessment, 5,* 55–70.

Luborsky, L. (1962). Clinicians' judgments of mental health: A proposed scale. *Archives of General Psychiatry, 7,* 407–417.

Luborsky, L. (1975). Clinicians' judgments of mental health: Specimen case descriptions and forms for the health sickness rating scale. *Bulletin of the Menninger Clinic, 39,* 448–480.

Luborsky, L., & Crits-Cristoph, P. (1990). *Understanding transference: The CCRT method.* New York: Basic Books, Inc.

Luborsky, L., Crits-Cristoph, P., Friedman, S. H., Mark, D., & Schaffler, P. (1991). Freud's transference template compared with the core conflictual relationship theme (CCRT): Illustrations by the two specimen cases. In M. J. Horowitz (Ed.), *Person schemas and maladaptive interpersonal patterns. The John D. and Catherine T. McArther Foundation series on mental health and development.* Chicago, IL: University of Chicago Press.

Luborsky, L., McLellan, T., Woody, G. E., O'Brien, C. P., & Auerbach, A. (1985). Therapist success and its determinants. *Archives of General Psychiatry, 42,* 602–611.

Luborsky, L., Singer, B., & Luborsky, L. (1975). Comparative outcome studies of psychotherapies. *Archives of General Psychiatry, 32,* 995–1008.

Maisto, S. A., & Connors, G. J. (1988). Assessment of treatment outcome. In D. M. Donovan & G. A. Marlatt (Eds.), *Assessment of addictive behaviors.* New York: Guilford.

Marks, I. M., & Mathews, A. M. (1978). Brief standard self-rating for phobic patients. *Behavior Research and Therapy, 17,* 263–267.

Marmar, C. R., Horowitz, M. J., Weiss, D. S., & Marziali, E. (1986). The development of the therapeutic alliance rating system. In L. S. Greenberg & W. M. Pinsof (Eds.), *The psychotherapeutic process: A research handbook* (pp. 367–390). New York: Guilford.

Marmar, C. R., Weiss, D. S., & Gaston, L. (1989). Toward the validation of the California Therapeutic Alliance Rating System. *Psychological Assessment: A Journal of Consulting and Clinical Psychology, 1,* 46–52.

Matarazzo, J. D. (1989). The reliability of psychiatric and psychological diagnosis. In J. M. Hooley, J. M. Neale, & G. C. Davison (Eds.), *Readings in abnormal psychology* (pp. 36–65). New York: John Wiley.

Mathews, A. M., Gelder, M. G., & Johnston, D. W. (1981). *Agoraphobia: Nature and treatment.* New York: Guilford.

McLellan, A. T., Luborsky, L., Cacciola, J., Griffith, J., Evans, F., Barr, H. L., & O'Brien, C. P. (1985). New data for the Addiction Severity Index: Reliability and validity in three centers. *The Journal of Nervous and Mental Disease, 173,* 412–423.

Meltzoff, J., & Kornreich, M. (1970). *Research in psychotherapy.* New York: Atherton Press.

Messer, S. B. (1991). The case formulation approach: Issues of reliability and validity. *American Psychologist, 46,* 125–142.

Michelson, L., Mavissakalian, M., & Marchione, K. (1985). Cognitive and behavioral treatments of agoraphobia: Clinical, behavioral, and psychophysiological outcomes. *Journal of Consulting and Clinical Psychology, 53,* 913–925.

Milby, J. B., Mizes, J. S., & Giles, T. R. (1986). Assessing the process of desensitization therapy: Five practical measures. *Journal of Psychopathology and Behavioral Assessment, 8,* 241–252.

Miller, R. C., & Berman, J. S. (1983). The efficacy of cognitive behavior therapies: A quantitative review of the research evidence. *Psychological Bulletin, 94,* 39–53.

Mintz, J., & Kiesler, D. J. (1982). Individualized measures of psychotherapy outcome. In P. C. Kendall & J. N. Butcher (Eds.), *Handbook of research methods in clinical psychology.* New York: Wiley.

Mintz, J., Luborsky, L., & Christoph, P. (1979). Measuring the outcome of psychotherapy: Findings of the Penn psychotherapy project. *Journal of Consulting and Clinical Psychology, 47,* 319–334.

Mizes, J. S., & Crawford, J. (1986). Normative values on the Marks and Mathews Fear Questionnaire: A comparison as a function of age and sex. *Journal of Psychopathology and Behavioral Assessment, 8,* 253–262.

Moran, P., & Lambert, M. J. (1983). A review of current assessment tools for monitoring changes in depression. In M. J. Lambert, E. R. Christensen, & S. S. DeJulio (Eds.), *The assessment of psychotherapy outcome.* New York: John Wiley.

Morrow-Bradley, C., & Elliot, R. (1986). Utilization of psychotherapy research by practicing psychotherapists. *American Psychologist, 41,* 188–197.

Mowbray, R. M. (1972). The Hamilton Rating Scale for Depression: A factor analysis. *Psychological Medicine, 2,* 272–280.

Mulsant, B. H., Rosen, J., Thorton, J. E., & Zubenko, G. S. (1991). A prospective naturalistic study of electroconvulsive therapy in late-life depression. *Journal of Geriatric Psychiatry and Neurology, 4,* 3–13.

Neese, R. M., Curtis, G. C., Thyer, B. A., McCann, D. S., Huber-Smith, M. J., & Knopf, R. F. (1985). Endocrine and cardiovascular responses during phobic anxiety. *Psychosomatic Medicine, 47,* 320–332.

Newman, F. L. (1983). Therapist's evaluation of psychotherapy. In M. J. Lambert, E. R. Christensen, & S. S. DeJulio (Eds.), *The assessment of psychotherapy outcome* (pp. 498–536). New York: John Wiley.

Nietzel, M. T., Russell, R. L., Hemmings, K. A., & Gretter, M. L. (1987). The clinical significance of psychotherapy for unipolar depression: A meta-analytic approach to social comparison. *Journal of Consulting and Clinical Psychology, 55,* 156–161.

Nietzel, M. T., & Trull, T. J. (1988). Meta-analytic approaches to social comparisons: A method for measuring clinical significance. *Behavioral Assessment, 10,* 159–169.

Oei, F. P. S., Evans, L., & Brook, G. M. (1990). Utility and validity of the STAI with anxiety disordered patients. *British Journal of Clinical Psychology, 29,* 429–462.

Oei, F. P. S., Moylan, A., & Evans, L. (1991). Validity and clinical utility of the Fear Questionnaire for anxiety-disorder patients. *Psychological Assessment, 3,* 391–397.

Ogles, B. M., & Lambert, M. J. (1989). A meta-analytic comparison of twelve agoraphobia outcome instruments. *Phobia Practice and Research Journal, 2,* 115–125.

Ogles, B. M., Lambert, M. J., & Sawyer, J. D. (1995). The clinical significance of the National Institute of Mental Health collaborative depression study data. *Journal of Consulting and Clinical Psychology, 63,* 321–326.

Ogles, B. M., Lambert, M. J., Weight, D. G., & Payne, I. R. (1990). Agoraphobia outcome measurement: A review and meta-analysis. *Psychological Assessment: A Journal of Consulting and Clinical Psychology, 2,* 317–325.

O'Malley, S. S., Suh, C. S., & Strupp, H. H. (1983). The Vanderbilt Psychotherapy Process Scale: A report on the scale development and a process-outcome study. *Journal of Consulting and Clinical Psychology, 51,* 581–586.

Orlinsky, D. E., & Howard, K. I. (1966). *Therapy Session Report, Forms P and T.* Chicago: Institute for Juvenile Research.

Orlinsky, D. E., & Howard, K. I. (1967). The good therapy hour. *Archives of General Psychiatry, 16,* 621–632.

Orlinsky, D. E., & Howard, K. I. (1986). Process and outcome in psychotherapy. In S. L. Garfield & A. E. Bergin (Eds.), *Handbook of psychotherapy and behavior change* (3rd ed., pp. 311–381). New York: John Wiley.

Parloff, M. B., Kelman, H. C., & Frank, J. D. (1954). Comfort, effectiveness, and self-awareness as criteria of improvement in psychotherapy. *American Journal of Psychiatry, 111,* 343–351.

Patton, M. J. (1991). Qualitative research on college students: Philosophical and methodological comparisons with the quantitative approach. *Journal of College Student Development, 32,* 389–396.

Persons, J. B. (1991). Psychotherapy outcome studies do not accurately represent current models of psychotherapy: A proposed remedy. *American Psychologist, 46,* 99–106.

Pfohl, B., Stangl, D., & Zimmerman, M. (1984). The implications of DSM-III personality disorders for patients with major depression. *Journal of Affective Disorders, 7,* 309–318.

Piotrowski, C., & Keller, J. W. (1989). Psychological testing in outpatient mental health facilities: A national study. *Professional Psychology: Research and Practice, 20,* 423–425.

Platt, S. (1981). Social adjustment as a criterion of treatment success: Just what are we measuring? *Psychiatry, 44,* 95–110.

Polkinghorne, D. E. (1984). Further extensions of methodological diversity for counseling psychology. *Journal of Counseling Psychology, 31,* 416–429.

Polkinghorne, D. E. (1991). Qualitative procedures for counseling research. In C. E. Watkins & L. J. Schneider (Eds.), *Research in counseling* (pp. 163–204). Hillsdale, NJ: Erlbaum.

Prileau, L., Murdock, M., & Brody, N. (1983). An analysis of psychotherapy versus placebo studies. *The Behavioral and Brain Sciences, 6,* 275–310.

Rakover, S. S. (1980). Generalization from analogue therapy to the clinical situation: The paradox and the dilemma of generality. *Journal of Consulting and Clinical Psychology, 48*, 770–771.

Rehm, L. P., Kornblith, S. J., O'Hara, M. W., & Lamparski, K. M. (1981). An evaluation of major components in a self-control therapy program for depression. *Behavior Modification, 5*, 459–489.

Reynolds, H. M., & Gould, J. W. (1981). A psychometric investigation of the standard and short form Beck Depression Inventory. *Journal of Consulting and Clinical Psychology, 49*, 306–307.

Riskind, J. H., Beck, A. T., Brown, G., & Steer, R. A. (1987). Taking the measure of anxiety and depression: Validity of the reconstructed Hamilton scales. *Journal of Nervous and Mental Disease, 175*, 474–479.

Robbins, L. N., Helzer, J. E., Croughan, J., & Ratcliff, K. S. (1981). National Institute of Mental Health Diagnostic Interview Schedule: Its history, characteristics, and validity. *Archives of General Psychiatry, 38*, 381–389.

Roberts, R. E., & Attkisson, C. C. (1983). Assessing client satisfaction among Hispanics. *Evaluation and Program Planning, 6*, 401–413.

Roberts, R. E., Attkisson, C. C., & Stegner, B. L. (1983). A client satisfaction scale suitable for use with Hispanics? *Hispanic Journal of Behavioral Sciences, 5*, 461–476.

Rogers, C. R., & Dymond, R. (1954). *Psychotherapy and Personality Change*. Chicago: University of Chicago Press.

Romano, B. A., & Nelson, R. O. (1988). Discriminant and concurrent validity of measures of children's depression. *Journal of Clinical Child Psychology, 17*, 255–259.

Russell, C. S., Olson, D. H., Sprenkle, D. H., & Atilano, R. B. (1983). From family system to family system: Review of family therapy research. *The American Journal of Family Therapy, 11*, 3–14.

Russell, R. (1994). *Reassessing psychotherapy research*. New York: Guilford.

Safran, J. D., & Wallner, L. K. (1991). The relative predictive validity of two therapeutic alliance measures in cognitive therapy. *Psychological Assessment, 3*, 188–195.

Sandberg, D. E., Meyer-Bahlburg, H. F. L., & Yager, T. J. (1991). The child behavior checklist nonclinical standardization samples: Should they be utilized as norms? *Journal of the American Academy of Child and Adolescent Psychiatry, 30*, 124–134.

Sandell, J. A. (1981). *An empirical study of negative factors in brief psychotherapy*. Unpublished Dissertation, Vanderbilt University.

Saunders, S. M., Howard, K. I., & Newman, F. L. (1988). Evaluating the clinical significance of treatment effects: Norms and Normality. *Behavioral Assessment, 10*, 207–218.

Schacht, T. E. (1991). Formulation based psychotherapy research: Some further considerations. *American Psychologist, 46*, 1346–1347.

Schacht, T. E., & Henry, W. P. (1992). Reaction to Lambert, Ogles, and Masters: "Choosing outcome assessment devices." *Journal of Counseling and Development, 70*, 533–534.

Scott, M. M. (1991). Naturalistic research: Applications for research and professional practice with college students. *Journal of College Student Development, 32*, 416–423.

Shaffer, D., Gould, M. S., Brasic, J., Ambrosini, P., Fisher, P., Bird, H., & Aluwahlia, S. (1983). A Children's Global Assessment Scale (CGAS). *Archives of General Psychiatry, 40*, 1228–1231.

Shaffer, J. W., Perlin, S., Schmidt, C. W., & Himelfarb, M. (1972). Assessment in absentia: New directions in the psychological autopsy. *Johns Hopkins Medical Journal, 130*, 308–316.

Shapiro, D. A., & Shapiro, K. (1982). Meta-analysis of comparative outcome studies: A replication and refinement. *Psychological Bulletin, 92*, 581–604.

Sharpley, C., & Cross, D. (1982). A psychometric evaluation of the Spanier Dyadic Adjustment Scale. *Journal of Marriage and the Family, 44*, 739–741.

Silverman, W. K. (1991). Person's description of psychotherapy outcome studies does not accurately represent psychotherapy outcome studies. *American Psychologist, 46*, 1351–1352.

Skodol, A. E., Rosnick, L., Kellman, D., Oldham, J. M., & Hyler, S. E. (1988). Validating structured DSM-III-R personality disorder assessment with longitudinal data. *American Journal of Psychiatry, 145*, 1297–1299.

Smith, M. L., Glass, G. V., & Miller, T. I. (1980). *The benefits of psychotherapy*. Baltimore: Johns Hopkins University Press.

Snyder, D. K. (1981). *Marital Satisfaction Inventory (MSI) manual*. Los Angeles: Western Psychological Services.

Snyder, D. K., Wills, R. M., & Grady-Fletcher, A. (1991). Long-term effectiveness of behavioral versus insight-oriented marital therapy: A 4-year follow-up study. *Journal of Consulting and Clinical Psychology, 59*, 138–141.

Sorensen, J. L., Hargreaves, W. A., & Friedlander, S.

(1982). Child global rating scales: Selecting a measure of client functioning in a large mental health system. *Evaluation and Program Planning, 5*, 337–347.

Spanier, G. B. (1976). Measuring dyadic adjustment: New scales for assessing the quality of marriage and similar dyads. *Journal of Marriage and the Family, 38*, 15–28.

Spanier, G. B., & Thompson, L. (1982). A confirmatory analysis of the Dyadic Adjustment Scale. *Journal of Marriage and the Family, 44*, 813–823.

Speer, D. C. (1992). Clinically significant change: Jacobson and Truax (1991) revisited. *Journal of Consulting and Clinical Psychology, 60*, 402–408.

Spielberger, C. D. (1983). *Manual for the State-Trait Anxiety Inventory STAI (Form Y)*. Palo Alto, CA: Consulting Psychologists Press.

Spielberger, C. D., Gorsuch, R. L., & Lushene, R. E. (1970). *The State Trait Anxiety Inventory Self Evaluation Questionnaire*. Palo Alto, CA: Consulting Psychologists Press.

Spitzer, R. L., & Endicott, J. (1978). *The Schedule for Affective Disorders and Schizophrenia-Change version* (3rd ed.). New York: Biometrics Research, New York State Psychiatric Institute.

Spitzer, R. L., Endicott, J., & Robins, E. (1975). *Research Diagnostic Criteria (RDC)*. New York: Biometrics Research, New York State Psychiatric Institute.

Spitzer, R. L., Williams, J. B. W., Gibbon, M., & First, M. B. (1989). *Instruction manual for the Structured Clinical Interview for DSM-III-R*. New York: Biometrics Research, New York State Psychiatric Institute.

Strupp, H. H. (1981). Clinical research, practice, and the crisis of confidence. *Journal of Consulting and Clinical Psychology, 49*, 216–219.

Strupp, H. H., & Bloxom, A. L. (1975). Therapists assessment of outcome. In I. E. Waskow, & M. A. Parloff (Eds.), *Psychotherapy change measures* (pp. 170–188). Washington, DC: NIMH.

Strupp, H. H., & Hadley, S. W. (1977). A tripartite model of mental health and therapeutic outcome: With special reference to negative effects in psychotherapy. *American Psychologist, 32*, 187–196.

Strupp, H. H., Hadley, S. W., & Gomes-Schwartz, B. (1977). *Psychotherapy for better or worse: An analysis of the problem of negative effects*. New York: Jason Aronson.

Strupp, H. H., Hartley, D., & Blackwood, G. L., Jr.

(1974). *Vanderbilt Psychotherapy Process Scale*. Unpublished manuscript, Vanderbilt University.

Strupp, H. H., Keithly, L., Moras, K., Samples, S., Sandell, J., & Waterhouse, G. (1980, June). *Toward the measurement of negative effects in psychotherapy*. Paper presented at the annual meeting of the Society of Psychotherapy Research, Pacific Grove, CA.

Strupp, H. H., Moras, K., Sandell, J., Waterhouse, G., O'Malley, S., Keithly, S., & Gomes-Schwartz, B. (1981). *Vanderbilt Negative Indicators Scale: An instrument for the identification of deterrents to progress in time-limited dynamic psychotherapy*. Unpublished manuscript, Vanderbilt University, 1981

Strupp, H. H., Schacht, T. E., & Henry, W. P. (1988). Problem-treatment-outcome congruence: A principle whose time has come. In H. Dahl, H. Kaechele, & H. Thomas (Eds.), *Psychoanalytic process research strategies* (pp. 1–14). Berlin: Springer-Verlag.

Suh, C. S., Strupp, H. H., & O'Malley, S. S. (1986). The Vanderbilt process measures: The psychotherapy process scale (VPPS) and the negative indicators scale (VNIS). In L. S. Greenberg & W. M. Pinsof (Eds.), *The psychotherapeutic process: A research handbook* (pp. 285–323). New York: Guilford.

Tanner, B. A. (1982). A multidimensional client satisfaction instrument. *Evaluation and Program Planning, 5*, 161–167.

Taylor, J. A. (1953). A personality scale of manifest anxiety. *Journal of Abnormal and Social Psychology, 48*, 285–290.

Tingey, R., Burlingame, G. M., Lambert, M. J., & Barlow, S. H. (1991, June). *Recent empirical developments in clinical significance*. Paper presented at the Society for Psychotherapy Research, Wintergreen, VA.

Tracey, T. J., & Kokotovic, A. M. (1989). Factor structure of the Working Alliance Inventory. *Psychological Assessment, 1(3)*, 207–210.

Trull, T. J., Nietzel, M. T., & Main, A. (1988). The use of meta-analysis to assess the clinical significance of behavior therapy for agoraphobia. *Behavior Therapy, 19(4)*, 527–538.

Wallace, C. J., & Haas, B. J. (1983). Assessing outcome in chronic populations treated in day-treatment programs. In M. J. Lambert, E. R. Christensen, & S. S. DeJulio (Eds.), *The assessment of psychotherapy outcome* (pp. 99–131). New York: John Wiley.

Waskow, I. E., & Parloff, M. B. (1975). *Psychotherapy change measures*. Rockville, MD: National Institute of Mental Health.

Weed, L. L. (1969). *Medical records, medical education, and patient care: The problem oriented record as a basic tool*. Cleveland: Case Western Reserve University Press.

Weissman, M. M., & Bothwell, S. (1976). The assessment of social adjustment by patients self-report. *Archives of General Psychiatry, 33*, 1111–1115.

Weissman, M. M., & Paykel, E. S. (1974). *The depressed woman: A study of social relationships*. Chicago: University of Chicago Press.

Wetzler, S. W. (1989). *Measuring mental illness: Psychometric assessment for clinicians*. Washington DC: American Psychiatric Press.

Whisman, M. A., & Jacobson, N. S. (1992). Change in marital adjustment following marital therapy: A comparison of two outcome measures. *Psychological Assessment, 4*, 219–223.

Whitt, E. J. (1991). Artful science: A primer on qualitative research methods. *Journal of College Student Development, 32*, 406–415.

Wilkins, W. (1979a). Expectancies in therapy research: Discriminating among heterogeneous nonspecifics. *Journal of Consulting and Clinical Psychology, 47*, 837–845.

Wilkins, W. (1979b). Getting specific about non-specifics. *Cognitive Therapy and Research, 3*, 319–329.

Williams, S. L. (1985). On the nature and measurement of agoraphobia. *Progress in Behavior Modification, 19*, 109–144.

Wojciechowski, F. L. (1984). *Double-blind research in psychotherapy*. Netherlands: Swets & Zeitlinger.

Wolf, M. M. (1978). Social validity: The case for subjective measurement or how applied behavior analysis is finding its heart. *Journal of Applied Behavior Analysis, 11*, 203–214.

Wolpe, J. (1982). *The practice of behavior therapy* (3rd ed.). New York: Pergamon.

Woodward, C. A., Santa-Barbara, J., Levin, S., & Epstein, N. B. (1978). The roles of goal attainment scaling in evaluating family therapy outcome. *American Journal of Orthopsychiatry, 48*, 464–475.

Ziegler, V. E., Meyer, D. A., Rosen, S. H., & Biggs, J. T. (1978). Reliability of videotaped Hamilton ratings. *Biological Psychiatry, 13*, 119–122.

Zimmerman, M., & Coryell, W. (1987). The Inventory to Diagnose Depression (IDD): A self-report scale to diagnose major depressive disorder. *Journal of Consulting and Clinical Psychology, 55(1)*, 55–59.

Zimmerman, M., Pfohl, B., Stangl, D., & Coryell, W. (1986). An American validation study of the Newcastle Diagnostic Scale. *British Journal of Psychiatry, 149*, 627–630.

Zuckerman, M. (1960). The development of an affect adjective checklist for the measurement of anxiety. *Journal of Consulting Psychology, 24*, 467–462.

Zung, W. W. K. (1965). A self-rating depression scale. *Archives of General Psychiatry, 12*, 63–70.

Zung, W. W. K. (1971). A rating instrument for anxiety disorders. *Psychosomatics, 12*, 371–379.

Index